THE STOPPING PLACES

The Stopping Places

a Journey through Gypsy Britain

by

Damian Le Bas

Chatto & Windus
LONDON

3 5 7 9 10 8 6 4 2

Chatto & Windus, an imprint of Vintage,
20 Vauxhall Bridge Road,
London SW1V 2SA

Chatto & Windus is part of the Penguin Random House group of companies
whose addresses can be found at global.penguinrandomhouse.com

Penguin
Random House
UK

First published by Chatto & Windus in 2018

penguin.co.uk/vintage

A CIP catalogue record for this book is available from the British Library

ISBN 9781784741037

Typeset in 11/16 pt Bembo Std
by Integra Software Services Pvt. Ltd, Pondicherry

Printed and bound in Great Britain by Clays Ltd, Elcograf S.p.A.

Penguin Random House is committed to a sustainable future for our
business, our readers and our planet. This book is made from Forest
Stewardship Council® certified paper.

MIX
Paper from
responsible sources
FSC
www.fsc.org   FSC® C018179

In memory of my dad
Damian John Le Bas
1963–2017

Contents

DJLB 2018

⌇ = ROUTE

THE HIGHLANDS
SCOTLAND
Skye
The Tinkers' Heart
Blairgowrie
THE LOWLANDS
Stirling
The Thieves' Road
Romannobridge

Appleby Fair

Blackpool Sands
THE NORTH COUNTRY
ENGLAND

Bala
WALES
Kingsmeadow
In between we went to Les Saintes Maries de la Mer
Marshland St James

THE EAST

NORTH
WEST ◁◁ ◇ ◇▷ EAST
SOUTH

Boscastle
THE WEST COUNTRY
THE SOUTH COUNTRY
Fulham
Harlow
Gravesend
Bodmin
Winchester
Gipsy Hill
The Flamingo Club
St Germans
Haldon Hill
Brandeau
Horsmonden
Bridie's Tan
Furzey Lodge
Home (The Yard)

Nan's Places: Messenger's Meadow
Hartley Park
Butler's Down
Shalden Green

The Stopping Places

There is a road that runs from the salt coast of Sussex, back to the green hop gardens of rural Hampshire. It is an old road, a road of black and white; a road composed of many roads. Some of them have half-memorable names: the Valley, the Long Furlong, and Harting Down, a hill of many stags. Most have no name but a faceless coda of letter and number: the A27 westbound, the A286 out of Chichester, the B2141 from Mid Lavant to Harting. But in me all these disparate roads add up to just one: the road from the world I grew up in, to the world of wagons and tents that passed in the decades before I was born.

It was a road we took twice a week throughout my childhood, from the yard where we lived to a cobbled old market town called Petersfield. We had a 'pitch' there – a spot on the main square where four generations of my family would take turns to stand out in all seasons and sell bunches of flowers. We made the journey in a growling old white Ford Transit van, lined with rattling plywood and heavily laden with flowers. There were boxes of daffodils packed squeaky tight; tall green buckets of chrysanthemums, yellow and copper and pink; stargazer lilies that burst into purple and white streaked with orange. There were little black buckets of freesias, their buds like fruit humbug sweets sucked to a tiny, bright core. Spray carnations, the white ones frill-edged with light red, yellow ones tinged with peach. Ferns in dark greens jostled against the million tiny white stars of gypsophila.

In one corner of the van were stashed the less interesting tools of the trade: cellophane, secateurs, reams of tissue-thin wrapping paper in pale pastel shades, and boxes of tape and elastic bands to hold all our arrangements together. And I learned the jargon and abbreviations of the trade – the long, plummy, tongue-twister names of flowers truncated to working-class forms: 'spray cars', 'daffs', 'sprig of gyp', 'pinks', 'chrysants' and 'stocks'. And occasionally we'd use our own words when we didn't want customers listening: '*Kekker*, they're *dui bar* a go.' '*Atch* on, the *mollisha's dinlo*.' '*Kur* the *vonger* in your *putsel*.' '*Dordi chavi, mingries akai*.' I had no idea where these words came from, or why we understood them and almost nobody else did. But I'd learned not to use them at school. If I did, a long silence would follow, turning my mood from light to dark, and I would feel lonelier once the silence had passed.

I had already been making this journey for years before I began to think about how it had started. Of course, we went to Petersfield to sell flowers, but why there? Why this twice-weekly trip, an hour each way, to a little town miles from where we lived? Why didn't we just sell flowers closer to home? We had smaller pitches in other towns, too, dotted around the vicinity: Lancing, Broadwater, Emsworth, Godalming, Selsey. A roll call of places that no one outside the region had heard of. But there was something special about Petersfield. I could tell that my elders all felt it; they looked forward to going there more; there was anticipation each evening before we set off.

On the way, my elders would point and nod at empty spaces by the sides of the road, flat areas on verges and slightly raised banks, vacant pull-ins and lay-bys, and make comments as if things were there, things that I couldn't see. The references were muttered and coded, their significance unclear to a child's ears, but they stood out against the rest of the conversation like a broken trail of breadcrumbs in the mud of the woods. 'That was where Uncle and they used to stop, look.' 'I can still see me granny sat there.' 'Cousin's lay-by, look, Dee.' I tried hard to tune in to the meaning, but never felt brave enough to ask what these phrases meant. They were glimmers of another world, but it felt as distant as the stars. I knew the places they were pointing out had something to do with the time they were 'on the road' – most of my family were settled now, living in houses or caravans and mobile homes on private bits of land. But in spite of my interest, I wouldn't ask questions. Twin dictums ruled over my child-hood, austere morals that had survived the transition from nomadic to settled life, remnants of a less indulgent, almost bygone time. One was a saying I've heard many people use: 'Children should be seen and not heard.' Another was specific to my family and their relations, and was drummed into me as the only right way for a child to behave when in company: 'Keep your eyes and ears open, and your mouth shut.' And while I was a young boy, when it came to this half-secret world, that was just what I did.

Alongside selling flowers, the family had roofing and car-breaking businesses. We had a big field and a 'yard', a word that seemed to mean a place where all things might, and did, happen. Terriers, geese and perturbed-looking cockerels roamed in between the legs of cantankerous horses. Stables were stacked full of the musty paraphernalia of horsemanship, flower-selling, roofing and car respraying. Bits of cars lay everywhere, named as if they were the parts or clothes of people or animals: bonnets, boots, seats, wings, belts. There were brass-handled horsewhips, jangling harnesses, buckets of molasses-sprayed chaff and milled sugar-beet, bales of sweet-smelling fresh hay. But all of this old rustic stuff was stacked and wedged in amongst the hard and greasy gear of the family economy: gas bottles, blowtorches, leaky old engines, spray paint, rolls of lead, felt, and seemingly infinite stacks of every conceivable type of roof tile. A heavy boxing bag swung with barely perceptible creaks, keeping time in the half-light of the dusty old garage.

There were caravans there that we sometimes lived in and out of, especially in the summer. We never considered this odd, even though we also had a big house on the land that my grandad had built with his men. And there always seemed to be heavy and dangerous things lying close to hand, with names that sounded like the hard noise they would make against flesh: bats and grub axes, claw hammers, club hammers, 'four-bi'-two' offcuts of wood, bits of scaffold pole. When people visited, they'd speak politely, with deference to Grandad who ruled this domain that was half Wild West, half-wild West Sussex. The hard stuff of motion was every-where, though we were settled: cars, tractors and trucks, some brand new, others eaten by weather and time; horses, ponies, traps, sulkies and carts; scattered wheels and bolts from Ford and Bedford lorries. And, hung from a barn door like a pair of swords and scabbing to ochre with rust, there were two axles rescued from the ashes of the last wagon owned by our family.

We had a name for ourselves: Travellers, which was always pronounced with just two syllables – *Travlers* – as if to differentiate it from the regular sense of the word. In our case, it didn't just mean anyone who travelled around, regard-less of their race: to us it meant our people specifically, the Romanies of Britain. The first Romanies probably arrived on the British mainland towards the end of the fifteenth century, and had been a contentious presence ever since. At first they were believed to be Egyptians – some claimed to have been the Dukes or Princes of 'Little Egypt' – a term that would morph into 'Gyptians', 'Gypcians' and eventually 'Gypsies'. Over the years, in England and across the Old World, other theories for their origins arose. The Elizabethan playwright Ben Jonson referred to them as 'Moon-Men' in a play; others suggested the Gypsies were a lost band of Jews, or conversely, that their ancestors were survivors of the destruction of Sodom and Gomorrah, or the fabled lost city of Ur of the Chaldees. A connection to the Sigynnae – a tribe of charioteers mentioned in Herodotus – was suggested, based on a similarity with the Romanian word for Gypsies, *Çigany*.

Since most Gypsies seemed to be semi-perpetual wanderers, some thought they might be the last of the Druids, or priests of the old cult of Isis; perhaps even the sons of Cain, expelled from the biblical Garden of Eden and fated to wander the earth. In a similar vein, and because so many Gypsies worked as blacksmiths, a myth arose – both inside and outside Romany culture – that they had been cursed to roam for having forged the nails that crucified Jesus Christ. A few theories came nearer to the truth. There were educated guesses that the first Gypsies were the ten thousand musicians given as gift to the ruler of Persia by an Indian Emperor in 439 AD, as described in the epic poetry of Firdausi. Less glamorously, some suggested they were descendants of emigrant *Sudras*, members of the Hindu worker caste.

Wherever the Gypsies went, they took with them their strange tongue, Romani, and it was through this that the mystery of their origins was solved. An eighteenth-century German linguist called Johann Rüdiger overheard Gypsies talking, and was struck by the similarity of their speech to Indian languages. Although he was not alone in noticing this,

6

Rüdiger was the first person to put his observations to a systematic test. He translated a selection of phrases from Hindustani – as Urdu was then called – into German, then spoke the German versions to a Romani woman called Barbara Makelin. She then explained to him how she would say those sentences in her own language. Not only did many of the words match, but the grammatical similarities were so close that there could be no doubt: Romani was clearly an Indian tongue. Features it did not share with Hindustani, including the use of a definite article, had been picked up during the Gypsies' westward journey.

In the case of the Gypsies' word for 'the', it had been appropriated from the Greek language during their time in the Byzantine Empire. Later linguists, including the so-called 'Romany *Ryes*' – *rye* being the Romani word for a gentleman – such as the English writer George Borrow and the Irish academic John Sampson, would identify layers of borrowings from Persian, Slavic and Romance languages in the Gypsies' speech, using these to trace a philological map of their long road into the West. English Romani had German-derived words in it, like *nixis*, meaning 'nothing', and *fogel* for 'smell'; and the dialect of the Gypsies of Wales had a unique layer of Welsh. As for the name of the Romanies, it was derived from their own word for 'man' or 'husband', *rom*, and it had nothing to do with Romania, which got its name from the Roman military camps which once filled its territory. The Gypsies called their language *Romanes*, an adverb meaning 'like a *rom*'. To '*rokker Romanes*' meant, simply, to talk like a Gypsy and not like a *gorjer* – a non-Gypsy. And this is what my family were doing when they spoke to me in our secret language in the little market square of Petersfield.

Theirs was a culture in love with clear distinctions; with wanting to believe that a crisp, clean border exists between the black and the white, the light and the dark. For the Gypsies of Britain, black-and-white (and occasionally brown-and-white) animals seem possessed of a special importance, a different aura. It is thought that this stark differentiation in the colouring of an animal's feathers or fur symbolises the separation of good and evil, and whether or not this is true, it is consistent with the Gypsy tendency to polarise: to draw a stark dividing line. With the exception of the magpie, with its cackling voice and ambiguous, fey reputation, an animal dressed in starkly contrasting dark and light colours means good fortune to a Traveller. Piebald and skew-bald cobs – black-and-white and brown-and-white patched, respectively – are amongst the Travellers' favourite horses, and various explanations are tendered for this. It is widely believed that in days gone by, breeding 'coloured' horses would put off the army from taking them, because of the Establishment's long-standing preference for horses of solid colour. But it's likely that the division of darkness and light in the colouring also plays at least some role in the Gypsies' preference.

Travellers sometimes refer to the pied wagtail as the 'Gypsy bird', and used to believe that if you saw a wagtail then you'd bump into fellow Gypsies later that day. Not only is the wagtail black and white, but it's also one of the smallest birds that often walks instead of hopping along the ground, which gave the Travellers another affinity with it in their long past as largely pedestrian nomads before the acquisition of engines. To this day, whenever I see a Dalmatian, I remember the old line Mum taught me when I was little: *If you see a spotted dog, spit for good luck.* I raise my hands up to my face and spit a barely detectable, ceremonial amount of saliva onto the fingertips of each hand, then clap my hands together twice.

This love of binary clarity extends to people: in the old Romany tradition, you can only call yourself a true Romany Gypsy – one of the *kaulo ratti*, the black blood – if all your ancestors, as far as you know, are of the tribe. I can trace my Romany ancestry back at least six generations; I was brought up to know the Romani language; to learn the old tales and to keep the *Romanipen* – the cleanliness taboos of the old-fashioned Gypsies. I was raised, and still live, in a Romany psychological realm; a mental Gypsyland. But I have both Gypsy and non-Gypsy blood and so, in many Travellers' eyes, I do not have the right to call myself a true-bred Romany. It does not matter that there is no such thing as a racially pure Gypsy: over a thousand-year migration it is virtually impossible that there will have been no mingling in the line. The mixing in my family had happened within living memory, and this meant I was at best a *poshrat* – a mixed-blood Gypsy – and at worst a 'half-chat *gorjie*' or, as a friend once memorably put it, a 'fucked-up half-breed'.

I do not look like most people's conception of a typical Gypsy, my blue eyes and fair hair belying my origins, my picture of myself. My identity was inside me and the outside didn't match up. It imbued me with a tetchy defensiveness, and a resentment of people whom I then believed had simpler ethnicities: Scottish, Nigerian, Han. I felt so close to my roots, and especially to the Romany women who'd brought me up – my mum; her mother, Gran; and Gran's mother, Nan. But this seemed to count for little in a world which, for all its modernity, still believed in labels like 'half-caste', 'full-blood' and 'mixed race'. Later, as a teenager, I started carrying photographs of darker-haired family members in my wallet, to challenge the disbelief of those who thought I was lying about my Romany background. I lived in a world that wasn't sure if I really belonged in it, and so I wasn't sure either. Regardless, it was where I was. Our family were the mistrusted local Gypsies, the bane of the decent, upstanding Parish Council. We were 'gyppos', 'pikeys', '*diddakois*', 'them lot'. Locally, we were infamous. The divide was crystal clear.

Compared with the insults and slurs, the words 'Romanies', 'Gypsies', 'Travellers' were dignified, and we used all of them interchangeably. The greater part of our family owned their own yards and bungalows, but the name 'Travellers' still seemed to make sense. There were wheels everywhere, and we were always on hair-trigger alert to hook up trailers and go when the need arose: we drove miles for a living, even further to the fairs, and had family who lived on the road. Still, the word 'Gypsy' wasn't often heard back then. When it was, it was usually as part of a story about the old days, where someone had shouted out 'dirty Gypsies' and nine times out of ten a fight had ensued, which the 'dirty Gypsies' – who, in my grandad's words, were 'rough, tough and made out of the right stuff' – almost always won.

In spite of my confusion over who I really was, I loved our world. It felt as though we did whatever we wanted: rode ponies, rode quad bikes, poured petrol on huge stacks of wood ripped from building jobs, and burned them as kestrels rode currents of air high above. Sometimes our relations would come from their scattered homes across the south coast, and join in. I noticed the features that picked them out against the backdrop of everyone else in the world: the massive gold rings and tan boots, or *faunis* and *chokkers* as we called them; the 1950s hairstyles; the trucks that they drove, sporting chrome horseshoes, miniature boxing gloves and – in a little gesture to a different kind of masculinity – their daughters' or granddaughters' baby shoes hanging from their rear-view mirrors.

And there were the different faces. Not all, but most of them, looked very different from the surrounding families in this very white corner of the country: the South Downs, built on oceanic chalk. They had darker skin, harder features. Their eyes seemed forever a-squint from natural forces, perpetually half-closed to keep out the smoke and the sunlight, the rain and wind. The men had big arms and hands, often big bellies too. They spoke in gravelly, lilting tones, in a continuum of accents that weren't from round here – more rural, farmerish, sometimes very West Country, occasionally with a hint of Australian. The corners were softened off consonants; vowels were blended into instantly recognisable diphthongs, 'oe's and 'ae's. And always their speech would be peppered with our secret words. I learned more every week, and made lists of them. *Shushi* and *shero* for 'rabbit' and 'head'; *waffadi* and *wudrus* for 'sickly' and 'bed'; *jukel* and *jigger* for 'dog' and 'door'; *lowvul* and *loovni* for 'money' and 'whore'; *gilly* and *geero* for 'song' and 'strange man'; and *vardo* for 'wagon', sometimes 'caravan'. For certain things there were several words. By my teens I knew four Traveller words for 'punch', five for 'money', and seven for the 'police'.

When Traveller friends or relatives visited they would bring tales of the special places linked to our family – a roll call of place names, most of which I'd never visited, that were burned onto their consciousness like a network of unseen roots that made them who they were. Shalden Green, Pagham's Copse, Shripney Corner, Jack's Bush, Messenger's Meadow ... A list of locations as meaningless to most people as the shipping forecast is to the non-fisherman. Still, hearing them so many times, I couldn't help learning the names; knew them by heart, though I couldn't be sure if I'd ever seen any of them. Were any of these the places that had been pointed out to me on the old road to Petersfield? Which ones were still there? Had they all been built over?

Did they have any meaning for me? I learned that there was a name for all of these sites, a way that my family referred to where they had lived. They called them 'stopping places', or *atchin tans*.

My great-grandmother on my mum's side, Nan, told me what the 'stopping places' were. She explained they were the diverse places where she and her family used to live, in the days of the wagons and 'bender' tents. On occasion they would be there for years, other times just a few days. Often they had permission, granted by a farmer they worked for or some kindly landowner. Sometimes they had no permission and had to lie low. Some *atchin tans*, were places of happiness. Nan described Messenger's Meadow as a miniature land of perpetual summer, all yellow with buttercups, edged by a crystal-clear stream. A place of tap-dancing on old boards and playing the spoons and harmonica, an enchanted corner of England. Other places, I learned, had been very different. Butler's Down sounded the worst: an isolated hilltop exposed to perennial storms, the tormenting night-voices of crows, and the hell of the mud and the cold, the hunger and the rain.

As for the wagons and tents themselves, I was told how these could be of various kinds, depending on the family, their customs and the extent – or modesty – of their wealth. The traditional Romany tent, the 'bender' tent, was a rounded structure made of long, thin hazel ribs, which were inserted into holes in the ground and tied together in a series of intersecting arches. It was then covered in waterproof canvas, or – if none was available – heavy blankets greased to keep out the rain. They varied in their complexity, from small and simple ladybird-shaped domes to longer, double structures with an open space in the middle for a fire, and a wigwam-like open flue above to let the smoke escape. One way of identifying Gypsy families in old census entries and birth certificates is by the frequent references to them dwelling 'under canvas', which meant that they were living in bender tents.

For over three hundred years following the coming of the Romanies to Britain the bender tent was the typical dwelling, as it had been of the isles' indigenous nomads since long before. In spite of this, it was the horse-drawn wagon that would come to be synonymous with Gypsy culture, and to this day it remains many people's image of the authentic Romany accommodation. The first wagons were simply bender tents placed on top of flat carts or 'trolleys' to keep them off the cold, wet ground: a cheap innovation that led in time to the creation of bespoke living wagons. The most common type of wagon to this day, the 'bow-top', is a development of this theme: a canvas roof over a hemisphere of arched ribs.

Other kinds of wagons soon followed. The 'ledge' wagon had staggered sides – ledges – that broadened out towards the roof, creating a little extra living space for the family inside. Some models had the specific needs of certain trades in mind: the 'brush' type wagon was made with sets of external racks and rails for storing and displaying the brooms, baskets and brushes that its owners made and sold for a living. But one of the most popular types was the 'Reading' wagon, named after the town where it was invented. It had a relatively simple box-like structure, but its high, flat wooden sides were harder wearing than the canvas shell of a bow-top: for most Gypsy families it was the practical choice, and it was a Reading wagon in which my nan was born.

Romanies (as well as other ethnic nomads like the Yenish of Central Europe) also lived in wagons in nearby countries, including Germany, Switzerland, Holland and France, but the art of wagon-making unquestionably reached its zenith in Victorian England, an era that Travellers call the 'wagon time'. Family firms arose who became famous for their ability to construct the finest 'vans': H. Jones of Hereford; Thomas Tong of Bolton; William 'Bill' Wright of Rothwell Haigh, near Leeds. At first almost all of these firms consisted of skilled non-Romany carpenters and wheelwrights who were shrewd enough to capitalise on the Gypsies' and Showmen's desire for expensive mobile quarters, but later some Romanies mastered the trade, notably the Gaskin family.

Over time the design of the wagons became increasingly elaborate. For the right price, wagons could be commissioned with ornate cut-glass and hand-etched mirrors; bevel-edged carving and painted scroll-work; polished brass gas lanterns; exotic ceiling upholstery; and fitted wrought-iron 'queenie' stoves, tiny but perfectly suited to warming the small interior. Eventually, gilding the outside of the wagon – painstakingly, with gossamer-thin gold leaf – became standard practice. The

Romany wagon soon evolved into a symbol of the lusted-after aspects of Gypsy life: its freedom and colour. It grew to be one of the most romanticised accommodations in the history of humanity.

It was the custom to burn a wagon when its owner died – due to the belief that a dead person's possessions were infused with their presence, and keeping them would therefore extend and nourish grief. This only added to the wagon's mysterious and unattainable aura, and, in the end, its cash worth: today, fine examples often command the price of real estate. But the wagon began as a pragmatic solution to the difficulties of nomadic life. A contemporary caravan, its gleaming white body engineered from the latest metals and plastics, is simply a modern response to the same old problems. To the Romanies, the painted wagon piques memory, nostalgia and pride, which is why so many still keep them, and sometimes commission new ones to be made. But as a Gypsy dwelling, it is no more authentic than a brand new twin-axle trailer, and requires a great deal more maintenance. Whether two hundred or two years old, a living van's job is to keep out the rain and the cold.

Through everything my family told me, a dichotomy of summer and winter ran like a seam in old rock. The road could be heaven and hell; there was dark; there was light. I registered this, but as a young child I had no thought that any of this could impinge much on me and my life. I didn't know the *atchin tans*. I wanted to know them, but I wasn't sure how I ever could.

When I was ten years old, one of my classmates got wind that my family were Gypsies. He wasted no time making sure all the other kids knew, and when the teacher's back was turned he quietly said to me that I smelt of cow-shit because I was a Gypsy. It was one of the first times I'd heard anyone use the 'G' word. I told the teacher, who shrugged and did nothing. I got in a fight after school, and my dad spotted it from afar and came running to pull me out. He carried me home on his shoulders, and I felt less sure-footed after this, as if I might not be able to last in school; as if the world might shift and I would fall. I drove with my great-uncle to the fields where he kept his cob horses. We fed them and watered them, picked blackberries and sloes, hunted rabbits. There was light in these places, and solace. I found myself pulled ever more towards them, especially since the bullies had tagged me a dirty Gypsy at school.

But there was no question of me leaving school early – as many of my relatives had – because my parents believed in education. Alongside doing typical Traveller jobs – selling flowers and labouring – Mum and Dad were both artists, and had managed to go back to college and get their degrees after interrupted schooling. They saw that I was bright, and Mum had a friend whose husband had gone to a nearby boarding school called Christ's Hospital, and who suggested I might benefit from going there. There was no way on earth that we could have afforded to pay, but they did offer schol-arships. Mum sat me down and we talked it all over. I could go up there, take the entrance exam, and then, if I passed, decide whether I wanted to go. I sat the paper, and managed to win a full scholarship: if I chose to attend we would have to pay nothing at all.

The family was split. Nobody had ever done anything like this before, gone to live – whilst a child – somewhere else. But then, in what seemed half a miracle, Mum also managed to get a job at the school teaching art part-time. This softened the blow, but the consensus remained that this was a weird and unwise move, and that unforeseen harms might befall me. Yet I had some idea, dim and distant, that education was what I needed, and lots of it. And so that was that. Off I went.

I worked hard, mostly, and things seemed to go well. The dark fear that my roots would be dug up and used as weapons against me began to subside. But there were close shaves. A teacher got hold of a newspaper cutting that showed Mum at Appleby Horse Fair wearing traditional Romany clothes – long skirt, plaits, fancy creole gold earrings – standing next to a bow-top type wagon in red, green and gilded gold. He pinned the article onto a noticeboard in a busy corridor, got a bollocking from the deputy head, and all was calm again. Then there was a one-off tense moment two years later, when a kid twice my size, who had grown up around Travellers, spotted that I was wearing a buckle ring, a dead giveaway to those in the know that its wearer is a Gypsy.

'What are you wearing that ring for?' he said.

'What ring?'

'That fucking ring. That's a pikey ring. What you wearing it for?'

I was scared, partly of him, but mostly that this might set off some bad chain of events that would lead to the end of my time at boarding school.

I fudged a response. 'My dad got it off someone,' I said. 'Why, what is it? What's pikeys?' I held just enough courage together to look him straight in the eye as I played it naive.

'Fuck it, don't worry,' he said.

That was the last time that 'pikeys' were mentioned at school, but I had already realised that the land I lived in would never allow me to forget that it saw the Gypsies as a people apart, but equally that my life's path might have diverged too much from them for me to be seen as one of their own. Equally, I knew that my Gypsiness would never leave me: that every time someone said 'gyppo' or 'pikey' within earshot, I'd still get that terrible feeling, like a physical punch in the gut. I dreaded being asked if I was a Gypsy or not, but it was a question that was unlikely to go away. If I wanted to stay sane, I would have to find my own answer one day, and make my peace with it.

In the holidays I still went and sold flowers with the family, and occasionally laboured on building and roofing jobs with my mum's brothers. I loved flying about down the old country lanes in vans and trucks – always Ford Transits, the Traveller's choice – in a daily cycle of hunting for cash, girls and laughs. I smoked fags and laughed nervously as my uncles hollered and ululated at hapless pedestrians. They drove with great skill, blended with the kerb-mounting style of a maniac breed. I got to know landlords and barmaids. We buttered them up, anything to secure better service or access to free drinks or long, deferred tabs. Charisma was key: it was how Traveller men got things done. All in the moment, and making the world burst with laughter and fall for their tricks. And wherever they went, they never forget the old stopping places that lay beside the hedgerows, stabbed like splinters between roads and fields, between highway and countryside. My uncles still knew where they were, although they had hardly stopped in any of them. I tried to remember them all. I tried to absorb it all into myself, sensing that I might need this information in some distant time of crisis, poverty or adventure.

Now, though, I had one foot in a different place. Not only was my ancestry tainted: my education was changing me too. I worried about consequence, shied from using the Romani language in public. I doubted whether I still belonged in the Traveller world, though I so badly wanted to. On one occasion, a cousin caught me down the yard on the phone to my girlfriend, talking in more cut-glass tones than the ones that I spoke in at home, crossing Ts, hanging Gs. He shouted, 'Oh yes, hello, I'm Damian Le Bas, yes, I'm too bloody good for you lot,' in an absurdly posh, brigadier's accent that, for him, summed up my betrayal, before walking off in a rage. I put the phone down and tried to run after him to explain, but he got in his van and sped off. I was desolate. What was this world that refused to just let me belong? Would I ever find some way to be English, educated, but a Gypsy? I couldn't even be sure where the crux of my discomfort lay, and I wondered how many people on earth felt torn in different directions the way I did. If there was an answer to all this, it lay far off, and who knew where. The stopping places of my future, some resolution to the unease: these were far out of sight.

One day, when I'd just turned sixteen, I was sitting in a van outside a Travis Perkins builder's merchants while my uncles went inside to buy sand and cement. My phone rang, and I knew by the area code that it was school: they were going to tell me the results of my GCSEs. I breathed in deeply and listened as the lady's voice read them out slowly. I had got nine A stars and one A. I said thanks, put the phone down, then hollered out in a mixture of shock and relief as I slammed my fist up into the roof of the van. A few moments later, I realised what these results actually meant: I would stay at school and do my A Levels now, and eventually go off to uni like everyone else there. Another five years of half-in, half-out. Until this moment I had tried to fool myself that I could return to the Gypsy world as if nothing had happened, as though this time spent somewhere else were a slight aberration that time would wash out.

I was living in a trailer when I got into Oxford to study theology, and Oxford was also the place where I first encountered the enormous wealth of books about my people. Up until this point I'd found that libraries lacked almost any materials about Romanies. In the Bodleian library, by contrast, there were dozens of volumes stretching back hundreds of years. They made constant reference to India, and to the customs which had defined my childhood, especially that of avoiding *mokkadi* – unclean – habits, which include mixing articles related to the body with those used for preparing food. This was why we boiled our tea towels and dishcloths on the hob and never put them in the wash with our clothes; why animals must not share a bowl or a meal or a kiss with a human. I read about the customs of bringing a dead person's body back to their home, the vigil of 'sitting up' awake with it for nights on end, and opening the windows and curtains when the body was taken away to be buried to let their soul out. Things began to make sense: why my mum stopped to have her picture taken with Rajasthani dancers in London, and felt an affinity with them, their clothes and their style; why some of my relations were dark-skinned: 'black-faces' as Travellers call them, an affectionate term that sounds harsh to outsiders who don't know that being 'real dark' is often a mark of great pride amongst Gypsies.

I learned about the contact and intermarriage between the Romanies and the ethnic nomadic peoples of Britain and Ireland, particularly Irish Travellers. I was surprised to learn the etymology of *Needies*, a favourite term of self-reference among the Romany Gypsies of the south, used only amongst themselves. I had always thought it was a reference to the old days of hardship in wagons and tents, as in 'the poor and the needy'. It turned out it had nothing to do with needing anything, but was in fact a word from the Gamin – the old Celtic tongue of the Irish Travellers – made by reversing the consonants of *daoine*, the Irish word for 'people'. I smiled at the thought of how certain Romany people – who can sometimes be as prejudiced against other Travellers as anyone else – would react if they learned this.

All this made me feel I was part of something far-flung and mysterious, a diaspora scattered across the wide earth out of the East that few knew anything about. Not all Gypsies yearned for India – some did not even believe their ancestors had originated from there at all. But others, like Clifford Lee, who had accompanied a 1970s *National Geographic* expedition retracing the migratory route of the Romanies back to the subcontinent, spoke of it as their spiritual home – 'that fabulous land where my forebears originated'.

When I read these books about Gypsies, it often felt as though something was missing. The more I thought about it, the more I realised it was the stopping places with their secret names that often returned no results when I looked them up on the internet. The *atchin tans* were what rooted my family here, there, wherever they'd been. They gave the lie to the notion of Gypsies as footloose and clueless marauders, moving in arbitrary fashion from place to place. The reality was the exact opposite. They frequented these places with good reason, and that reason was usually work, or the fairs, or their family.

How far all this might be connected to some sort of inherited wanderlust, I had no idea. But I knew that without a sense of the individual people and where they and their language lived, and had lived, there could be no understanding of who they were as a group. Without visiting these locations, I couldn't hope to understand who I really was, either: so crucial was the role the stopping places had played in shaping the characters of the people from whom I had come. These sites rooted the people I knew in reality, in the geology of their environment.

They bound them to the crops that grew out of the earth, and to the people who farmed them.

In places, the hops and potatoes were to the Travellers like buffalo were to Sioux hunters or oil to Texans: they were why the Gypsies were there; in some eyes, why they *were*. Alongside the particular roadsides of each place and the tenderness, or malice, of the local people, police and councils, these things tied them to the seasons and weather, the accents and dialects, the regional customs and ballads and by-laws, and the folklore and ghosts of a place. I began to wonder if the *atchin tans* were the missing key to understanding the psyche, the soul, of my people. It was all reducible to a simple truth: you can never understand Gypsies unless you understand where they live, and where they have lived. In my work as a journalist, people told me the reason Gypsies were unwelcome everywhere was because they did not belong anywhere. And the stopping places proved that this assertion was a lie.

Gypsies have always been abstracted from our environment, or placed in one that doesn't reflect our reality. The Gypsylorists had always managed to find their favourite Gypsies in the finest of wagons on beautiful windswept heaths, by the shores of picturesque Welsh lakes, or slumbering in first-class tents among sheltered dunes. Eighteenth-century landscape painters placed Romany families in the gently cupping roots of great willows and beech groves. Later, the painters Dame Laura Knight and Sir Alfred Munnings depicted 'their' Gypsies at country fairs, dressed in elaborate clothes, smiling and smoking cigarettes, dancing: at leisure.

It was not that all this was untrue, but it was askew, lopsided. It was only a part of the picture. The rest was the reality I knew, partly first-hand, partly from the smoke-dried memories of my relatives. Yes, the Gypsy reality was partly composed of fairgrounds and showgrounds, picturesque lakeside halts, sheltered commons, bright heaths. But it also comprised frozen copses and hilltops. Old maintenance roads with potholes and bad light. Scrap yards. Council waste ground. Lay-bys near the edges of tips. Slag heaps and drained marshes. Fen ends. Chalk pits, yards and quarries.

These are the stopping places, these fringes and in-between places. They are the places that nobody lives except Travellers – or nobody but those who share ancient connections with them: gamekeepers and poachers, scrap-metal men, horse-women, rangers and shepherds. They are the old nomad's haunts of the island. Many are smashed and built over; some – magically – are more or less just as they were in centuries long past. They form the hidden Gypsy and Traveller map of the country we live in: the bedrock of our reality and, perhaps, the antidote to unending cycles of romanticisation and demonisation.

A plan was beginning to form within me, to visit these places, to live in them in my own way, and see what I might learn. Perhaps I might even solve the bizarre contradiction of Britain's love affair with caravanning, camping and 'glamping', and its hatred of those who were born to this life, and who largely inspired its adoption as a non-Gypsy pastime. As one Scottish

Gypsy Traveller put it, 'There are eighty thousand members of the Caravan Club, but I'm not allowed to travel?'

There is more to this Gypsy geography than a list of physical places. The stopping places themselves are an outgrowth of something non-physical, something that is ancient, unseen yet important; precious and reviled, envied and feared. This thing is the Gypsy belief – the core belief of the culture – that it is possible to live in a different way; in your own way, part of the world, but not imprisoned by the rules. That you can know the ropes and yet not be hemmed in by them. That you can dwell alongside the mainstream, whilst not being part of it. Otter-like, you can live in the bank of the river and swim and hunt there when you need to, and then climb back out with equal ease and alacrity. There is no better symbol of this belief than the network of *atchin tans* laced across Britain; they are historical, topographical proof that the Gypsy philosophy has existed here, that it still does, that it still can.

I began to ask Gypsy friends and relations about stopping places. As soon as I started asking questions, it became clear that this map was bigger and more complex than I could have imagined. Half a millennium of Romany life in Great Britain had bred thousands of *atchin tans*, of which I could only hope to visit a tiny fraction. They wrote themselves out slowly in dendritic structures as I spoke to the people who'd stopped there – wagon painters and musicians, farm workers and florists, wealthy horse dealers who owned big plots of land; and also the roofers, tree surgeons and block-paving men who are more common nowadays. First they'd mention the main stopping places, where much work was done, where they'd stayed for months, known a kind farmer, where babies were born. Then others would crop up: 'A few days there, oh yep, that's right, we stopped there for the night, what a *mullerdi* place.'

I would even find a few of my own *atchin tans*, mentioned to me by no one, sniffed out as dusk came down or seeming to beckon to me through rain, the last secret fruits of a free way of life that is no longer meant to be there. I learned how each place was defined by the season, could be heaven or hell or a slow purgatory of damp, simply due to the month. Through my searches, I'd find that a few stopping places still held an enticing magic, seemed enchanted by slow interactions of Gypsies and locals; of history, weather and time. The little tin church in the woods near Bramdean in Hampshire. The area around Bala Lake in North Wales, last redoubt of the oldest form of the Romani language to survive in Britain. The shifting sands of Blackpool's south shore, a haunt of the old fortune tellers. Rommanobridge, on the road up to Stirling, where two clans of Scottish Gypsies once drew swords and fought to the death. And the Tinker's Heart of Argyll, where the travelling people of Scotland were wed at the crossing of ancient roads.

Other places had simpler links to the Travellers, and were less easily romanticised. The sides of the M1, the A1, the A303 and the M25 are peppered with modern-day *atchin tans*. They are sites with access to opportunities to earn money, and – being less desirable to non-Gypsies – also the sorts of locales where less cash is needed to set up a camp. Such places symbolise the misunderstood truth of many Traveller lives, which is that they are neither permanently nomadic, nor ever truly static. Howbeit these yards provide a base, the highway is right beside them, ready for the times when family ties, work, a wedding, a funeral, the fair season, beckon. Councils refer to them as 'sites close to the key regional transport corridors, favoured by Gypsies and Travellers'. Travellers call them 'handy, being right by that main road'. Handy, yes, but still handcuffed to tragedy. Every family is haunted by stories of relatives, too often toddlers, who have been knocked down and killed by their literal closeness to roads.

As for my route, it would be influenced by all of these factors, a brew of influences from the nuances of Gypsy history that wafted me this way and that, until finally I'd join the dots and see how our dispersed and often deeply localised history might be fitted and overlayed onto the atlas of Britain.

From the beginning, I knew when I went on this journey that I would have to spend my nights in the *atchin tans*. There would be no point in simply visiting these places, getting back in my motor, and leaving. That would be no different from seeing them as everyone else did: nothing but places, some empty, some not, but all of them lacking a crucial thing: a memory of myself living there, even if only briefly. That would mean eating and sleeping in them, sometimes washing my clothes there, sometimes going back a few nights on the trot. The Scottish mountaineer and writer Nan Shepherd wrote that 'no one knows the mountain completely who has not slept on it', and I believed the same would be true of the stopping places. Unspectacular compared to snowy peaks or ancient lochs, the *atchin tans* nonetheless have something in common with these features of the landscape, in that they are often seen, but rarely dwelt in or on for any great length of time. Spending the night there would be my means of getting back on the curious wavelength of the old stopping places, to understand if there was some quality they all shared, beyond what they were used for. Was there some essence of a 'Travellers' place' that set it apart from somewhere that was just a mere parking space for the night? I had to experience the *atchin tans* at their darkest and deepest, when they were most likely to give up their secrets.

I needed to get to the stopping places, so I needed to get on the road. It was the road that connected the whole picture up, and where I might at last find out where I belonged. It was the long trail of Romany history, that ran from the place where I'd joined it in the deep south of England, to the corners of Wales, and the lowlands of Scotland where a Gypsy presence in Britain first enters the record of history. I would begin at my story's beginning, branching far out from the haunts of my family, eventually tacking my way northwards to the spot that had witnessed the entrance of Romany people on the cultural and physical landscape of Britain.

By the end I hoped to answer the questions that had been following me, on and off, all my life. What is left of the stopping places? Where are they? Who used to go there before, and who is there now? Why have I always felt it was crucial to remember them? What might we learn from them? What redemption might lie there, in a country that still passes new legislation aimed at ending the Traveller way of life? Is it still possible to live on the road? Was the end of the old Gypsy life a tragedy, or was it a case of good riddance to an irredeemably hard and pitiless life on the edge? Above all, I hoped to resolve the biggest question: the question of myself, whether I could make my peace with Gypsy culture and its love of a clean, stark line. My conflict seemed to echo the wider tension between nomads and settled people that lives on in contemporary Britain. The strife between the Gypsies and the *gorjies* might never be stilled, but in the stopping places, I hoped I might find the strength to dissolve – or accept – these old divisions that ran through both the country and myself.

But I didn't yet have all the equipment I needed to do anything about it. I had a degree, which helped me to read the books, but I hadn't received the certificate Travellers prize above all the rest – my driving licence. I needed a van – a Ford Transit, of course – which would enable me to spend long enough in these places to soak up any lessons they might have to teach. Once I had passed my test, got my van and kitted it out with the essentials of life on the road, I knew exactly where I needed to go first: to my nan, and then on to the place where for her, and so also for me, all of this had begun; a place near the old roads where we drove, years ago, with our van full of flowers and memories.

2

The Ghosts

Messenger's Meadow, Hartley Park, Butler's Down, Shalden Green

I am sitting at Nan's old kitchen table, the same table that has been here all my life. It's always here when I come back, no matter where I have been or how far I have roamed. It stows away flush next to the wall most of the time, but when needed its two sides flip up and lock into place so everyone can get round it for Sunday dinner. Nan is nearly ninety now, but every Sunday she still does a full roast with meat, stuffing and five or six different vegetables, and there's always one thing on the plate that reminds us where we came from: a Traveller's speciality, alongside all the typical English fare. This is usually a steaming, suety pudding of some kind, maximum calories for minimum cost, cooked in a clean tea towel tied up with string and simmered away for hours on the hob. It's either a 'meat pudding' – chunks of beef and offal boiled in a bowl-shaped casing of suet and flour – or a 'rasher pudding', made of streaky bacon rolled into a foot-long sausage-shaped dumpling case. Stodgy and wet when first cooked, bacon pudding soon settles into a harder form that can be sliced and taken on the road.

Back in the days of fieldwork, it was an ideal portable food: tasty and calorific, with plenty of salt to replace lost sweat. Nan lives in a bungalow now – she has been settled for nearly seven decades. With every passing day the time of the wagons and tents fades further into the past, accessible only through the memories of the oldest ones, like her.

It is late in the summer, and a small glass bowl of lime-green cobnuts, the first of the season, sits on the pristine kitchen tablecloth. I've just been outside 'spivving' the van – brushing and hoovering it out, washing down the ply lining, then restacking all my gear: cooking stuff, water jack, generator and petrol; bedding and clean clothes stowed away under the bed with my wash-bowl, as far away as possible from all the items relating to food. As I nurse a cup of tea, my mind fumbles for words to explain to Nan that I am about to go on another one of my journeys – except this time I'm even more cautious than usual, because this time it's no ordinary trip. This one is a quest for the Travellers' road. The old road. Her road. And the more I think about it, the more I realise I'm half a *dinlo*.

Dinlo – one of the Travellers' favourite words. It's both noun and adjective, and when people translate it they usually put 'fool' or 'foolish'. But its remit is wider than that. To say 'the *mush* is a *dinlo*' can mean that someone has got no common sense; that they wear strange clothes or – as it means in my case – that they have lost their grip on the most sensible way to live. Spending a year of my life obsessively tracing the places where Travellers once dwelt, and sleeping in the back of a

Transit van – I am well aware that this qualifies me as a *dinlo*. But that is what I've decided to do, so I tell Nan about it, hoping to get some sort of blessing for this bizarre undertaking of mine. But instead Nan makes us both a red-hot cup of tea, sits down opposite me, and starts talking as though I have already explained my intentions. She does this a lot. A glance at my face seems enough to tell her what she needs to know, and prompts the wisdom that I need to hear.

'The trouble is, mate, if you wasn't brought up like it, you'll never take to life on the road. There's no way you'd suffer it.' It's a gentle warning, but a warning all the same.

'See, we never knew no different than to be sat round the fire, sleeping in the tents, going and having to ask people for water. Some people wouldn't give you a cup of water, never mind let you fill up a churn to take back to the tents. And me dad was like a sergeant major, he wouldn't have no messing about in the morning, you couldn't lay in bed, there was nothing like that. Soon as he was up you had to get up, have yourself a wash; even if you had to break the ice on the water to have a wash, you still had to do it. He wouldn't let you touch nothing until you'd had a wash, washed your face and hands, wouldn't let you touch no cups or nothing until you was clean. And where we never had no toothbrushes or nothing like that, the best you had for your teeth was a bit of ash out the fire – we used to rub that into our teeth to keep 'em clean. Must have worked though, eh, mate, I've still got all my bit of teeth now – look. But we hardly never had no sweets and that did we, not like they got now.'

It doesn't take Nan long to paint a pretty convincing picture of why life on the road was tough, harder than most people now would be able to handle. I don't know why, but when she's talking about the old times, I always picture my spine being made out of plastic, like a cheap plastic knife, while hers and her brothers' were made out of iron or steel, forged in moonlight and storm. I snap out of the vision, and just as the picture is getting bleak verging on black, Nan turns, a light enters her eyes and a sadness at what we have lost in transition to living in comfort, in streets, behind brick walls and glass.

'But the thing is, mate, people used to help each other then. Didn't matter if they hardly had nothing, they'd share their last bit of food with you if they knew you was hard up. They helped bring up the kids, more or less looked out for each other, you know. And the best was the old nights at hopping time, having a sing and a dance on an old bit of board. I used to dance and play the spoons, we used to make our own entertainment. There wasn't nothing else to do, was there? We used to get round the old fire and have an old laugh and a joke. And see, nowadays you wouldn't get nothing like that. Travellers won't help each other. They wants everything, don't they? Money and holidays and that. Foolishness. All nice things at the end of the day, but they can't bring you happiness.'

Nan is spooling it out as she has done a thousand times, the old paradox that we have heard about all of our lives. The hardship of old times, versus the sense of togetherness which Travellers have lost. The gratitude for comforts that not long ago were undreamed of and unheard of, set against the moral corruption, unhappiness and constant malaise that have come from an overfast integration into the *gorjies'* consumerist world.

The word *gorjies* comes from the old Romany word *gadje* or *gadzhe*, and though its form has mutated with time, its meaning's the same: the non-Gypsies, outsiders, the people-who-aren't-us. For centuries, politicians had guessed that if Gypsies could be settled in regular housing, then within a few short generations they'd be just like everyone else. There would be no need for a word for outsiders, because we would be just like them. But that isn't what's happened. Many Gypsies now live either in housing, or on permanent caravan sites, not in meadows or lanes or lay-bys or by the sides of old tips. And yet they are still what they are, changed in some ways, but different enough to draw the old line between themselves and the *gorjies*.

I sometimes wonder what Nan thinks I am. Of course I am her great-grandson, born from her line, flesh and blood. But I'm not what she calls a 'true Traveller'. Aside from my mixed roots, I wasn't born to that life: I arrived into a changed era, one of stability, stasis, hot running water, and Christmases stacked with teetering piles of presents. The Romany bloodline never dies out. But the life of the Traveller changes, sometimes so much so that you could forgive the outside world for thinking the people themselves have vanished.

When I first got engaged to my wife Candis, an actress with Romany blood from the Traveller heartland of Kent, Nan was happy and cuddled me up. But she also waited until we were alone to tell me that under no circumstances must I try to move Candis into a caravan. 'You wasn't brought up like we was, mate,' she reminded me, 'but you did live in a trailer, when you was younger. If that girl ain't lived like it, she'll never get on in a trailer.' I listened, but wondered how hard it could actually be. Everyone lives a bit rough sometimes, I told myself. Cand lives out of a rucksack when she's on an acting job, water bottle poking out of one pocket, toothbrush in the other. Isn't trailer life basically the same thing, only endured for longer? And isn't it somehow more noble, and hence easier to bear? Isn't it just a bit closer to our roots?

But Nan was never wrong about the basic stuff of life, and anyway, this wasn't the first time I'd been warned about life on the road. A cousin of mine, who'd brought up her first child in a trailer without running water, had told me the same. 'It's one thing when you're fifteen, using that as a bedroom to run in and out of,' she said. 'But you just try eating and sleeping and cooking and cleaning, and raising a child in one, all through the seasons ... ' She didn't finish the sentence, but left the dare hanging in the air, knowing that nobody really gets it until they have done it. And by now, Nan and the rest of the family knew I was going to do it, *dinlo* or not. And they knew where I'd start: at Nan's places, the stories of which had filled my childhood. The ones orbiting Petersfield, and the belt of land circling the small town of Alton.

Unlike the famous New Forest that lies to its south, the area around the little Hampshire town of Alton is not well-known. It does not have a name that is mentioned in faraway places, printed on mass-produced postcards and sent round the world.

With its sparse network of scattered farms, fruit plantations, and outlying hamlets and villages, it would seem to most people to be a nondescript part of the countryside, a bit of rural England that's not really special in any particular way. But for the local Gypsies, my family among them, this area does have a name. It's a name that reminds us why this place is special, and why it is special to us. We call it the Hop Country.

Hampshire is not as well known for its hops as Kent, the famed 'Garden of England', where every late summer a flock of occasional workers from east London and its surrounds would come down for the hop picking. Working-class families all round the region tell tales of this time, when a wage and a holiday still coincided for some people, who were only too happy to pocket some cash for a break from the grind and 'the Smoke'. Kentish museums make a fuss of it. Small-print-run history books pick it out as a happy and picturesque industry. Even today the old oast houses poke their bright white cones from stacks of old red brick, as if the buildings themselves are proud, their noses held high in the air. Kent's hops are folklore where Hampshire's aren't. Hampshire's hop gardens are not much discussed. But they are in my family. Somebody mentions them almost every day. They keep cropping up.

Hopping time, without doubt, was the central point of the Gypsy calendar, at least in the south. Seasons revolved around September, not Christmas or Easter or the school summer holidays which variously seemed to play that role for the *gorjies*. September was the happiest, most carefree time of the year; the time when even the most strait-laced house-dweller might experience a pang of jealousy at the sight of the Gypsies, their cash-in-the-pocket economy, and how they spent almost all daylight hours outside when England was at its most languid and balmy and beautiful. They were earning good money: experts by inheritance, and by experience, at the gathering in of the hops through cold mornings and baking, outstretched afternoons. The Travellers had swagger then, too. They'd been working for months, might have bought some flash clothes. They were darkly tanned, and their skins shone with the luck of the sun. Winter was so long gone as to be half-forgotten. Who wouldn't want this version of Gypsy life?

I've never been hop picking, but the old job cast a long shadow, and I grew up there. By the time I was born, none of us picked hops for money any more. But once, when I was about six years old, we were on the way back from buying chrysants from a grower when Gran spotted a big vine of hops growing wild on a tall wire fence. We did a quick U-turn in the van and pulled over, grit under the tyres, pale gold dust puffing out behind us in miniature clouds. I jumped down from the van and went toddling across to the fence. They lifted me up and said, 'Here, Daney Doodles, just get one of them hops and rub it in your hands.' I pulled off a hop, looked at it, saw how it was so delicate, like a pine cone made of interleaved layers of crêpe paper, light, slightly cold, and as green as a sprout. Then they put me back down on the floor and I started rubbing the hop back and forth between my palms. It looked dry on the vine, but now it was moist in my hands, separated to brownish-green rubbings, a dampness half-water, half-oil.

'Now smell that,' said Grandad. I brought up my hands to my face and breathed in. I have never forgotten the smell. It was green. It was fresh. It was different from all other plants. It was sugary-sour. It smelled like something precious. I wanted to lock it up somehow and take it back with me, even though I had no idea what hops were actually for. Grandad took out a small folding knife and reached up and cut off a section of vine two feet long. It was smothered in hops. 'Here y'are,' he went, and gave it to me. It was my bit. I held on to it tight. They cut a few more lengths of vine and then we got back in the van. 'Now you know what hops look like,' said Gran. 'And isn't that a good smell.'

Nan made me a hop-pillow, too, a tiny square cushion stuffed full of dried hops that Mum would tuck in next to my pillow, the silent music of the smell of them encircling my head as I slept. The hops are supposed to aid sleep, and Travellers also believe that their smell brings on an appetite for food. 'Used to make you so hungry, the smell of the hops in the fields,' says Nan. But at least this was hunger in a happy time, a pang in the midst of fast business, a seller's market for farm workers' labour, and the busiest, most jovial part of the Travellers' year.

Nan starts up the familiar roll call of the stopping places where they had camped with their wagon and tents for generations. Messenger's Meadow, Butler's Down, Picket Twenty, the Lunways ... I register them all, but as always it's Messenger's Meadow that gets my attention. It is the one she mentions the most. Such an English name, so familiar:

the unhurried, light-heeled sprung rhythm. It exists on no map, is listed in no feudal ledgers, and I have never been there.

Nor do I have a clue where it is: I can picture it, though, like a memory, sloping and yellow with buttercups. Nan tells me how she and the family were stopped there when war was declared; how a girl in long petticoats came running over the field to say England was fighting the Germans. Even these days, when anyone mentions the war, it's the first thing I see, this place that's as far from a war as it was from the city. From the outset, it has been at the top of my list: the first place I have to head for in the van.

Messenger's Meadow was named for its owner. Mr Messenger was a farmer, well trusted by Gypsies because he employed them, with seasonal camping as part of the deal. Nan has only described Mr Messenger to me once. We were having our toast and tea in silence one overcast September morning, when a vision seemed to pass before her eyes. All of a sudden, she was back there in the 1930s:

'Old Mr Messenger lived with his mother, you know.' Her eyes narrowed a little, as if trying to focus the picture. 'They had one of the *eddest* houses we'd ever seen, massive it was. He was a tall man, ever so tall, and he always carried a long old walking stick. And he always had a fag on his lip and a drip on the end of his nose. And he used to pull up with his dear old mum in the car, a real big car with this thing like a bonnet pulled over the top. And the boys used to holler out, "Look up, here comes old Drip Nose in the motor!"'

I check the location of Messenger's Meadow with Nan, then walk outside into the late August warmth. It's still summer, but I'm nervous about the idea of sleeping in the van. The back looks about as homely as a giant toolbox, simple plywood lining over cold-looking blue steel, and I haven't put anything in the back except a sleeping bag, some sandwiches, some water for me and the van, and a change of clothes for the morning. I am unsure what I really need, if I have prioritised things correctly, but eventually I slam the door shut and drive to the garage to fill up the tank. Then I head west out of Worthing, retracing the same old road we always took to Petersfield Market. Once I get there I plan to head north for the town of Alton, stopping along the way at another of Nan's old stopping places, Hartley Park, before moving on to the little village of Holybourne just outside Alton to find Messenger's Meadow. If there's time, I'll also go to the family graves, and perhaps to the loneliest *atchin tan* of the lot, old Butler's Down. Like Mr Messenger, Old Butler was a farmer who the family worked for. I've heard even less about him, but the memories of being camped up on his windy hill in the winter storms are enough to make Nan shiver, even now.

I call into a supermarket to buy some yellow and white chrysanthemums in preparation for visiting the graves of Nan's parents and grandparents later on. Driving over Harting Hill on the approach to Petersfield, I pass the old improvised jail at its foot, where my nan's uncle Whistler was once locked up. It's a well-worn family story, but when I asked Nan why they imprisoned him there, she kept a poker face and said, 'Well,

I expect he did something they didn't like.' But Nan does remember how, unusually amongst Travellers, Whistler had a great ginger beard. I picture him spending the night hemmed in amongst the cold brick walls. He died sometime in the '30s, while still a young man.

I drive north along the old Selborne Road towards Alton until I find Hartley Park, also called Hartley Common, surprised to find that it comes up on the satnav. It's an anonymous, flat, sunken field by a farm business centre on the thin River Wey. I pull up and stare for a while at this boring expanse of grass. The road at my back is busy with the this-way-and-that whoosh of cars. In Nan's time, whole families of Travellers swore that they'd seen a spectral coach and horses crossing this park. The thought of spending the night here makes me uneasy, bland as it looks by day. Within moments I've jumped back in the van and driven off, telling myself that I'm sensible, it isn't the ghosts, it's the fact that the lay-by is shallow and that I'd be too close to the moving traffic. That's true. But it isn't the only reason I'm leaving: at this early stage on my travels, I'm nervous about stopping anywhere, and especially daunted at the prospect of spending the night near Hartley Park. I wouldn't need to see the ghosts to find myself afraid.

Nan's stories are full of ghosts, which means that whichever way I turn on my journey, they will be there with me. In their attitude to ghosts, the Travellers share much with everyone else, but they also have a cache of their own particular spooks. Alongside long-fingered Jack Frost, the pale Victorian girl long lost in the woods, and the usual mixture of headless horse-men, spectral coaches and phantom hounds, there are others which seem to exist only for us. As a kid I was warned to stay in my bed at night for fear of the Toady-ode, a curious and undescribed menace which I imagined as an evil pumpkin that walked on two horrible green slimy arms. In the wagon time my relatives had been terrified by the sound of fifty squealing pigs on a strong storm wind at Jack's Bush, an *atchin tan* on the road down to Salisbury. They'd seen the devil in the middle of the road as a ball of fire that vanished in front of their eyes.

When I reach Messenger's Meadow, it's nothing like I expected. It seems too close to the village of Holybourne, too flat and flowerless; green and empty. It was meant to be the most beautiful patch of pasture in the world, and here it is, no more than a normal field by the side of a normal road. It fills me with nothing at all, and feels like a poor beginning to my quest. I stand and stare, trying to see what I can learn. There is a sign warning people not to tamper with the earth. Be aware, there are Roman remains in the soil: important ones. I look for the stream where the Travellers used to draw water, cool in every season, so Nan said: watercress grew in its shallows, a sign traditionally taken by Travellers to mean the water is good to drink. I also heard the old ones say that if you see a frog going in and out of the water then it will be safe for drinking, but I can't test any of these theories because I can't even find the stream. Pleasant as the surroundings are, it makes me feel lonely and stupid – *divvy. Dinlo.*

I walk down a dirt trackway dividing the meadow from its neighbour. It is arced over by sycamores and alders, a cloister-like passageway. Among the trees, small birds jump and flit as they sing: my mood is lightening as I work my way into the place. There is a gap in the trees at the path's edge, and I go through it. The next field along looks more like my idea of a stopping place: high hedgerows, hollowed and sheltering, offer a place where tents could hunch and wait out winter storms. But I'm seeing with modern eyes, trailer- and house-bred, pampered, unused to spying out *atchin tans* where I might stop. And I can't get the van anywhere close to here. I wonder where Mr Messenger's house is, whether his family might still live there. Whether they might remember mine.

In lots of rural locales, these Traveller–landowner relationships go back generations, families of farmers and Gypsies who knew each other's names, the faces of each other's children. They mucked in to the same rural economy. They depended on each other. It's possible that whole dynasties of Gypsies got their English Yeoman surnames in this way. What their names were when they set out on rough barques from the coasts of Norway, Holland and Germany, who knows. But soon 'Mr Boswell's Egyptians' were just called the Boswells, the Lees, the Penfolds, the Lockes, and so on. It's tempting to draw a close parallel with slave surnames in America, but it's doubtful that the matter is as uniform or simple as that. The old Welsh Traveller family called Jones, for example, are supposed to have gotten their surname from the marriage of Alabaina Wood, a Romany girl, to a man called Jones – apparently known as *o baro gajo*, 'the giant *gorjie*'.

I spend a while longer walking around the fields, breathing in their air, in search of a different taste, a different smell. Then I sit down in the shelter of a tumbling hedge of brambles, and decide I can't stop here. There's time left in the day, and other places I need to see.

East of Holybourne, along a narrow hedge-sided road, is the tiny village of Binsted. Four generations of Nan's family lie buried in the churchyard there, which they'd pass by every year on a well-worn circuit of hop picking, hedge laying, ditch clearing, and 'stone picking up' – the back-breaking job of removing troublesome rocks from arable fields. As a little boy, up there for funerals, I could see we weren't drifters or wanderers who belonged nowhere. We were tightly attached to these places, like everyone else.

I drive to the churchyard and pull up outside: as soon as I cut the engine, the place is silent, and I am an interloper in a place I don't belong. I reach across to the passenger seat for the flowers, then walk slowly towards the graves of Nan's parents and grandparents and stand there surrounded by birdsong, hearing familiar names, and picturing faces I only know from fuzzy old black-and-white photographs. I imagine them laughing, the men knocking back pints of bitter: they would have been happy at this time of year, August, with 'hopping time' just around the corner.

Many Travellers won't drive past someone they know without calling in, briefly, for tea. It would be bad luck, tailing you like a shade up the highway. And for some of us, the same principle goes for the dead. Our extended families fan out beyond life's end, reaching long fingers of Romany presence deep into Britain's graveyards and churchyards. All cultures honour their dead, but the Romany tradition demands a heightened and cultured morbidity. The first time I watched *Who Do You Think You Are?* on television, I was amazed at how little people seemed to know of their family pasts. As a small boy I stood with my mum while she gently placed carnations into a square marble vase on my great-great-great-grandfather's grave. He had been dead over fifty years by the time I was born – there is no date on the simple wooden cross that adorns his grave – but in our family memory it might as well have been last year. Their bodies aged and tarnished, but the memories did not.

Nan's grandad is buried a mere few yards from the tomb of 'Monty': Field Marshal Bernard Law Montgomery, 1st Viscount Montgomery of Alamein, KG, GCB, DSO, PC, one of the greatest combat heroes in British history. Monty's huge stone sarcophagus casts a long shadow, but the cross on my forefather's grave pokes out of it and into the sunlight. I slide the plastic sleeves off the bunches of chrysanthemums, and tease the elastic bands from off their stems, then place them one by one in the small stone vase on the grave. I do the same at Nan's parents' grave, then go to the tap and fetch water to fill up the vases, poured from a four-pint milk container that's been left by somebody else.

Two Gypsy mantras come to my mind. The first I have heard many Travellers say: 'We don't think we're better than anyone else. But we also don't think anyone's better than us.' A favourite phrase of Nan's follows: 'We all end up in the same place, all boxed up, at the end of the day.'

I drive away from Binsted to Butler's Down, angry at myself for going back and forth instead of keeping to a neat, circular route. Butler's Down lies even further away from the traffic of twenty-first-century life than Binsted. It sits half a mile back from Holybourne church, and rises up windswept and lonely out of the land. I walk up the hill slowly, crows cackling after me, and in places the mud seems to grab and clutch my boots: even in summer, the ground remembers to live up to its treacherous reputation. This is a place where Nan still returns in bad dreams: it's an exposed spot, high and right out in the wind, with only a small copse offering paltry shelter. 'We had a terrible life,' Nan told me once, whilst remembering the camp at Butler's Down. 'We was like slaves, really, mate.'

I stand still for a while in the ocean of wind and picture them carrying churns full of water uphill. If times were tight and there wasn't a churn or a water jack, they'd have to take buckets instead, with nothing but a few sprigs of young ash leaves in the top to keep the water inside. It was a precarious job which nobody wanted and everyone still had to do. If they tripped and spilled the water at any point on the long walk back to the tents, it was miles back to beg for more, and in all likelihood the person in charge of the water would think you were lying and be disinclined to have mercy for your mistake.

I trudge back down the hill, past apple trees gnarled into claws by the winds of previous winters. There's no way I'm stopping here, but the light is fading. The next place will be my lot.

Shalden Green is the last *atchin tan* I find, out north from Alton, the most isolated of all the places so far. As the sun goes down I trundle towards it along an old lane, lined on one side by a very old-looking flint wall covered in dark moss. Nan was born here in January 1927, in a Reading wagon caught in a snowdrift. The doctor walked miles from the little town of Alton to deliver Nan. 'He said to me dad, you've got a baby girl, now make me a nice cup of tea,' as she always says: a rare happy memory from a time when a winter birth often meant the death of a Traveller child.

I can't be sure that I've found the right place, but it seems as though it ought to be here. A ditch, about two feet deep, has been dug around its perimeter, between the verge and what is now the brambled ground where I suspect the wagons used to stand. A height restrictor ('pikey barriers', some people call them) overhangs the way in. Most of the *atchin tans* look like this now: restricted access, used for nearly nothing. Fastened against the people who, for many generations, had made them their occasional homes, where fires once burned and people tap-danced and sang.

To my surprise, the stopping place is now home to a single Highland cow, massive, long-horned and orange. It's so far south of its native habitat I see it as an omen though its meaning is unclear. It stares at me across the ditch as it stoically chews the cud. I stare back and take some photos as the sky begins to lower, darkening, spoiling my pictures. Static is palpable in the sky. As I get back in the van, I notice a sign on a fence post: 'YOUR DOG COULD BE SHOT IF FOUND AMONGST LIVESTOCK.'

Behind the storm clouds, the sun is lighting a final, thin red charge along the blurry line of the autumn trees. I think of Nan's first night on earth a few yards from this spot, nearly ninety years ago, couched in a wagon beneath the falling snow. No snow is falling now, and the air is still and warm. I crawl into my sleeping bag and roll up a pair of jeans for a pillow. The storm that seemed to be threatening does not arrive, and the place is soundless. In spite of the feeling of trepidation that comes with spending this first night in the van, I huddle against the cool air, and eventually fall asleep.

3

The Gypsies
Gravesend, Horsmonden

It's the first day of autumn. I've just pulled over to the side of the road, and plucked a sweet chestnut leaf from the grille of the van. A few miles back, driving, I watched it fall down from its tree and into our path. It fell in a long, lilting zigzag; I noted it, drove on, forgot it in a moment. But now I've pulled over and here it is, stuck in the grille. I am suddenly sad. Autumn's not here in full, but it must have arrived. I am holding it here in my hand, like a parchment letter announcing its coming, blown here from a faraway land.

It's only September, but when the clouds pass the sun there's a nip in the air. Then the sun spills back out of the sky, generous as a harvest, and brushes the thought of winter away for a while.

Once I've stretched my legs I return to the van and before long we're moving again. My wife Candis sits in the passenger seat, a little folding mirror cupped in her palm in front of her face. She stares into the mirror like it's a portable oracle, wide-eyed, as her other hand applies thick black mascara to her lashes with deft little strokes. I'm scared when Cand's doing her make-up. The thought of hitting a pothole, slamming on the brakes or swerving to miss a pheasant makes me prickle with fear. We're living pretty rough; the least I can do is provide a smooth drive so she can do her make-up en route. I drive well under the speed limit. A black BMW drifts out behind me, gains speed, drifts back in, does it again. Eventually it overtakes, angry that we are so slow in its hurrying world.

Candis is from Kent, but not the same Kent that we are driving towards. She is from Gravesend, in the north of the county, a town on the River Thames where it widens out, twenty-five miles or so east of London.

With its nearby motorway and high-speed train to London's King's Cross, Gravesend should be a major commuter town, but it isn't: the morbid name and low-down-the-estuary status combine to frighten people from elsewhere in England, yet it remains a traditional first stop for newcomers to the UK. Recent decades have seen large numbers of Sikhs arrive in Gravesend, where they have built the largest Sikh temple in Europe. Since then they have been followed by East Europeans, including the Roma.

I have managed to speak to Roma people in Gravesend a few times. Normally it's the kids who will talk; they are more curious and less cowed by the questions of strangers. One night I was waiting in the street next to my friend Tegh's car, rolling a cigarette, when three boys came up on bikes to admire the ride.

'Whose car is that?' says the eldest, talking in Romani to his mates. I know that my grammar is bad but I answer him anyway.

'*Lesko mobili*' – His car, I say. I nod in the direction of Tegh, who is Sikh, and looks far more like a Rom from Eastern Europe than I do. I look nothing like these Roma kids, but here I am speaking their language; my friend looks a lot more like them but does not speak a word of it. We must make a funny combination. One of the boys gets nervous and instantly pedals away; but the other two stay, and the eldest one speaks again.

'Where are you from?'

'*Akathe. England.*' – Here. England, I say, pointing to the ground at my feet.

'*Rom san?*' – You are Roma? he asks.

I continue in faltering Romani. 'I am. You know there are pale Roma here?'

'I know. I know ... ' His voice trails off. The conversation is weird, or my grammar is bad, or I am too white. Whatever it is – most likely, a touch of all three – I can see the curiosity fade in his eyes, and reticence starts to replace it.

His friend says, 'Let's get out of here,' or something similar. They've switched to a language I don't understand, most likely Slovak. They get back on their bikes and speed off up the street.

I think back to my earliest recollections of hearing the Romani words. The sun is out. I leave my little three-wheeled bike on the patio and toddle into the kitchen. I climb up to sit on a chair, and my feet don't reach the floor. Nan describes the dinner she's cooking: '*mass, canni, puvvies, shok* an' *coggi'* – meat, chicken, potatoes, cabbage and swede. '*Kushti*,' says Nandad – lovely. Steam rises from the pots into the bright air.

Exchanges like this, simple Sunday conversations about good food, do not get heard by people outside the family. When non-Gypsies do hear Romani spoken, it's more likely that it's being used to conceal something. This is one reason why the Romani language has a lengthy association with dodgy dealings. It seems obvious that any criminal who speaks a second language is going to use it to make himself harder to catch. But in the Gypsies' case it is often implied that the language itself is a criminal thing; that it exists to be the tongue of thieves. In September 2011, BBC News ran a story entitled *Gypsy dialect in the spotlight after Kent court case*. It began by pointing out – accurately enough – that words like 'chav', 'mush', 'cushti' and 'wonga' were Romani words 'that have embedded themselves into the English vocabulary'. (The character of Del Boy from the TV show *Only Fools and Horses* wasn't a Gypsy, but his use of Romani words testifies to the influence of Gypsy culture on the London working class.) The article continued:

But few people would guess their origins belong to a sixteenth-century Romany Gypsy dialect still spoken by some travellers today … sometimes called 'rokker' after the Romany verb to talk … It has been recently put under the spotlight during the trial of a drug-dealing gang in Kent. An expert had to be called in to give the jury an overview of the dialect used by two of the defendants who were later convicted.

Referring to modern 'Angloromani' as a sixteenth-century dialect is curious: it's like referring to Scottish Gaelic as a fourth-century language, instead of simply 'a language'. But in spite of its flaws, the news report flows back into my understanding of the brief conversation with the Gravesend Roma kids. Our language, or languages, conspire to tell a tale of something important: Kent's recent Romany immigrants are exactly that, its *recent* Romany immigrants. Whilst it is impossible to say exactly when the first Gypsy set foot in Kent, we can surmise based on the recorded presence of the Romany language in nearby Sussex by 1542 that there were Gypsies there by the first half of the sixteenth century. Kent's latest Roma arrivals, all of them housed and speaking two or three languages fluently, seem so different from their paler and often trailer-dwelling English Gypsy neighbours that you could be forgiven for failing to see a connection at all, as some on both sides do. But these two groups, in one degree or another, are descended from the same nomads who left Rajasthan in the eleventh century AD.

Not everybody believes this, of course. North Kent is a hotbed of a curious English pastime: moaning about Gypsies whilst simultaneously denying they're Gypsies at all. The line usually doled out in the pubs and clubs of Gravesend is that while there are definitely 'true Gypsies' out there, most of the people in the town who profess to be Romanies are really 'what we call pikeys'. 'They like to call theirself Travellers, but they ain't proper Gypsies at all'. Always fascinated by ethnographic expertise, I sometimes ask the people who make this claim which 'pikey' families they're talking about. I am offered surnames like Eastwood, Ripley, Fuller, Baker, Coates, Friend, Jones and Vine, all of them Romany families as 'proper' as any other.

The Kent we are heading to now is a different place entirely from the riverside Kent of Gravesend. This is the Kent of strawberry farm and orchard, far from the sea and the lumbering Thames, from where London with its glass towers cannot be seen; where its fusty, diesely air can't be smelt. Horsmonden is in south-west Kent, smack bang in the Weald by the old road from Maidstone to Lamberhurst. A back-world of the south, land of brambles and dragonflies. This is the Kent that was once called the Garden of England: not just for its neatly kept hedges and fields, but, as my late friend Simon Evans – musician, broadcaster and friend of the Gypsies – explained, because Kent was the county charged with the feeding of London: it was therefore also the 'market garden' of England.

In this context, the village of Horsmonden – which is where we are headed – is something of an anomaly. It had more to do in the past than the growing of fruit, hops and vegetables. It was once home to ironworks, is the site of an important mediaeval foundry, and in the more distant past had been known for its horsemen: the name Horsmonden is derived from the Anglo-Saxon for 'horse farmer's valley'. So it seems appropriate that it should be the site of one of the bigger Romany horse fairs in the south-east. When I was little I remember some Travellers calling it Horseman's Den: a mishearing, yes, but an apt one that tunnels by accident into the deep history of the place. And I like to think that at least some horseshoes must have been made in the days of the ancient foundry.

When I was small, Horsmonden was a typical Travellers' horse fair. This meant that most people weren't actually there for the horses. It's true that a core of those who came, mostly men but quite a few women as well, were 'proper horse people'. They came towing their 'boxes' with strong cobs standing inside, tethered in the half-light; their two-wheeled sulkies – light trotting carts with a seat big enough for one or two people – and their harness, head collars and whips. They left trails of horsemanship in their wake: odd strands of straw here and there, and small piles of horse shit. But most people weren't of this ilk. They came from far and near to the fair, and they weren't interested in any equine displays. If they were, then it was simply because they provided an authentic backdrop. What they were interested in depended on the individual: but mostly, they were interested in each other.

The young came along for the 'sparkin'': an old Travellers' word for flirtation. It captures the static and fizz of brash, nervy teenage attempts to strike up a romance. 'Sparkin'' goes hand in hand with the crackle of sultry skies in the summer and autumn, weather that heats up the body and threatens hot rain. At the fairs I'm reminded that we are a small and conservative people, who still think young marriage is better than cycles of heartbreak and tearful confessions. We depend on the horse fairs to meet. It is a quirk of our scatteredness: a few hundred thousand people at most, flecked across Britain's damp islands, and we meet mostly at weddings, funerals and fairs. The horse trade has its ups and downs – as I write this, it's down, the worst in my lifetime. But the fairs will persist, because their purpose goes beyond trade. When the days are hot and tanned skins gleam with sweat in the sun, it's clear once again that horse fairs are shop windows for young brides and husbands. They always have been. This much, at least, is gospel, and proudly announced to journalists and inquisitive souls who come asking questions about the culture. But not every dalliance ends in a marriage, and rumours occasionally flare of unauthorised, ultra-brief flings at the fringes of fairs: dangerous liaisons that lead to bad names, fights, or worse, feuds that run on and on.

For the not so young, what they seek from each other is something subtler, less clear to outsiders, but an equally powerful draw down the road to the fair. I suspect few would want to explain what it was, for fear of sapping its power by giving it voice. What the fairs offer is a chance to track the progress of our lives; to reminisce about previous years when we trod the same field, but equally to remark on how far we have come; to exchange a joke, or even simply a wink, with our contemporaries, a look that says 'remember how we were, and look at us now'; a glance that honours the past and present and future. People come there with their children, and possibly also their grandchildren. Dressed to the nines in Harris Tweed jackets and tan brogue boots, or calf-high riding boots for the women, with the 'littl'uns' safely couched in prams covered by lace parasols, we browse the markets and waft amongst the attention of our peers, never staring, but always aware that everyone's here on parade. We polish and dress up our lives for the day and compare them to the lives of others, affirming their context, confirming their meaning. The fairs are where we remind ourselves who we are. It's not that we don't keep being who we are in between – of course we do. But the fairs provide a special concentration of Traveller experience; a tincture of what it is to be a Gypsy. At a horse fair we get to see, just for one day, what life would be like if the world shared our Gypsy priorities.

And then there are those who despise both horses and the fairs. For some families, the horse had its day a long time ago. I once asked my mate Charles if he and his family used to go to the fairs up north, which is where he comes from. He looked at me as though the question was perverse. 'We don't mind a day at the races, but Damian, can you see me or me dad, or any of us here, fucking about with horses? My great-great-grandad was a proper Gypsy man, and he was driving a Rolls-Royce a hundred year ago.' He finishes up with a dig at the South Country Travellers: 'The way you lot carry on, sometimes you'd think news of the combustion engine never got that far south.' I laugh, but beneath the friendly smiles, an ember of the old north–south rivalry gleams.

Back in the 1980s and '90s, a big part of the draw of Horsmonden Fair was the market, especially for women. Travellers have always had a love for certain goods that are otherwise

quite hard to come by in day-to-day life. Some have a practical association with caravan living, such as highly polished
stainless-steel water jacks, wash-bowls and churns. These are
essential kit if you don't have running water in your trailer.
They keep water cold; they last years and don't tarnish; they're
easy to clean, and when buffed and shined they broadcast your
cleanliness like an advertisement, glinting with silvery light.
Then there are the stalls selling crystalware, glasses and fruit
bowls and statues, and 'flash' china dinner sets and tea services,
made by traditional porcelain firms like Royal Crown Derby,
Royal Worcester and Aynsley. These are coveted not just for
their cash worth, but the way they reflect the wider Gypsy
and Traveller look. Few companies actually make things with
Romany people in mind. Instead, a Gypsy aesthetic has been
woven together from various items that match the tint and
tone of our view of the world: generous gilding; plates finished
with still-life paintings displaying the wealth of the harvest;
scroll patterns and diamonds and droplets like golden rain.
Other popular items are lace – tablecloths and net curtains,
especially – and white muslins for drying the dishes. The taste
for these things is partly born of sheer habit; partly the way
they allow no mistake to be made when it comes to their
cleanness. A dark dishcloth might mask a number of sins, but
a white muslin speaks for itself.

Finally there are the elaborate outfits for small children: 'grown
up'-looking three-piece tweed suits, braces and caps for the
boys; fancy lace-trimmed dresses of silk and smocked fabrics
for the girls. Other trends have peaked and passed on since I

was a kid. Mohair jumpers with embroidered patches of silk and pearlescent fabric were in then for girls, and some of the boys wore trilby hats and little leather jackets that have since gone out of style. All this stuff drew the custom of Travellers from all over the region, but it was of no use to a kid, and there were rarely any stalls selling toys. A horse fair is one of those things, like the taste of beer, or an hour spent admiring a view, which a child simply cannot appreciate. It's funny to think nowadays of how I'll drive five hundred miles to a horse fair that, once, I'd have done anything in my power to avoid.

I didn't look forward to horse fairs back then. I loved our own horses and ponies, but there were so many at the fairs that their glory was sapped: my favourite animals became a crowd, no different from people. The big horsemen bred so many cobs that not even their children could have names for all of them. And there was little else at these events to interest a child: besides the few stalls that sold ice creams and candyfloss, I never saw anything at them I wanted. Once in the early '90s, Dad went up to Appleby Fair with Grandad, Nandad and some relations and friends. He returned with a plastic bag for me: inside was a Dracula action figure, blister-packed on a piece of coloured card. I thanked Dad for it, then took it into my bedroom and cried: not because I didn't like it, but because it showed how much he loved me. I thought Dad must have wasted his whole weekend scouring the place to find me a present, the only toy at the fair.

Some fairs have many names. The Great Dorset Steam Fair is popular with Travellers for its classic cars, lorries and the odd heavy horse. It's a sprawling tapestry of fields full of everything that exists in the countryside edgelands. There are fat-scented burger vans, tack stalls and tents full of chromed-up post-war heirloom motorbikes. Vast 'auto jumbles' cover whole fields. They are graveyards for cars, infinite boxes of nuts and wing mirrors and pistons that smell of rain after a dry spell, picked over by old men with gazes like vultures and untranslatable mindfuls of engines and gears. The main attraction is the funfair itself, partly powered by Victorian Showmen's steam engines, gilded and burnished and smothered in twisted brass. Their keepers wear flat caps and overalls, shovelling coal in the fiery maws of their treasured machines alongside their sons and grandsons. Endless market stalls flap in the dust of the Dorset crosswinds. The fair takes place not far from the Dorset town of Blandford Forum every September. Nobody but the organisers seems to refer to it by its official and cumbersome name, the 'GDSF'. To us it has always been 'Blandford'. To Showman families who had been going there decades, it was called 'Stourpaine Bushes' after a spot further west where it used to be held. A few attendees called it 'Tarrant Hinton Fair', after the rustically double-barrelled name of the nearest village. I once met an old timer there who simply called it 'the *Fair*', with a growling emphasis that seemed to suggest all other supposed 'fairs' were but pale imitations. He had silver sideburns that stuck out an inch from his face, and had been going there for years with his Scammel 'mechanical horse' – a bizarre-looking early tractor from the 1930s. It looked as though the front of an American streetcar had been surgically cut off and stuck on the three-wheeled chassis of a Robin Reliant. His 'horse' was burgundy-coloured, with an immaculate new paint job. I remember reckoning at the time that he was the oldest farmer I'd ever met, and this weird machine could well have belonged to his grandfather. It was surprising to think that the mechanisation of agriculture had begun so far back in the past. To Travellers it was the still-recent scapegoat for everything: the amoral and inevitable creeping phenomenon that had robbed us of our place.

As we near Horsmonden we come to a T-junction, guarded by an old phone box half lost in the claws of the hedgerow. I pull over to get a better look at it. Long years of uneven sunshine have marbled its reds, which are flaking in places, oddly pristine in others. One side is still in good nick, but the other side's windows are smashed out completely, aside from a few tiny lingering teeth of dull glass. The hedgerow is piling up to the top like a breaking wave, and a bramble has started to take over inside. I gingerly pick up the heavy black phone and put it to my ear, consulting its entrails of wire. The distant continuous bleep is still there, like an archive recording of the moment England's heart rate failed. I replace the phone on its hook and close the door, suddenly spooked by this thing that is smashed but still works, a survivor from some other time, still clinging on.

We had set out too late. By the time we get to Horsmonden the sun is beginning to hang in the west and the crowd has started to thin out. The fair takes place on the village green, a square of grass not much more than half an acre. Proud old English houses press in tightly on two of its sides. The main roads on the other two sides aren't wide, either, so the arrival of a few hundred Travellers has transformed the village. While the villagers' cars appear to be tucked away on their drives, the roads are lined with spotless pickups and vans, perching two wheels up on kerbs and grass verges. Almost all of them bear some small sign of customisation – chrome covers on door handles; leatherette bonnets; a sun visor above the windscreen like the ones kids wore in the '80s. A few policemen and women are standing around in pairs, arms folded or hands clasped in front of them as if they were fringe presences at a wedding. The men wear tall helmets, the women wear caps, and they all sport the same bored, time-to-go-home-now faces. I can see in their eyes that it's just been a run-of-the-mill horse fair: most likely nothing has happened, except horses standing and eating and shitting and Travellers mooching about with their families. If something had kicked off the atmosphere would be different. More police would be here, looking more vigilant. Maybe a journalist might have turned up. At Horsmonden nowadays, such things are rarer than rare. It's linked to the fact that everyone here is stone-cold sober. Every pub in the village is closed.

Not long ago, Kent was infamous among Romany people for the 'NO TRAVELLERS' signs in its pub windows. Unlike the oft-referenced 'NO BLACKS, NO DOGS, NO IRISH' signs of the '60s, they were still around when I was a kid, and are occasionally still seen today. They crop up with the frequency of bad storms: here in a Wrexham bar in 2008; there in a Blackburn ice rink in 2012. In 2013 Traveller activists had to request that one be removed from a pub just off London's Holloway Road. Pub landlords often launch 'common sense' defences of the signs. They argue from the manager's discretion to refuse service and, when expedient, that 'Travellers' clearly refers to a 'lifestyle' and not to a race.

In 2000, the then Home Secretary Jack Straw signed an order to ban Horsmonden Fair after locals claimed it had outgrown the village. His decision followed remarks he had made about Traveller criminality on BBC radio the previous year. 'Many of these so-called Travellers seem to think that it is perfectly OK for them to cause mayhem in an area, to go burgling, thieving, breaking into vehicles, causing all kinds of trouble, including defecating in the doorways of firms and so on, and getting away with it,' he said. There were protests and the following year the fair was restored, but after a different fashion. Nowadays there is little to draw those who aren't into horses. The market is gone, bar a few stalls that sell tack and harness, and a couple of converted trucks selling chips and other fast food.

I amble up to a burger truck manned by three women who look as though they're ready to pack up and leave. The oldest one, piercing blue eyes and no make-up, hair tied back into a cascade of silvery curls, steps forward to serve me. 'Yes, my young man?' She's a Traveller, she's got the old twang in her voice. I order a cheeseburger and a can of Coke, hand her a fiver. Without needing to look, she slides a metal spatula under the sizzling patty. There is a slicing sound of steel on griddle before she flops it into a cheese-lined white bun, then nods in Candis's direction.

'Nothing for your lady? You're an 'andy chap, ain't ya!'

'She'll have to fight me for it,' I say.

'Well, go on then, get your shirt off and get in the middle of that green!' She gestures with the spatula at a space between a few horseboxes. Everyone laughs. I take my greasy dinner and we walk off to have a look round what's left of the fair, but it's slipping away into the evening before our eyes. A broad-shouldered man in a green tweed body-warmer over a T-shirt encourages a black-and-white mare up into one side of a partitioned horsebox. The other side's empty. He lifts up the tailgate and closes it, takes out a big wad of notes, counts out a couple of hundred quid and hands it to his boy. They part without words, then get back into opposite sides of their truck and roll off, leaving nothing but pressed grass tyre tracks in their wake.

I am back at the fair, and this time I am ten years old. We've had to park at the foot of a hill, but my great-grandad's legs are bad. He asks me for a hand and leans on my shoulder as we make our way slowly up. He's doing his best, with a stick in one hand, but I'm not a big child and I struggle to aid him. I'm not even sure if I'm helping: his weight is cumbersome, and I am weak. Up we go anyway, an odd couple, sixty years apart, one struggling with his youth and the other with his age. We get to the top, though, and he quietly says he is sorry and then, 'Thank you, my mate.' Proud to have managed to help him get where he is going, I push my skinny chest out and am strong for the rest of the day.

My great-grandad – whom we called Nandad because he was married to Nan – had one sole obsession in life, and that was his horses. Aside from family photographs, the only figurative depictions in his home were equine: paintings, china figurines, and two great, heavy horse heads carved from oak that he and Nan used as tables to rest their teacups on. He had a chest of drawers full of video tapes of the fairs: Wickham, Stow-on-the-Wold, Horsmonden, Ballinasloe over in Ireland, and the daddy of them all, Appleby in the far north. They were all about two hours long, shot on unstable home video cameras, with no editing but the haphazard cuts of the pauses made by the cameraman. The footage was scratchy and riven with lines, and the poor sound quality made it a challenge to concentrate.

There was no context or storyline either, simply a pixelly logo on the title screen that confirmed, in spite of the terrible quality, that this was a product someone had actually made. The film itself would be one or two hours of men and horses standing around in cordoned-off market-town streets, with a rider or driver occasionally trotting by to loud shouts of 'Ayayayayay!!' The eras were different – the '70s ones featured braces and flared cords and mutton-chop sideburns; the '90s ones silk shirts and greasy pop-star-esque mullet haircuts – but the pattern was always the same. As a young kid I found them so boring I struggled to be in the room while these tapes played. But Nandad loved them, and we never stopped buying them for him until he at last lost interest in the weeks leading up to his end.

Where the rest of the world saw a crowd of anonymous horses, munching the grass of a verge with all the interesting-ness of a passing cloud, he saw his passion kaleidoscoped into fractals of thrilling complexity. The build of each colt, its poten-tial, its strength; its balance; the hidden coiled spring of its speed; the stance of the mares and their hips, how they'd carry a foal with great trouble or sauntering ease. He could judge the fetlocks of the colts when they were no more than misty little wisps of hair that wafted off the backs of their ankles like threads of spider web, and see which ones would transform in a few short years into glorious pearlescent feathering that would give majesty and kingliness to the young stallion in his bucking and muscle-bound pomp. The rest of us had all 'been round horses', but Nandad was 'horsey', a proper horseman who knew breeding and 'stamp' – character and stance, temperament, things that only came out with time. He traded in futures: could spot the potential in stick-legged foals, knew the fey gaits of those that were simply too weak: liabilities in the long run.

But I had to read all of this in his face, in the focus and stare of his eyes, and the weighing-things-up cog-work that was ticking behind them. He never said much, not wanting to come across as a showing-off, know-all type like some other horsemen. But he was serious, his seated reflection a-glint in the glass and mahogany cabinet filled with dozens of treasured and blemish-less Beswick china horses he'd acquired over dozens of years. The horse was inextricable from his soul. In ancient times he might have been called *graimengro* – horseman – or possibly some subtly different form with a localised drawl. Sometimes I wish I had told him that, and asked him what he thought of those noble words, lost in a time when the piston surged ahead of the strutting cobs he had loved all his life. For his part, Nandad never left the epoch of the horse – it was a better time, a simpler time, a time in which he fully belonged, and he drove his van slowly, apparently reluctant to go any faster than the speed of a good trotting cob.

A Gypsy's attachment to the idea of the horse can survive the indefinite absence of the real thing. Concrete horses' heads adorn the gateposts of many a Romany's home – including Nan's – regardless of whether the occupants have owned a horse in years. The old set of family harness – dried and brittle through want of use, and too far gone to be healed even by the magic of expensive neatsfoot oil – still hangs on a peg in the garage and will probably never be sold. Out of sight most of the time, revered and useless, it is held in its place by a superstition so old that nobody feels the need to express it in words. When I was small and we lived only yards from our animals, Dad would sit drawing sketches of Grandad's horses all evening, even after he'd spent hours mucking them out, smoking cigarette after cigarette as he tried to master the circles of their pectorals and rears, the knobbled lines of their legs in shifting, restless strokes of pastel and charcoal.

Dad became a full-time artist but when he was younger he'd try his hand at whatever work was going to make a few quid, including selling flowers on one of the family pitches, and doing the odd bit of roofing. I remember him wincing with pain one night as he drew the horses, his right palm recently gashed by a falling slate – someone had thrown it from the roof and, for a laugh, shouted' 'Catch!' To their dismay, Dad had looked up too late and instinctively caught it. He didn't draw as many animals later on, working mostly on old maps instead, but he still had tattoos of horses on his chest, his arms and legs, totems kept under wraps most of the time, but Dad knew they were there, like his memories of them snorting and munching alongside our chalet as I slept in a little basket on the floor. Many people love horses, but for the Gypsies there was more: not only the carts they depended on for their liveli-hood, but their homes themselves were once designed to be physically attached to a horse, the wagon shafts gently curving as if they remembered and yearned for its muscular shape. The names of the horses who pulled the old wagons and flat carts – Dolly, Janey, Jimmy, Baby Boy – are recalled with emotion as if they were part of the family, which is unsurprising, because without them, my family would have gone nowhere.

I finish my burger and amble around the fair. I see a face I recognise: a wealthy Travelling man in his seventies who's an old friend of the family. He owns shops and land all over the south and is respected as a 'dealing man' whom you wouldn't want to cross: Grandad once told me he 'ain't backwards in coming forwards', a euphemism for someone who understands how to use his fists. I catch his eye and am just about to say, 'Alright, uncle?' when he breaks eye contact and walks straight past. I can't tell whether he's being funny or simply doesn't recognise me without my elders around. Nobody in the world except me knows that this has just happened, but I am *ladged up* – ashamed – all the same. Some sort of spell has been broken, and the motors are pulling off quickly now. Soon they'll all be gone.

After a while there's just one pickup left. It's brand new, sitting high on big wheels, 'fully loaded' with extras, parked right in the centre of the green. It is surrounded by men, magnetised to this final stand of the fading fair, all ages, all well groomed. The smooth runs over the rough and tough.

One aspect of the Gypsy look always seems to stay the same, though the shirts and blouses loosen and tighten over the years, and the cuts of the dresses and trousers shift and alter. What doesn't change is the clean-cut, pristine, box-fresh style, with nods to the 1950s, typified by the wet-look, swept-back hair-styles of a large number of the men. It goes hand in hand with the politics, the morals, the atmosphere; with a clean-cleft gender divide; with the songs of Elvis, Patsy Cline, Dolly Parton and the Arizona gunfight-balladeer, Marty Robbins. It is a playlist for hard-up lovers, for outlaws slung in the jailhouse, and it echoes through the memories of every Gypsy wedding for fifty years.

The fading of the 'wagon-time' intersected with the mass availability of radios and affordable record players, whilst petrol generators and the batteries from lorries and pickups offered the portable electricity needed to run them. Where previously traditional singing accompanied by the fiddle, squeezebox and spoons had ruled the day, alongside step-dancing to hornpipe rhythms on old salvaged bits of wood, the Gypsy baby-boomers threw their arms and hearts wide open for yodelled railroad blues, rockabilly and country-and-western music. Post-war Americana, especially that which came from the southern states, chimed with the Gypsy experience more than anything that was being produced in Britain at the time. Rich but samey voices sang of heartache, horses, open spaces, wagon trains and trucks and plains, harsh lawmen and their brave but outnumbered Indian quarries, all camped out under the stars. It began a trans-continental attachment that's been there all my life, and which, in spite of my will, I can't shake off. Search for 'Gypsy music' on the internet and you'll hear the enticing sound of guitars from Spain to Belgium, Russia to France; the cimbaloms, violins and mournful double basses of the Carpathians. But that wasn't what Gypsy music meant in my world. It was Romany women filling amber-lit nights in pubs with Anne Murray's 'Snowbird', and men in boots and braces crooning Jimmie Rodgers's laments for lonesome trains.

The men have formed a last stand of the fair, and they're having a deal. I can't yet tell what it's for – it could be the truck they're gathered around – but it's got them excited.

One shouts out, 'Go on, *chavi*, give him the deuce!'

Another, 'Go on, *del* him the two hundred quid back.'

The deal has stalled over 'luck money'. Once a price is agreed, there's another negotiation over how much cash the buyer should get back in his hand for good luck. It's a customary denouement of which the culture cannot let go. There is an old aversion to paying the full advertised price for anything, and the bigger the item, the bigger the buyer's distaste at having to cough up the lot. Even when the price has been agreed in a deal, it's still seen as 'the price' and the buyer therefore wants something back in his hand to sweeten it up; to show that the seller isn't begrudging or overly miserly. This is 'luck money', and I doubt it will ever die out amongst entrepreneurial Travellers. It's a haggling culture, and failing to barter is seen as out of the ordinary, and possibly a sign of weakness.

The seller's reluctant, though. He waves a hand up as if to call off the deal. This elicits a minor uproar. 'Ahhhhhh, come on, *mush!*' And 'Ah, don't be a *minge!*' This is the final moment of the fair, and a non-end to this deal would mark a bad start to the dark half of the year. There is slapping of backs and laughter and shouts of 'Come on.' Then at last the seller says, 'Ah fuck it, go on then,' and reaches an arm alongside the bright gleam of the truck in the faltering sun. There's a slap and a shake of the hand and a cheer mixed from words: 'That's it!' 'There y'are!' 'That's the way!' and the like. Laughing, the men turn their backs and walk off in their twos and threes, towards all the directions of the compass. I don't see anybody get in the truck, yet it starts with a thrum and drives off all the same. Last to walk away, slowly, are two old *mushes* – I see them smiling and chuckling, shaking their heads. They know the deal.

Seeing the two old men reminds me of how the old men were when I was small. Most of them were physically feared as late as their seventies, which enabled them to act as guardians of the mood. They 'wouldn't suffer no messing', which meant they made sure that laughing and joking didn't veer off course into crudeness or disrespect. In spite of their age, their judgements were not to be taken lightly. As Travellers look on at the world from their perch at the rim of society, so I remember Nan's brothers at weddings, sitting around tables at the edge of the dance floor like arbiters of the peace, staring out with grim expressions from under the brims of their trilby hats. They say the last thing a footballer loses is his touch, which remains long after his joints and his fitness are gone: likewise, an old Travelling man might have diabetes, arthritis, poor sight, but if he's within range his time-hardened fists and quickness practised over the decades might still catch and shatter a mouthy fool's jaw unawares. Many drunk young fellas have come unstuck against a man three times their age. I was always taught to beware a left hand outstretched towards your chest, as if in a friendly or calming gesture. It could be a boxer's touch in disguise, the gentle move of a serious man who's already lost his patience. Once the leading left hand gets its distance, then the right will find its mark, regardless of whether the puncher is old, or even going blind: it won't make any difference if he's seen it all before.

The green is now empty of horses and vehicles, but a few stragglers remain. Cand and I are sitting on a bench at the edge of the green, shaded by huge oak trees. Some small boys are messing about with their horsewhips and half-heartedly playing chase. I notice there are a few bits of rubbish strewn around: paper bags smeared with ketchup, Coke cans, polystyrene cups, plastic cutlery. Then, as if my thought itself had summoned her, the silver-haired woman from the burger truck strides up and asks the young boys to clear up the mess that's been left. Her request is firm, but delivered as though it's quite clear this is something they'll be proud to do.

Whips in hand, they quickly jog round and pick up the last flecks of litter. In a few minutes there's nothing left but odd wisps of hay and straw, amid horse manure strewn about in patches like abandoned games of bowls. The burger truck's packed up and gone. As we walk back to the van, the local kids gingerly roll up on pushbikes, reclaiming the green before dusk, for another year.

4

The Darkness
Gipsy Hill, Fulham

It is full-blown autumn: the leaves of the horse chestnut are copper-coloured and curled. I pull up in Rosendale Road, Gipsy Hill. The second I cut the engine, a conker falls down onto the roof of the van with a donk. I move forward a few yards, out of reach of the tree. There's a postbox, a sports field down in a dip to the right giving green reflected autumn light, space and air. This is one of those precious London streets with no road markings: they're already rare and will soon be extinct in the wild. The road has speed humps that will limit the pace of the night-time traffic: this is a good stopping place.

My mate William told me a while back that he thought there were people living here in campers or horseboxes, and that he'd seen rubbish build up and get cleared, in a manner somehow suggestive of nomadic living. There are two vans just ahead of me, one 'Luton'-type with the front of its box body jutting out over the cab, and one regular camper, twenty years old, but still clean. I can't see anyone around.

I could knock on the doors of these vehicles. But I won't. I'm still at the stage where I wouldn't want anyone knocking on mine.

I'm getting used to living in the van, and with every passing night I care less whether anyone sees me going in and out. I am more afraid of stopping in the city, where signs, lines and the agents of authority seem to be everywhere. But I rationalise my fears: you are just another bloke going in and out of a van, and even if someone is suspicious, what are they going to do? The van itself changes a little every day as I adjust it to my needs. I've put up a thermal curtain behind the seats, which makes the back private, and keeps the warmth of the day locked in for a little bit longer at night. Everything has its exact place, religiously stowed so I can find it easily, especially in the dark: torches, matches, water, spanners, gas canisters, kitchen roll and bleach wipes for mopping up spillages. If I misplace something I get angry and swear. Most importantly, I keep my earplugs under the pillow. They deaden the sound of the rain just enough to make it possible to sleep. Each morning I wake, shave, tidy up and get in the cab with my cup of tea. Sometimes I am surprised that people don't seem to notice the difference I feel in myself. Every day I appreciate more and more why all nomadic peoples have a word for 'outsiders'.

It is hard to be a Traveller in London, though. Our family sometimes used to drive up in the early hours of the morning to buy stock from the Covent Garden flower market, but they departed as soon as they could from this place where red and yellow lines run freely down almost every road, horizontal banning bars in the colours of animal warning. They are the hieroglyphs of a world that has no time for nomads, and they signal this by championing motion. The lines aren't there to prevent you moving, they're there to prevent you stopping, and a nomad is defined not by the travelling, but by the living of domestic life outdoors, and often by the sides of roads. Hence these lines are gutters of possibility, draining away the thought of a different life. They carry a thick and barren message sealed in weatherproof paint. This is no place to be a Gypsy Traveller. I can't light a fire or sing or play the spoons. I could do these things, I suppose, in defiance of the fact that I simply don't want to do them here. The fire would get me arrested, and as for the singing and spoons, there are too many people around. Or so I tell myself. It is just as likely to be cowardice that stops my tongue and interrupts my rhythm.

But for at least two hundred years leading up to the 1860s, the hilly area east and south of Brixton was a favourite haunt of Gypsies – hence the names of 'Gipsy Road' and, more famously, 'Gipsy Hill'. Prior to the opening of Gipsy Hill railway station in 1856, this was a remote area, close and yet still far away from the low, black lands of London proper. Long ago, it lay within Brixton Hundred, historically the north-eastern corner of the county of Surrey. From the seventeenth century, until deep into the Victorian age, Gypsies were part of the great 'inferior class' of London. From time to time the authorities would attempt to improve their condition which they did by brutally razing their homes to the ground. The process is still happening now across south London, including on the Heygate Estate five miles north of Gipsy Hill. The area around the Heygate was once a stopping place called Lock's Fields – a marshy, open expanse that now lies buried beneath the hard streets to the south of the New Kent Road. An ancestor on Dad's side – my great-great-grandad – once traded horses at the famous Elephant and Castle donkey market. By coincidence, Cand's great-grandad, a general dealer who made good money in coal and various other businesses, used to drive up there to sell his wares. Perhaps they might even have shaken hands on a sale, for all I know. I don't have a picture of my great-great-grandad, so when I drive through the place I'm forced to make do with clichéd imaginings of flat caps, long coats, pocket watches and leading reins with jangling clips. Later on, driving down the nearby Albany Road, I see the words 'NO TO SOCIAL CLEANSING' spray-painted in silent blue capitals on an isolated section of weathered and damaged concrete wall.

On 11 August 1668, the diarist Samuel Pepys wrote of a visit to the (by then already well known) Romany community living in Norwood. Londoners would often traipse down to the camp on Sundays to look at the Gypsies and have their fortunes told. Unfortunately, while his wife went, Pepys himself didn't go, something that irritates me every time I read his diary entry, wondering in vain how he might have described what he saw. 'This afternoon,' he writes, 'my wife and Mercer and Deb went with Pelling to see the gypsies at Lambeth and had their fortunes told.' And we get nothing more.

The tale of the Norwood Gypsies is taken up by W. H. Chouler, a mid-twentieth-century journalist and local historian, in his pamphlet *Tales of Old Surrey: Myths, Legends, Folk-lore and Ghosts.* Like any good spooky rendering of the past, Chouler's story swings from the probable to the fantastical. He observes that 'many strange tales have been told' of the power of Margaret Finch, the most famous of the Norwood Gypsies who once told the fortune of King George III. Her birth date is uncertain, but she died in October 1740, and was variously claimed to be one hundred and eight or one hundred and nine years old. The shack in which she lived survived until 1808, when a series of enclosures finally brought an end to the Romany presence on Gipsy Hill.

Like many mediaeval and early modern witches or 'cunning folk', Finch was supposed to have had 'the power of transforming herself after nightfall into anyone she wished ... her favourite character being that of a hare'. There is an echo here of the trial in 1662 of Isobel Gowdie, a Scottish woman suspected of practising witchcraft. It is not known exactly why Gowdie made the confession, which was reportedly achieved without the use of torture. She may have been suffering from mental illness, or have actually believed she was capable of metamorphosis. In any case, she claimed that in order to switch her form, she would say the words:

> *I shall go into a hare*
> *With sorrow and sych and meickle care*

And I shall go in the Devil's name
Ay while I come home again.

In Nan's time, the Travellers still believed in witches, but they were less likely to be described as shape-shifters than simply those with a gift for predicting the future. Nan tells me her great-aunt was well known in this respect. Some people avoided her entirely, worried she'd bring them news of a future they did not want but couldn't avoid: better to meet your fate in ignorance than worry about it uselessly. She once predicted that one of her nephews would get three years in Borstal, and when he did, it seemed to confirm that she had at least something of the craft of a witch. It's possible that the accuracy of her forecast was not as remarkable as people thought: this was a typical Borstal term at the time, and she'd no doubt seen other boys get sent down, and simply observed it. Nan's mother, for her part, was sceptical of the idea that Travellers – especially those who were living in relative poverty – had supernatural powers. She summed up her reasoning with a saying: 'If people was witches, they'd witch theirself better off.'

There's a description in Chouler's pamphlet of the Norwood Gypsies' lodgings which rings true with the usual, gradual shift in the character of long-inhabited camps. They change at an imperceptible speed from temporary to semi-permanent sites. Gipsy Hill was:

the haunt of a special gypsy tribe, who every summer pitched their blanket tents beneath the trees on the

Common there ... Soon the tents gave way to wooden huts, each one having on its door a horse shoe nailed with its points upwards. The gypsies loved horses and put great faith in these shoe-charms. They believed anything belonging to a horse was an antidote to the Evil Eye, and that as it was made of iron, it was hated by the forces of evil.

I picture the yard back home, its stables and wooden barns made out of salvaged telegraph poles, their eaves and clefts home to families of swallows and pied wagtails. My grandparents have nailed horseshoes to the uprights of almost all of these outbuildings. Fixed to the grille of my van is a steel horseshoe enclosing the simple motif of a horse's head in profile, facing the wind and all the reflected colours of London's sunlight.

Not everything in these stories fills me with warmth, however. They symbolise the pincer of demonisation and romanticisation in which the Romanies seem to be permanently trapped. The Gypsy men were 'rogues and vagabonds and thieves' who 'looked the part ... their long, black locks, tough as horse hair, hung down over brown unwashed faces, tanned with sun and wind, while their eyes shone out beneath bushy eyebrows'. The fortune tellers themselves were 'ugly old women'. 'Strange as it may seem,' Chouler writes, 'the uglier and older the gypsy woman, the more famous she became.' Here we have, in a few short sentences, a good number of enduring stereotypes and slurs: similarity to animals; uncleanness; and an ugliness to which non-Gypsies are implied to be somehow immune. There are references to 'hooked noses', which cause me to reach up a hand and stroke my own.

Also, like the majority of people – to this day – who write about Gypsies, Chouler follows the custom of writing the word 'gypsy' without a capital letter. This may seem harmless enough, but the habit of spelling our name like this is connected to the tendency to see us as a counterfeit race. It chimes with his implication, along the lines of earlier writers, that it was a combination of dirt and the work of the elements that gave the Gypsies their darker-than-average hue. It was even sometimes believed that Gypsies had dyed their skins with walnut juice in order to give the appearance of racial difference, a charge that dripped with the dark old sap of spying and skulduggery. The same accusation was made of the Babington conspirators, who had planned to replace Elizabeth I with Mary, Queen of Scots. Like them, the first Romany people in England had been – at least outwardly – Catholics, and it's possible that this ancient air of Popish untrustworthiness has never been fully forgotten by Protestant England.

The proceedings of the Old Bailey from 1674 to 1913 are speckled with references to London's Gypsies and Travellers. There's a website that explains why they were 'over-represented in the proceedings': they formed part of 'what many contemporaries considered a dangerous and crime-prone "residuum"' which seeped back into the city at autumn following the end of the temporary farm work. It goes on, telling how 'in a working class mirror to the elite's "London Season", October and November saw hundreds and thousands of men, women and children returning to the capital from hop picking and market gardening, from touring the fairs and tramping in search of work'. It was a yearly migration from the city to the countryside and back that continued, for some, right up to the 1950s.

A list is preserved of most of the major Gypsy haunts, as told to the court. These were Seven Dials, around the church of St Giles in the Fields; Lock's Fields in Walworth; many scattered encampments in Battersea and Wandsworth; and, in the west, the impoverished and semi-industrial Notting Dale. This last area – now part of the Holland Park neighbourhood and home to some of the most expensive properties in London – was once a notorious slum full of brickworks and potteries, known as the lower-class counterpart to nearby Notting Hill. Last of all there was Norwood, the famous Gipsy Hill itself, home at that time to perhaps the biggest Romany camp within sight of the Thames. London, so comprehensively shut against the contemporary Traveller, supplies one of the longest checklists of historical *atchin tans*.

It is surprising then that not many Gypsies were convicted of vagrancy in London; but for those who were, the consequences were dire. In the summer of 1695, a sixteen-year-old Gypsy boy called Francis Buckley, 'of the Parish of St. Mary Islington', was arrested for felony. The reason was 'that he being above the Age of 14 years, was seen to wander up and down from the 10th of June to the 12th following, calling and counterfeiting himself to be an Egyptian'. Bizarre as it seems that you could be charged with both being and pretending to be an Egyptian, this is exactly what happened.

'The Evidence for the King was very positive,' say the proceedings, before taking a turn for the surreal, complete with bizarre echoes of the trial of Christ.

They did hear him say he was an Egyptian, and king of the Egyptians. He was taken in a Barn, at Hampstead, covered over with Straw, and two Egyptian Women sitting upon him; and they being made to rise, they discovered his Legs, and so pulled him out of the Straw. There was found upon him a Pistol ... He had a Mare likewise hard by that was worth 20 pounds. The Prisoner had little to say, but that he never declared he was an Egyptian. The Evidence fully proving it against him, he was found guilty of Felony.

On 28 August 1695, Francis Buckley was sentenced to hang. And as I read these words, my moonlit Transit van becomes a temporary chapel dedicated to the memory of his death.

Daytime, seven miles to the north-west. I've pulled over in Fulham but can't stray far from the van as it's permit-only parking. A moment of calm as I stand among concrete blocks of flats. Balconies jut out from their sides like awkward modifications. Down below, I'm leaning against my van in the slanted sun, smoking the last of a prison-thin rolled cigarette.

A Roma family spill from the doors at the bottom of one of the towers, slapping each other on the back, and talking loudly in Romani as if there is no one around to hear. They're dressed to the nines, the older women in frilled tops and long skirts; the men in smart shirts, black slacks and pointy patent-leather shoes; the teenage girls in big pink and red dancing dresses with bright, shiny hems.

This family isn't dressed up like this on a chance afternoon just because they are wild and flamboyant Gypsies: they're being filmed for a music video. The crew stand around with their cameras and mics, wearing scruffy T-shirts, shorts and trainers; with week-long stubble, tape measures and duct tape strapped to their belts. I'm working on the video, too. I've been driving the crew and kit around, and I'm doing a piece of poetry for the intro. I've got one foot in each of these two very different camps.

With my kestrel-faced Scandinavian looks, the Roma family don't have me down as a Gypsy. I'm camouflaged and ignored, until I respond to a rhetorical question flung up in the air in the Romani language.

'*Aide, chavalen!*' – Come on, young Gypsies! – shouts a girl of fifteen or sixteen. She is wearing a red-and-gold dress full of layers of sequin-edged ruffles.

'*Avav, phena!*' – Here I come, sister! – I reply.

I am met with some quizzical looks: the family have been speaking in Romani for a few minutes, and are now rewinding the tape in their head to find out if I might have heard anything I shouldn't have.

The girl and her sister go quiet, waiting for their mother to make the first move. She is her daughters fast-forwarded two decades: slower moving, but with a piercing wit in her eye that tells me she could sense an untruth like a cloud passing over the sun.

'*Rom san?*' – You are Roma? she asks me, stone-faced.

'*Rom sim.*' – Yes, I am.

'*Wacho jives!*' – Good day!

Now I know from their accent they're Polish Roma.

'*Katar avilan?*' – Where are you from? she asks.

'*Katar England.*' – From England.

'*Thaj tire vitsa?*' – And your people?

'England.'

'*San rommado?*' – You're married? she asks.

'*Awa, bibi. De pansh bersha.*' – Yes, aunt. For five years.

She smiles. I am doing my best, but my 'international Romani' still isn't great after a decade of trying to learn it. I accidentally used the English Romani word for 'yes'.

'*Chavensa?*' – With children?

'*Na. Nai man.*' – No. I have none.

Now the eyebrows are rapidly raised. A man my age married that long and still childless means one of a limited number of things in the conservative Romani mindset: I am unlucky, or a closet gay; or either I or my wife, or both of us, must be barren. When I'd been married two years and Cand still wasn't pregnant, a Serbian Romani friend of mine offered to make me some ancient Gypsy-recipe herbal teas to help get us reproducing. The idea that anyone might deliberately wait to start a family bleeps only faintly on the outer rim of the radar of possibilities; and in any case, it would be inadvisable to admit to that. It begs the question, why has he waited? What's his agenda? Can he be trusted around my daughters?

One of the daughters takes this as a cue to move forward and tease me, to the amusement of everyone there.

'*Kamav tut.*' – I like you. She moves closer. '*Muk tiri romni! Av mansa.*' – Leave your wife! Come with me.

'No.'

The mother decides to change tack and test my credentials. She switches to English and calls out, 'Dance with me!'

She flicks her hands up to either side of her head as her shoulders and feet undulate back and forth in rivulets of motion.

'*Na, bibi.*' – No, aunt.

She tries again, grabbing my hands.

'*Na khelav akathe, akana.*' – I am not dancing here. Not now.

She stamps her left foot. Shakes her head, speaks over her shoulder to her daughters. '*Nai Rom. Gadjo si.*' – He's no Gypsy. He is a *gadjo*.

She chucks the insult in the air like a gauntlet, giving me one last chance to redeem myself. I don't take it.

I've been here before. On other occasions I've given in, clapped hands and danced, but something has changed, and I have decided today I'm not moving my feet. On the one hand, I'm jaded from decades of Romani people asking me to prove my ethnicity, which I reckon is largely because I've got fair skin and blue eyes. They don't seem to ask the dark ones, or maybe I simply don't notice. On the other hand, I refuse to play Gypsy in a way which misconstrues the kind of background I come from: a hinterland of hard and serious horsemen, builders and matriarchs who, if they danced, danced only when they actually wanted to, laughing at weddings or drunk in the old village pub. The idea of snapping straight into a jig in a London street in broad daylight would have any one of my people confused. With my right thumb I rub the underside of my grandad's old solid-gold saddle ring on the wedding finger of my right hand, and the hardness of it reminds me what I am, makes me strong and set in my ways like a column of stone.

The exchange has attracted the attention of a young Polish Roma man in his mid-twenties, who seems intrigued by my party-pooper English Gypsy demeanour. He strolls over with an older man wearing a cardigan, slacks and winkle-picker style shoes – his father or uncle, I guess – who although short exudes a head-of-the-family air. My friend Jake Bowers walks over to join us. Jake, a master-of-all-trades Romany man who is well known as both a journalist and a blacksmith, is working as a producer on the music video. He ambles up, wearing the trademark cheeky smile and relaxed shoulders of an accomplished 'fixer' – someone who can charm cooperation out of the most awkward people in the world.

The older man in the winkle-pickers talks first. 'So, you are Traveller. *Romanichel.*'

'Yes, you know that name.'

'I do know it.'

He mentions someone in his family who has married an English Gypsy girl.

'So there's more of that going on now?' asks Jake.

'Of course!' says the old *mush*. 'Gypsy is marrying Gypsy! We are all Gypsy.'

Jake laughs. 'Yep, that's true.'

'But you English Gypsies, I think you are not having *kris*?'

'No, we don't have it. Not any more,' says Jake, and I add, 'We leave, or we fight.'

A *kris* is a Romany court, convened to settle a family dispute without taking recourse to violence. The practice is common in Central and Eastern Europe, and in its émigré Romany communities. But if it was ever the norm among British Gypsies, then it has not been within living memory. In our world arguments are often resolved by somebody leaving and the relationship being severed. If this doesn't happen, then there will almost always be a fight. In the best-case scenario, it'll just be a fair fist fight, nice and clean, one on one, with a referee to see fair play and as few spectators as possible to get sucked into the row. It can be between two men or two women: it's usually men, but not always. These things are often organised quickly in a place right out of the way, so the law is unlikely to be an issue; plus, some police officers I've spoken to even seem to have a *laissez-faire* stance on it, possibly because they have seen worse ways of ending a row than a bare-knuckle fight. Worst-case scenario, it will not be clean and it will not be fair, and the more people that get involved, the more likely that is. If weapons come into it, then the police are especially likely to show an interest. After seeing a few family feuds that have turned into this, I have at times thought that we might have done well to keep hold of the *kris*. But we didn't.

'Yes, like the French Gypsy, some of them,' the old man goes on. 'They fight also, I think.'

'Yeah, I've heard that,' I say. French Gypsies have been known to storm police stations if one of their own has been harmed – a rare thing elsewhere.

'But they are still speaking *Romanes*,' he says. 'You English Gypsy, you lost the language. It is bad.'

Jake and I look at him, neither frowning nor smiling, but silent and still.

'But it does not matter. You are Gypsy!' He grins, slaps his leg, and says, 'Come! The girls dance.'

He hands me a CD, motioning that I should put it on. I walk over, lean through the van window and slide the disc into the stereo, turn it right up. Gypsy Klezmer-inspired pop music blares out, bouncing and guttering off the vast concrete blocks around us. The CD occasionally skips. Nobody seems to care.

The dancing starts and the old *mush* walks off to watch from close quarters. In his wake the young man now pipes up: like us, he would have been reluctant to talk freely while an older Gypsy man had the floor.

'I know some Travellers, man, they're alright, you know.' He's got a proper modern London twang, totally different from the thick Polish accent of the older man.

'Yeah. Some of us are and some of us ain't!' says Jake. We all laugh.

'You married?' I ask him.

'I was, man.' He smiles on one side of his face. 'Got married young, innit, got kids, we got divorced a couple of years ago.' Me and Jake nod our heads, taking it in. He looks twenty-two, maybe twenty-three at the most: young to be married at all in present-day Britain, never mind a dad already two years divorced.

'We get on alright, though. Stayed friends. It's good for the kids, know what I mean? I got a girlfriend now, she's an English girl. Not Roma. She's wicked though, man. Life's alright.'

I notice that he doesn't say his girlfriend's a *rakli* or *gadzhi*, both terms for a non-Roma woman, younger and older, respectively. They're supposedly neutral, but in reality each carries a slightly pejorative air. I think Jake notices too. There is a bit of a change in the air. There's a saying among the Roma: *Chi perel I phabaj dur katar o kasht* – 'The apple doesn't fall far from the tree.' That may be so, but when one apple falls and rolls a little, it might plant a tree somewhere else.

Maybe there is such a thing as a supranational 'Gypsy community', but it's not often seen or felt. Mostly, we still go about our lives within our various breeds, or what the academics call 'Romany subgroups'. But occasionally there'll be a wedding across a divide, or an NGO will organise a conference aimed at improving Roma and Traveller access to school; or the Gypsy Pentecostals will set up a Christian festival, with a big top standing in for a church and thousands of trailers and vans gathered round its canvas walls in the name of Jesus. This music video we're working on is an example of something similar.

English Gypsies and Polish Roma are involved together, with a shared interest: in this case, all of us are getting paid. There is no shame in admitting this: in fact, one thing that almost always unites us is our refusal to work for free. The idea of working 'just for the love of it' is madness to most Gypsies, and I never felt further away from my roots than when I was doing an unpaid internship at a magazine in Notting Hill. I kept it close to my chest and away from most of the family, and even though I knew it was doing me good, every second that I was there I still felt half a *dinlo*.

But every meeting of different Romany tribes is stippled with little touches of antagonism. The silk of the simple 'Romany nation' narrative snags on the thorns of real life with its jealousies and fears. Xenophobic quips fall out of the sides of suspicious mouths, half jokey, half barbed. 'What do this lot know about horses? Probably rather eat a horse than ride it.' 'How can they be Roma when they do not even speak our language?' 'They are too pale to be Roma.' 'They are too dark to be Travellers.' And so on.

Since I was small, the number of immigrant Roma in Britain has grown, and grown rapidly. In 2013, Salford University delivered a detailed report on the status of Roma immigrants, estimating that at least 200,000 were now living in the UK. Many of their children were either born here, or brought here when they were so small that they can't remember living anywhere else. 'The Roma community' is not the most useful term for describing these people, since the Roma in Britain come from several countries – the Czech Republic, Slovakia, Poland

and Romania are the main ones – and various tribes who often have little to do with each other. The different groups' names give a clue to their origins: historically, the Kalderasha were cauldron-makers, from Romanian *cåldare* or 'cauldron'; the Lovara, most likely horse-breeders, the word *lo* being an old Hungarian word for 'horse'; and the Ursari, originally known for the training of bears.

In Romanian territories, the majority of Gypsies had been slaves from practically their first entry into the land. Slavery was not abolished in Romania until the mid-nineteenth century, by which point it had been practised for well over four hundred years. An infamous newspaper advertisement printed in 1852 offers for sale 'Gypsy slaves ... 18 humans, 10 boys, 7 women, 3 girls – in good condition'. Most Gypsies were the property of Boyar aristocrats and the monarchy, who were largely free to do with them as they pleased: Romany girls were frequently offered as gifts to nobles for sexual entertainment, and children born of these rapes became slaves themselves, subject to the same abuse. Married couples were separated from each other to be sold. Technically it was forbidden to kill a Gypsy, but the Orthodox church was unlikely to interfere in reprisals, since it owned large numbers of Romany slaves as well.

Punishments for disobedience were varied and severe. In 1736, a runaway slave was caught in the German-speaking area of Siebenburgen. After his feet had been burned with lye, his lip was cut off and he was forced to cook and eat it in the presence of his owners. The history of Gypsy enslavement has been detailed by the Romany academic and historian Ian Hancock in his book *The Pariah Syndrome*, and the European Union has funded initiatives aimed at improving public knowledge of this history.

Slavery had a corollary in the form of 'Gypsy hunts'. The phenomenon spread across Europe, preceding the Holocaust and persisting into our own time. In November 1835 a 'Gypsy hunt' in Jutland resulted in over two hundred and sixty 'kills', including 'a Gypsy woman and her suckling baby'. In 2008, a Hungarian neo-Nazi gang embarked on a thirteen-month-long spree of violence with automatic weapons and explosives, in which they killed six Romany people and wounded several others. Among their victims was five-year-old Robert 'Robika' Csorba, shot to death on the steps of his home alongside his father Robert, after whom he had been named.

I have seen rapid change among the Roma in Britain in recent years. In 2009 I ran some art workshops with Czech and Romanian Roma kids who went to a state school in Hammersmith. Not all of them spoke English, and those who did clearly preferred to speak Czech, Romanian or Romani. Six years later I ran a film workshop at a school in Derby and all the Roma kids – though some were struggling academically – were fluent in English; some of them had been born here. It warmed my heart to think that the Gypsies were coming to Britain again, as my ancestors had in centuries long out of reach. But not everyone is so happy about it. In 2013 the former Home Secretary David Blunkett predicted there would be a riot because of interracial friction involving the Roma in Page Hall, Sheffield, and nearly provoked an actual riot in the process. I was interviewed about it on Radio 4's *Today* programme. When the presenter, Justin Webb, asked me why the Roma immigrants had come here, I said, 'That's not a question I can answer in simple terms, because I don't know them all.'

Back in 2000, my mum and dad drove down to Dover, carrying parcels of food and bedding. They were going to help a contingent of Gypsies from Eastern Europe who were stuck at migration control. I remember back then how surprised the family were by this. Mum explained to everyone that they were 'Travellers', like us, proper 'black-faces', and was met with suspicion. Some people had never heard the word 'Roma' before; others knew they existed, but couldn't see much of their own entrepreneurial, trucks-and-trailers, boxing-and-tarmacking culture in these people. In any case, the Traveller attitude to helping other Gypsies is mercurial. If a Traveller walked into our yard from his broken-down car – which has happened before – we would give him a hand with his vehicle, maybe some food and a nice cup of tea. If he asked for money, though, he would receive a different response, underpinned by doubt as to whether he'd ever lend money to us.

I leave London during a break in a week of rain. Cand is away on a job so I've come back to the yard to give the van a clean and get some supplies – gas canisters, bungees and clips, some oil for my generator. Unglamorous essentials I don't want to buy on the road so have stockpiled at home. I pull up outside my trailer. It's twenty-four feet long and barely seven feet wide, but compared to the van it is a palace, and fully deserves the name stamped and gilded on its prow: the 'BUCCANEER'. The cold winter light glints off the cut glass of the mirrors inside. I glance inside at Mum's two silver horse statuettes rearing up off the mantelpiece, in between ornately framed pictures of her and Candis smiling, both taken in summer. The burgundy carpet with its ornate paisley patterns looks warm and inviting, and the little Crown Derby plates on the rack make me hungry for hot toast and tea. I walk up to the trailer, hear the familiar 'tunk' of my boot on the steel step. Unlock the door, boots off on the mat, go inside. Shut the door behind me.

Before I can sit down I'm seized by the cold. I exhale suddenly with the shock and huge clouds of my breath fill the chill, hanging air. I'd had the heating on full in the van as I always do in the winter, bingeing on cheap hot air. In the trailer the undisturbed atmosphere has gone tomb-like with cold. It doesn't take long for a caravan to be utterly gripped by this weird, spooky, unlived-in ambience. I reckon it would take far longer for a house. Nature seems to know that the walls of the trailer are thin and vulnerable.

When I pulled up I'd noticed a puddle of water under the Buccaneer, right in the middle. My heart sank and I instantly tried to forget that I'd seen it. A puddle of water under a trailer, particularly an old one like mine, is not something that the person who lives in it wants to see. The ground underneath a caravan, especially one that's been sitting there for a while, is usually bone dry. The rain can't get to it, apart from the bits nearest the edges which get some run-off from the sides and where weeds start to grow. But this puddle was smack bang in the middle where rain couldn't fall. I knew what it meant. We had carelessly pulled the trailer to a low part of the yard where water was collecting on the ground.

The trailer has tiny holes in its floor for aeration, little ones less than the width of a pencil. They are under the bunks and inside the floor cupboards. These aren't a problem if you've parked somewhere nice and dry. They are a problem if you haven't. Since the trailer itself is a relatively dry environment, water that pools underneath will be drawn upwards into the caravan by osmosis. This is why people who know their caravans won't buy one that's been parked on grass for any great length of time. Depending on how long the water has been there, the caravan might start to rot. The axles and the chassis will be alright, as they're made out of metal, but the bunks in most trailers are made from cheap plywood, which does the job and keeps down the overall weight. Over time, though, any damp will start to warp and rot the ply, and cause mould to grow on the undersides of the cushions. In winter there are few things more depressing than lifting up the cushion off one of your bunks to find mould growing underneath. It makes you wonder whether the underside of your life, the structure and the assumptions that underpin everything, are mouldy and rotten, like the hidden parts of your trailer. The air turns suddenly misty as tiny metallic green spores float through shafts of reflected light. It's beautiful for a second, and then you realise that you are breathing in spores in vast numbers. Then you start to cough. Then you curse bloody trailers. Then, if it's dry, you take the cushions outside and try to brush off the mould.

One minute I am remembering doing all this, the next I am actually doing it. I lift up the big cushion in the sitting area at the front of the trailer. Its underside is covered in a thin sheen of mould. I swear out loud. Useless. I don't even bother to look at the other cushions as I pull them all out. At least it's not raining. I prop them all up against one of the stables and tie a T-shirt round my face. I smack the cushions hard with a broom handle to get the worst of the mould out, then brush them off with a handbrush. The winter air is full of tiny eddies and rivers of spores, drifting like a million silent prayers. I stand still for a moment, admiring this delicate shimmering show, put on free of charge, just for me. Welcome home.

5

The Birds
Winchester, Bramdean Common, Furzey Lodge

The old van grumbles and growls through the mist, wending and winding along the wide old shallow delve of the dual carriageway. To the right, the faster motors fly past us like birds. The road spools out like a long black ribbon between two towns, and runs underneath the shushing limbs of a line of massive oaks. As the pulse and flow of the traffic buzzes the beat of human time, the boughs of the trees reach out overhead like the arms of priests, their hands permanently outstretched in gestures of blessing.

I am eight years old, squidged in on the passenger side between Nan and Gran, and I can smell the sweet smell of the Polo mints that they're sucking. I hear the mints knocking off teeth as they move, a muffled and echoey tip-tapping sound. We've left the town behind us, a jumbled pat of buildings, greens and shops, a tumble of hemmed-in life. Someone's life, but not ours.

Morning. Cand and I are stopping in Winchester, and I wake up early to a cold dawn pulled over with cloud. Naked and desperate birch trees spike upwards into the grey. Today we plan to head for Bramdean Common and the old Gypsy 'Church in the Woods'.

In Europe, most Gypsies are Christian, but Romany culture is not wedded to any of the great religions. In the Balkan countries, many Roma are Muslim, as are almost all in Turkey. The local majority religion tends to be absorbed without much fuss: lip service is paid to its rituals and major rites of passage, and individuals may worship regularly or be 'God-fearing'; but proselytising and strident adherence to creeds are not the norm. The recent surge in Pentecostal worship among English Romanies and Irish Travellers is an anomaly in a long history of standing aside from the rush of religious zeal. Nevertheless, holy places are treated with the kind of hesitant reverence that comes naturally to a superstitious people. Some, like the Church in the Woods, are even considered to be 'ours'.

I light my trusty folding gas stove and boil the water for tea. Opposite us, a concrete police station squats on a broad expanse of tarmac. Liveried vehicles wait silently in their bays, white vans on black ground. It reminds me of a Travellers' site. I pour hot water on the teabag as steam rises to meet my face.

In past centuries, Winchester was a name often feared by those on the fringes of rural Hampshire society. There has been a prison here for at least seven hundred years, and it was the location of the regional assizes, where Travellers charged with petty offences would come to receive their sentence. The Romany and Traveller Family History Society has published a pamphlet entitled *The Winchester Confessions, 1615–1616: Depositions of Travellers, Gypsies, Fraudsters, and Makers of Counterfeit Documents, Including a Vocabulary of the Romany Language.* It contains the earliest known example of the use of Romani words within English syntax, the wedding of the two languages in a form that would come to be known as *poggadi jib* – 'the broken tongue'. The linguist Yaron Matras notes that the form of Romani found in the Winchester confessions was 'said to be in use by a group of outlaws', who referred to a pikestaff as 'a swisht with a sayster in the end'; used the phrase 'coor the gorife' to mean 'goe beate the cow'; and the expression 'to be corde' with the meaning 'to be whipped'. None of these phrases would roll off the tongue as examples of modern-day Romanes, but they are eerily similar: only as different from their twenty-first-century equivalents as lines from Shakespeare might be from contemporary British English.

Nan's dad, my great-great-grandfather, once served a stretch in Winchester prison. Whilst there, he heard men being whipped with the cat-o'-nine-tails in distant parts of the jail. He said their screams and calls echoed around the old stone walls, and that he never forgot the sound for the rest of his life.

Cand and I are both wide awake now and we work quickly, packing the bedding and blankets away, and sweeping the van out with a small dustpan and brush. There's a chill in the wide, free air so we make some porridge, trying to get the amounts exactly right so there's none left over, which makes it easier to wash up. There's a bit too much but I force it down, trying to think of how I'll be glad of it later.

Once I've secured everything back in its place with bungee cords, we head out of Winchester east on the Alresford road. Just before the town starts to fade into countryside, Candis spots two teenage girls picking their way up a steep bank, a forgotten stripe of scrub-covered hillside, bramble-scape wedged between old residential back roads. The girls are moving across it slowly, raising their legs up in weird, looping, rhythmic high steps, as though they've evolved to get over the tangled ground. One of them carries a small hacksaw, the other one a nylon shopper bag that is full to the brim with thin logs. They must be collecting wood, harvesting heat from a place where nowadays no one else goes.

The speed limit increases from 30 to 40, then finally the white circle crossed by a black diagonal line that is meant to mean 'national speed limit for a single carriageway', but in reality means no one has a clue what speed they're meant to be going. Fields full of fluttering turnip tops ripple out from the sides of the road, dull under the overcast sky.

I make a right-hand turn late and swing round the round-about. We're pulled to the left in our seats. It's bad driving. Cand grits her teeth and throws me a dark look.

As a kid I enjoyed these brief moments in centrifuge. Most of my family tore round the roads like maniacs, throwing us about in our seats like punters on a waltzer. Most of all I loved going too fast over humpbacked bridges, and the fierce cold pull in the belly that went along with it. It made me shiver and tense my legs under the seat, excited to be living, happy to be moving.

★

We come to the crossroads at Bramdean in super-fine drizzle, the sparsest of rain, almost mist. The common is split into sections by narrow roads, and bordered on all sides by woodland. It rolls out before us, wide, green and glorious, like a Gypsy's promised land. Few people who aren't from here know of this place, and it's the only common in the south I can think of that's still open-sided and can be driven onto, without gates or ditches or stakes driven into the earth. Over the years I've been coming here I've discussed it with few people, wary that too many might come, that its spell will at last be broken by a new by-law.

The common is largely empty, except for two cars. I pull into a gravelly lay-by, then onto the grass. A Rottweiler comes prowling out from around an estate car that's parked nearby: I see it's on a lead, tightly held by a girl in her twenties. The dog snarls at us through the rain-spattered windscreen, and we decide to hang on for a minute before getting out. Rottweiler and owner walk off quickly across the common, but every few yards the dog stops and turns back round to bark at the van as though it knows something about us.

We get out and walk off south-east down an old lane, which is nameless on my digital map. We've already forgotten the dog and we listen for cars, walking on the rampart of leaf-mould and mud that's stacked up by the side of the road like a chocolate gateau. Without warning, the calm is destroyed as the trees on both sides of the road explode in a frenzy of jackdaws and crows. We look up and around the high trees for an explanation, but can't see anything. The crows settle back down. I wonder if the uproar was down to us, or something else. Maybe a hawk.

I always thought the word 'hawker' was linked to real hawks: birds of prey. Its etymology seems obvious, the keen-eyed salesman swooping in on a rookery of quiet cul-de-sacs, hoping to catch the old, the frail or the unlucky. The connotations are there, but I was wrong about the origins of the word: it probably comes from the Middle Low German verb *höken*, meaning to peddle, or carry goods on your back, and is originally linked to the bent-over posture of pedlars. Early mediaeval woodcut engravings of Gypsies tend to show them walking with sticks, and stooping under the weight of the packs on their backs: pedlars perhaps, or just poor. But the root of the word can't mask its menacing air, and the way it seems perfectly tailored to describe the exploits of the Gypsy conman, the prowling, perennial nemesis of suburbia.

The sign for the church is a green-and-white painted wood panel that pokes out from a gap in the wood's edge. It informs us that this is 'Upper Itchen Benefice Church', but nobody I've ever spoken to calls it that. It is 'the Travellers' church' or 'the church in the woods'; the 'Gypsies' church' or 'the little green church at Bramdean'. Each of these names conveys its beloved and tucked-away preciousness better than the official name on the sign.

In drier times you can park in an inlet of the woods, closer to the church. But approaching it now after three days of rain, I'm glad I had the sense not to try. Someone has attempted it recently, and the thick dark mud has been churned up into high, squidgy ridges. I can see where their wheels have spun, leaving smoothed and hollowed-out bellies in the mud as they've struggled to leave. We walk on, around the dark tracks.

The wood is bright with a gentle, airy light between the trees – most of them naked of leaves. As we walk on, I start to register the many different shades of green on the few plants that are still in leaf. The deep and dark greens predominate: the blueish-dark tinge of the bramble, and the holly, a similar blue-green, but vivid, standing out against everything else in its winter ascendancy. But there are other colours: the lime-like glow that shows in the veins of young ivy; the light and lonely summer pallor of bracken. Velveteen-metallic emerald moss coats the bases of the trees. The dark heart of the yew pulses through all its little green leaflets as though night-time is locked up inside and then seeps out by day. And my favourite – the million miniature palm trees of the rain-loving haircap moss, also known as 'Great Goldilocks' – like a tropical jungle in miniature under our feet.

For all these fleckings of green, the wood is still almost entirely brown, with long thin shards of grey-and-white sky biting down from above like fangs. I pick up a few dried leaves from my favourite types of tree – the oak and the ash. They are so un-leaflike already: brittle-burnished, paper fossil versions of their former selves. The oak leaves that lie on the forest floor are dark chocolate brown and plentiful. Their undulating sides curl in on themselves, like the little red cellophane Miracle Fortune

Teller Fish I had as a child. The ash's leaves have mostly died *in situ*. They lie at the bottoms of ash trees, in neat rows still linked to their branches, gleaming with the soft brightness of fresh copper pipes.

Ash is one of the preferred firewoods of the Travellers. I was taught from early childhood that it lights well without needing to be seasoned; that even freshly cut, it 'makes a coal' – burns slowly into embers, making it perfect for cooking. A cousin refers to it as the 'queen of the firewoods'.

We are near the church now, coming up to the little knee-high white picket fence that surrounds it. We soon find the graves Nan mentioned: a little row of them, almost completely covered with leaves. One tiny headstone bears a thick patina of grey lichens and green moss, and I guess it must be two hundred years old: going closer, I see that it's only been there twenty years. The dank air and the relative warmth have combined to claim it, already, as part of the woods.

Next to it are the graves of an old couple, born just after the First World War. Their headstones are shaped like toadstools, each with a little stone heart propped up at its feet. Wreaths were left here in the run-up to Christmas, their holly now blotchy and dark brown. It reminds me that Bramdean and its little church are sacred not only to Gypsies.

The wooden gate at the front of the church is tiny, child height. Between it and the church, a patch of early daffodils has sprung up, knifing through the thick winter mulch. A few crocuses are trying to get through, too. There is no 'dead of winter' here. A frostless Christmas has confused the woods, and a shadow moves over my heart as I think of the words 'false spring'.

An acrylic plaque set into the top of a short tree stump offers an unsentimental smattering of history. The church was built in 1883 at the behest of the rector, Alfred Caesar Bishop MA, so that the various people who came and went on the Common would have a place to worship: the 'commoners, charcoal burners and gypsy itinerants'. In the past, census-takers would often list Travellers as 'gypsies' or 'egyptians' by occupation: it wasn't their race, but their job, or rather a category of jobs well suited to wanderers. In one large camp you might have general dealers, chair bottomers, basket makers, knife grinders, and then a family listed simply as 'travelling gypsies'. The blurred distinction between lifestyle and race is as old as the word itself, and Gypsy/Traveller only became an unambiguous ethnic term on the census in 2011.

We go back round to the front of the church. It's locked fast, with a mesh grille over each of its little sash windows through which you can just about peep at its austere, dark wood interior. We walk round the structure. At a slow, almost prayerful pace, it takes us less than a minute to complete a circuit of the building. It is built from iron sheets painted more or less deep holly green, and skirted with wooden panels carved in a similar scrolled design to that common on Romany wagons, and painted white. The belfry is hollow, a six-foot spike perched at the front end of the pitched roof, and the small porch is built in the same simple manner. The solid oak door on its long fancy hinges is the most church-like thing about the place, except that – like the door to a wagon or trailer – it's narrow, barely two feet wide, very different from the portal-like doors of most churches. Two handrails run up to it either side of the small brick-built steps, a gesture of sympathy for the infirm. Above the porch and at each end of the roof is a little white cross in an angular Celtic style. All in all, it lacks any air whatsoever of an English church.

A phone number is provided for contacting the rector and church trustees, if you require any information. I can't imagine they get many calls and I don't intend to help change that. Whilst I'm sad that we can't go inside the church, maybe standing outside suffices. At Romany funerals, many of the mourners wait outside the church during the service, not just because of the lack of room, but because entering the church is not seen as essential. It's the fact that someone has died that matters, and that you have paid your respects by attending the day. Likewise, it's enough for me to know that I've been here, and that this place is kept in repair by quiet, benevolent presences – sylvan protectors – watching over the place. I reckon they know it is special to many, regardless of race, age or faith. I think of one of Nan's sayings, 'A little help is worth a lot of pity.' With this thought in mind I lay my hand on the church's cold green side a final time before we leave.

As we head back out of the woods and towards the road, the rain turns from a misty spray to a shower that taps on the waxed cloth of our coats. I spot two white signs, one nailed

high up on a tree, one hammered low into the earth: 'PRIVATE
– NO PUBLIC ACCESS'. 'PRIVATE LAND'. They are notices
of an otherwise invisible girdle, which divides the common bit
of the wood from the privately owned eastern part. More
capital letters; more big, bold warnings. They are defensive
charms, half-hopeful; the signs may be white, but the spells are
still painted in black.

We notice some light grey splodges in the grass beneath the
canopy of an oak by the side of the road: Cand walks over to
inspect them. They are pigeons, necks broken, some with their
chests pecked open in a white puff of down, like unscored
chestnuts burst on a fire. One has had its head torn off, the
work of a hawk of some kind, a diorama telling of the vicious-
ness of birds.

Twelve years previously: I am nineteen, back from university
for the Christmas holidays. I am walking with the men of the
family across another muddy field. In its centre is a makeshift
barn made from two modified shipping containers placed end
to end. As we near one end of the barn, there are noises. I can
hear snuffling and scratching, then the tentative clucking of
chickens. Before we get to the open doors a man steps out
onto the threshold in wellington boots and a long and freshly
greased waxed coat. He must have been in there a while because
his hair is dry, where ours is beaded and glistening with rain
after coming across the field. My relations say the man's name,
and he replies by saying theirs. The names double as greetings.
There's no need for superfluous pleasantries.

'Poxy weather, boys,' says the man in the greasy coat.

'Ain't it.'

I follow them in as they talk about gossip and work that does not concern me. 'So-and-so got three year.' 'Thingy's boy's doing a barn conversion over Ringwood,' and so on. We are all inside now, out of the rain.

The makeshift barn has been fitted with long rows of pens on the left and the right, either side of a narrow walkway carpeted with old rugs. I look down into one pen. A snub-faced bull terrier is lying down in it, surrounded by small squirming pups. They are half-blind and worming around, pining strangely, bewildered by themselves and their huge, tiny world. The mother looks up at me briefly with wet, glassy brown eyes, then drops her head back to the ground. I move on, by now fully tuned out of the men's conversation. Their words have drifted off down the walkway like a small cloud of flies.

I'm expecting to see some more dogs, but there aren't any. Instead, the next pen I come to contains a chicken: a cockerel, metallic orange in colour, a foot tall and half of him legs. He is standing up nearly as straight as a man, the most upright bird I have ever seen in my life. He lets out a long, slow thrum of a cluck and looks at me with his black-and-gold dinosaur eye. There is something perturbing about him, his thin frame and huge claws, his mohawk-style crest and the way he seems to be more legs than body. I decide to stop looking and move on, but in the next pen there's another one, almost twice the size of the first, with clawed feet like a miniature Tyrannosaurus.

His crest is far bigger as well, his beak thick and hard like the tip of a Stone Age axe. I reckon if he put his mind to it he could leap straight out of his pen and into my face and peck the eyes out of my head in a matter of seconds. He is a tall, skinny, copper-clad prince among birds, and he seems to know it. He stays on the spot as I stare at him, then bends his head down to rub at it with a talon of his lizard-like foot. He rears back up to his fully upright position, chest out, and throws me a glance with a round amber eye that seems to gaze at me straight out of the past. It's a staring contest, and I am losing it to a chicken.

I know nothing at all about cock fighting – my family's never been into it – but I know that the birds I am looking at are obviously fighting cocks. I have never seen chickens this tall, made up of nothing but sinews and talons and beaks and fierce eyes. They are wire and claw, stony pink and blue skin, rich dark orange feather and motley red crest, tough skin stretched tight over the bone. There's one thing they are not, and that's meat. They are chickens, but their destiny isn't the plate. In some secret locale – God knows where, and I don't – they will find themselves locked in a fight to the death, pecking at artery, neck, eye and chest until their blood starts to mix with the dirt. It is a terrible thought and I start to feel sick. I picture the scene like a nightmarish riff on a livestock sale: a circular dirt pit smothered in sawdust, its short, galvanised-metal perimeter fence buckling inwards under the weight of big men wearing flat caps and abattoir boots. It would take place wherever that sort of thing happens:

a big old pub cellar somewhere in the docklands, or a corrugated outbuilding of a farm miles out from the town.

The places I'd conjured in my head all had one nice thing in common, and that was that I had imagined them. They were unreal: venues from films and pub bores' tales. Suddenly the distance between me and such things has collapsed. I don't want to be here. I'm thinking about the library back at my college, about learning and ideas and books. The academic work I'm always moaning about no longer seems quite so bad.

Suddenly the slap of a huge hand on my back nearly knocks me straight into the pen with the bird. All the air rushes out of my chest and I spin round in shock.

'Fucking hell,' I cough out.

'You had a fly up your back, *mush*.' They laugh.

'Nearly *trashed* me to death.'

'Looked like you never clapped eyes on a chicken, bruv.'

'Ain't never seen one like that,' I say.

'That's 'cause there ain't none like that. He's the best one there is.'

'Yeah. He looks it and all.' I am trying to hold it together.

'Don't worry,' he says. 'I ain't gonna make you fight him.'

Yes, something about these birds scares me, but even for a fighting cock, the principal danger is man. The chickens are bred to attack each other, but it is men who force them to do so, and men who can kill on a whim, or to prove a point. I once heard a story about a young Gypsy man known as Bottlejack. Bottlejack's brother told me about how they once went to buy a motor from some other Travellers. This other family had fighting chickens on their land. Once the deal was done and everyone had shaken hands and was happy, Bottlejack walked up to the cage of the family's biggest bird and said, 'That's some cockerel you've got there, boys.' They replied, 'Yeah, he's our best one, *mush*.' At this, Bottlejack drew a catapult from his back pocket and fired a steel ball bearing at the bird, killing it instantly. He walked away, leaving its owners stunned. As they drove off, Bottlejack's brother asked him why he had shot the chicken. He said, 'I don't trust the likes of these. They're wild, they'd be liable to follow us back to our place and *chore* something. But now they think I'm proper *radgey*. They won't come up our place after that.'

At the common's edge, we walk past a woman and man busy in the side door of an American GMC camper van, parked under the gigantic black boughs of a rain-sodden oak. I surmise they aren't Travellers – they've got tourist stickers in their back window and they look too happy-go-lucky. I hold up a thin stick of dry brown ash leaves by way of a silent greeting, and the man says 'Hello!' in a loud, cheery voice. It puts a spring in my step, which lasts about five seconds until we're back walking on the grass near the van. I notice it's much wetter now than before: water slaps and slurps under our boots as we walk. This is bad. There'll be no use trying to drive straight out; the turf will turn into brown mousse under the spinning wheels. I go in the back of the van and grab my bag of cat litter, the secret miracle stuff for escaping the mud. I smear it round all four tyres and pour some onto the grass either side of each one. I get in the driver's seat and try to get moving in second gear, keeping the revs as low as I can, muttering useless prayers. It's no good: the common slopes up all the way to the road and my front tyres haven't got much tread. It's time for a deep breath and a think: there is no way I'm getting towed off an old Gypsy stopping place by an AA man.

It's getting dark fast so we can't hang around. Cand reckons our best bet is to forget about going forward and instead reverse down the slope. Then we can quickly swing round to face forwards and build up some speed before leaving the common at its lowest point, which happens to be where the couple with the GMC camper van are parked. We strap ourselves in and go backwards, gaining momentum before swinging round, then accelerating forwards with loose control as I keep in the highest gear possible, picking up speed. It's working, but it's suddenly clear that we're going too fast for the bumpy terrain. My heart pounds as I tell Cand – but more so myself – to 'hang on' as we fly towards a ridge in the grass at a good 30 miles an hour, which feels more like 100 on this surface. What's more, I can't brake in case we get stuck again. We're nearing the edge of the common now, and the strategy has worked: there's no way we can get stuck going this fast. Cand grins and waves as we hurtle past the camper-van couple, who press their backs against their vehicle and stare at us open-mouthed. We've been saved by concocted momentum. We're back on the road. And I've learned to avoid winter grass.

★

A week later. Cand's gone to stay with her mum for a few days so I am alone. It's gone midnight as I rumble along through the dark understorey of the New Forest. The clock on the dash glows a ghoulish green: it's 1:35 a.m. The night air is a dense, continuous mist of rain. No sooner do the windscreen wipers smear it away than it's replaced with a fresh galaxy of silver droplets that shine like beads of mercury in the reflected light of my headlights. I haven't seen another car for ages. I can hardly tell if I'm tired, or dreaming, or mad.

Suddenly there is a nondescript smudge of tan colour in the middle of the road. It grows and grows as I drive towards it, until it splits into two and I finally see what it is: a pair of small deer, antlerless, caught in the drizzly searching beams of my headlights. As I slow down the deer raise their heads and stare at the van, stock-still, until I roll to a stop. They look at me for a moment, then skip off into the bracken. I drive on.

Furzey Lodge is a tiny hamlet a few miles from Beaulieu, set deep in the New Forest. In our family, the name was pronounced 'Fuzzy Lodge', which made it sound cosy and safe, a warm haven quite unlike the prickly bushes of gorse to which the word 'Furzey' alludes. I came here once with Mum and Dad when I was nine. We took a detour on a trip through the forest and stopped to have our pictures taken with a road sign that said 'FURZEY LANE leading to FURZEY LODGE'. I knew that it had something to do with the family, years ago, but beyond that I didn't care. It was just a sign by the side of a road. All the same, I remembered it.

I'm tired and suddenly the turn into Furzey Lane is upon me: I didn't see it until the last second. I swing a right into the road, and am instantly faced by the massive brown square of a cow that almost fills my vision. I holler out, 'SHIT!' and swerve round, just missing it. Regaining composure, I look in my mirror and see it still standing there, huge in the dim red glare of my tail lights. The sight of the deer must have made me subconsciously think lightning wouldn't strike twice, that I wouldn't see anything else for a while. I was wrong. I continue, panicked. I just want to get off the road.

As I trundle down the lane, exhausted, its sides start to close in as the sense of wildness morphs into the unmistakable feeling of entering a village. The roadside heathers and ferns give way to a mixture of trees and houses: this must be Furzey Lodge. The trees are indistinct black shapes. They resemble Rorschach blots, their edges bleeding into outer space.

I come to a fork and hold left, too worn out to look at a map or try to figure anything out. Finally there is what looks like a small woodside car park, next to a lockable gate that leads into the forest. I roll to a stop, so tired I can feel every granule of grit being crushed by my tyres. I pull on the handbrake and clamber into the back of the van, not wanting to spend one second outside in the thick, wet darkness of night. I take off my boots and throw them down to the far end by the back doors. Without needing to look, I grab the matches from down behind the bed in the nook of the floor and the wheel arch. I light a cream-coloured church candle in one of my lanterns and turn my little Roberts world radio on, but in less than a minute I realise I'm finished. I can't even muster the will to get undressed. I flick off the radio and blow out the candle. As I sink into sleep, I wonder if this marks a victory against another fear, the opposite of my reservations about the city: an older human dread, of the dark in the woods.

I dream of the edge of the forest, the summer before.

My grandad, my uncle and I are driving along a dusty track a few miles off the M27. Just as the tree cover begins to thicken, we pull through a set of open gates into Billy's place. Billy is a well-known horseman, and every year he hosts a 'drive' through the forest, which often attracts hundreds of Travellers with sulkies and carts. He and his boys are also known for being able to handle themselves: his son was a successful professional boxer and held a world-title belt. Along with a set of stables for the horses, a big garden with a fountain centrepiece, and a good few acres of land out the back, there's also a purpose-built boxing gym on the property not far from the bungalow in which the family live. I can't help feeling jealous of Billy's place. It offers all the freedoms a Traveller wants – the space for horses and trailers; the hard ground as well as the grass – along with all the conveniences of settled life: security, privacy, home.

Billy comes out to greet us, flanked by two other Travelling men. He is wearing a clean white short-sleeved shirt, and a woven hat from under which his blue eyes stare at us like gun-sights. He is broad-chested and walks in a halo of strength that commands, and gets, respect. There is more to his aura than a boxer's toughness: he is a master of horses. If you can break the will of a stallion, dealing with men must seem straightforward.

As the three of them get near to us I can tell that something is wrong, and I hope it's got nothing to do with us. Billy explains that a family of Travellers have camped up next to a river somewhere in the forest. When questioned by the Forestry Commission, the father said he was on his way to take part in one of Billy's horse drives, using it as cover for pulling up in a sensitive spot. Billy doesn't know the man from Adam and is furious that he's taken such liberties; to make matters worse it sounds as though he might be Irish. The New Forest is an English Gypsy redoubt, and Billy is lukewarm on inter-tribal solidarity.

'If he tries to come clever, I'm strangling him,' he says.

Billy gets in his truck with the other two men and they take off at speed down the lane. My grandad, my uncle and I spend the time drinking tea and chatting on the terrace while the women do the same indoors. Within an hour the men are back, and Billy seems content with the outcome.

'Fair play to him, he hooked the trailer on and flew straight off,' he says. 'I told him not to use my name.'

I wake up to faint light drifting into the back through my technicolour patchwork curtain – a present from Mum – and the tin-drum thrum of a light rain shower on the roof. I slept deeply, not waking once, and I smile in relief. Right now, a decent night's sleep is more precious than rubies. Most midwinter nights something wakes me up: rain, or howling winds, or a bird or a squirrel on the roof, hopping and jerkily walking with echoing scratches. The earplugs help but they can't block everything out, and I wouldn't want them to: if something goes wrong I'd rather not be dead to the world.

Straight ahead are two thin holly trees: they are the same shape and height, but where one's leaves are spiky, the other's are smooth. I've read that holly only grows prickly as a defensive response to being nibbled by animals, which makes me wonder why the smooth tree has been left alone. Some Travellers call smooth holly 'blind holly', which suggests that the prickles are eyes, looking sharp. I look out of the driver's-side window and see a triad of ancient oak trees on the small village green. Nan's parents stopped here in 1917, when her dad had just been demobilised out of the army: he was wearing his military uniform on their wedding day, an image that flashes up in my mind every time someone claims that Travellers never fought for the country. The oak trees must have been here back then, already showing the sheen of moss round the bases of their trunks, and the boughs stretched out parallel to the earth in their postures of protection. I get out and trace my fingers over the crenellations of the bark, a representation of lost time cast in the ridged and wrinkled shell of the living wood.

I'm shocked to see that half an hour has passed without my noticing: mind wandering amidst vegetation, I have lost all track of time. I start making a cup of tea when I hear munching sounds. I turn to see a pony, a bit bigger than a Shetland, five yards away, happily stripping a bramble of its leaves. Another one walks up, then kneels down and starts to roll about on the ground, revelling in the earth. A robin bounces around them both, serenading the ponies with shimmering tweets.

Driving out of the village, I stop by a bungalow to take a picture of myself with the Furzey Lodge sign as proof of my visit, but quickly realise I won't be able to take a good self-portrait with my big, unwieldy camera. I notice the postman is slowly making his way down the road, pulling in and out of each drive like a bee visiting flowers. I decide I'll ask him to take a picture of me, but before I move to speak to him I hear a noise behind me and turn round to see an old man walking around the bungalow. He looks a little bit suspicious until I call out, 'Sorry to bother you sir, but would you mind taking a picture of me with that sign?' I always call people 'sir' at moments like this, a tactic I got from a school friend: it butters them up for requests.

The old man comes out through his gate and wanders slowly across towards me. His age might be anywhere between seventy and ninety, but I can't guess closer than that: he is still strong, wiry and broad-chested, five foot eleven, six foot. He is wearing a simple brown jumper with a navy-blue shirt underneath, and a grey checked cap similar to mine. As he gets nearer I see he has the rangy gait and tanned skin of an outdoorsman, and his face is clean-shaven, with two bright white sideburns that cut a clean line under his high cheekbones. His eyes are icy blue with tiny pupils at their centres. He still hasn't spoken, so I break the silence.

'Sorry, sir, it's just that my great-great-grandparents used to live here, you see, a long time ago.'

'Oh, right,' he says.

'So I just wanted a picture of me with that sign.'

'Who were they then?'

I tell him their names. Draw a blank.

'Don't know them names, I don't think.'

The postman pulls over and hands the old man his mail. The old man leans over to him, and whispers, 'All you ever brings me's bills!'

They laugh, then both say, 'See ya later!' and the postman drives off.

The old man tucks his mail under his arm and beckons me. 'Give us your camera, then. How'd you work this?'

He takes a couple of pictures of me and tells me, 'They probably ain't much cop,' handing the camera back.

He is about to walk away when I decide to have one last go at seeing what he knows about this place's history as a Romany *atchin tan*.

'To be honest with you sir, my family that lived here ... They were Travellers. I know they stopped here at least once. A long time ago.'

The old man's face loosens up like I've solved a great riddle.

'Oh, Travellers, was they?' I start to notice how similar his accent is to Nan's and her brothers. The piratical old Hampshire twang.

'Yes, sir. But they didn't stay down this way long. They moved up to Alton way and travelled round there for a lot of years.'

The wind is getting up and there's drizzle in it. The old man puts his head down and instinctively walks over to the side of my van, out of the way of the wind and rain. I follow.

'Well, a lot of 'em used to work round Alton, fruit pickin' and hop pickin' and suchlike,' he says.

'Yes, they did. I've never done work like that myself.'

The more we talk, the happier he seems to get. He speaks about local Travelling families, the Coopers and the Sherwoods and Sherreds; about how the forest used to be a happier place back then, before the Forestry Commission ruled everything, back when the place could look after itself. He disagrees with the idea of national parks, the funds they absorb and the way they seem to spend loads of money on huge river projects and don't 'let the wood earn its keep': as a young man he worked as a coppicer and lumberjack and saw how the forest ticked along by unregulated custom. I don't know whether I agree with him but I don't know enough to disagree either; plus it would be churlish to argue with a woodsman far older than me who'd just done me a favour.

He starts talking about the compounds, Thorney Hill, Shave Green and the others, where the Travellers were forced to move when it was made an offence to camp out in the woods as they always had. The first compounds were established in

1926 and I lament that it's been that long since Travellers enjoyed the freedom of the forest, but he leaps in straight away, correcting my amateurish and inaccurate outsider's history, and telling me there were still Travellers living in the woods near here when he first came to these parts in 1949. He explains that the end of the lane, where I stopped last night, is where the old stopping place was. My heart is instantly warmed at the thought that I had driven to almost exactly that spot in the drizzly winter darkness, and, whether it was by instinct or chance, it was there that I lay down my head for the night.

He asks me again for Nan's parents' names, and I can see that he's troubled at not being able to help me more.

'When did you say that was?'

'1917 was the last time I know for a fact they was here.'

'Well, that was before my time, see. But ...'

He turns to the open land to his right, and stretches a slow arm out towards the horizon. 'I can still see 'em where they used to walk across there, where they'd be going to work from one place to another, or whatever they were doing ... Nice people, all lovely people, the ones that I knew.'

I'm taken aback by his kind words. None of this is what I was expecting. 'Well, it's nice to hear you say that sir, 'cause I've heard about some rough ones as well, but there's good and bad amongst everybody.'

'Well, that's right what you're sayin'. But the Travellers I knew was all good, lovely people. And that's all I know.'

We shake hands.

'Good luck wherever you're flying off to,' he says, before insisting that if ever I'm down this way again, I should call in and say hello. He turns and starts to walk away, but ambles back to the van once more to say some final words. The forest is too expensive for working people now, he says, 'the old Travellers, and proper old foresters' like him: it's all 'money people'. He'd never be able to move here now. The only reason he's here is because he has already been here for years.

6

The Tongue

The Flamingo Club, Bodmin, Boscastle, St Germans, Haldon Hill

I leave the New Forest and drive up to London for the annual conference of the Traveller Movement, a charity which aims to improve the standing of Gypsies, Roma and Travellers in British society. I give a very short speech and mention that I'm on a weird quest round some of the old *atchin tans*, trying to unpick the riddle of why we are seen as belonging to nowhere. There's a break and as I am making myself a cup of tea, a Romany woman in late middle age with a kindly face, immaculate clothes and bright, twinkling eyes comes up to me with her husband.

'I just wanted to say I think it's good, what you're doing,' she says. Her name is Rosie: behind her shoulder, her husband nods and smiles, his hands clasped loosely in front of him like a friendly preacher. 'I've had a go at writing some of the old stopping places down here, look,' she says. 'I don't know if that's any good to you.' She hands me a folded-up sheet of lined paper and presses it into my palm. I unfold it. She has written the names of sixteen places where she used to stop, some with brief descriptions of where they are, ranging from the east side of the New Forest right down to the bottom of Cornwall. I thank her but she moves her hand in front of her face, as if batting away the suggestion that what has just happened is anything special.

That night I set off for Cornwall alone, wrapped up in a shawl-neck jumper, wax jacket and cap. Although I am driving, I've dressed for outdoors: I keep the windows open, letting the freezing sky flood into the van, needing the rush of the winter chill to keep me awake and alert. My head and torso are rigidly cold but a hot blast of air rushes out past the pedals and keeps my feet and calves warm. It's the right combination for distance. I feel watchful, like a hare in its winter seat.

In crossing from Hampshire to Dorset I have left Nan's territory behind. The sea-flecked finger of Devon and Cornwall was uncharted land for her, and she rarely even mentions it, except when, sitting and peeling potatoes, she breaks into the old tune her mum and dad used to sing together while they were making pegs:

> *The judge said stand up, boy, and dry up your tears:*
> *You're sentenced to Dartmoor for twenty-one years*
> *So dry up your tears, lad, and kiss them goodbye*
> *For twenty-one years is an awful long time.*

I imagine how their knives exposed the white of the hazel as its dowels were drawn along the blade: in the same way, Nan's knife brings the bright cream flesh of the potatoes into the light.

The cab of the van is like a wind tunnel, loud with the flapping sound of rushing air, but the roads are quiet. I am part of
a brotherhood of drivers whirring across the countryside in the
dark, their headlights lapping the road like yellow tongues. They
are people I don't know and probably never will, but if one of
us had an accident down a lonely back road, we'd rely on each
other for help, and more often than not I reckon we'd probably
get it. And yet we are also each other's principal danger, each
vehicle a weapon poised on a hair trigger of death. It is like
the camaraderie of soldiers, locked in a shared discipline, yet
each one posing a constant, imminent threat. I think of the
hitch-hikers I've occasionally picked up. They seem perturbed
at first to see a Transit van pulling over: is this a serial-killer
tradesman offering a lift? As they climb in, they are amused
and relieved to see that the passenger footwell is packed with
old books, then disturbed afresh as they notice the books are
all about Gypsies.

I pass Stonehenge on the right, though I can't see it in the
darkness. It is weird without the daytime queues of people,
understandably distracted by the most famous stone circle in
the world. The nearby roundabout is clear of cars. I fly through
the notorious bottleneck at speed, as if flouting an unwritten
law of regular travel.

A while later I realise I must have passed Totnes, where I
got married. Cand did her degree down there and fell in love
with the place, and it has long been a magnet to wanderers
who come for their different reasons. Some are drawn by the
town's alternative spirit, symbolised by its attempts to prepare

for a world that has stopped using fossil fuels, its tolerant attitude to caravan dwellers – there are well-established New Traveller encampments in the vicinity – and the fact that it has its own local currency, the 'Totnes pound'. Others go further, believing Totnes to be a place where leylines cross, built close to a lost Atlantean temple sacred to the moon. For a stretch of road I am accompanied by memories of Candis walking under the boughs of the ancient Dartington yew tree in the flowing red of her dress, the traditional colour of Romany brides before Christian white became the norm. The red symbolised fertility, health and luck: ember-hot counterpoints to my freezing and lonely present.

I get down to the Celtic Sea in one hit, five hours without stopping once. I step out of the van and onto the soil of Cornwall, a tongue of land stretching far out into the sea, under the twinkling light of the winter stars.

Folded up in my pocket is the piece of jotter-pad paper bearing Rosie's list of *atchin tans*. It symbolises a geography within a geography, Travellers' memories overlayed onto place names from the back of any ordinary British atlas: Copper Kettle, Ringwood; the Hump, Newton Abbot; Poor Fields, Taunton; Flamingo Club, Redruth. The last one is the closest, so I decide I'll go there first.

Before long I'm in the back of the van with the lanterns lit and the radio on. Within minutes the temperature has equalised with that of the world outside. I barely stay awake long enough to drink a cup of hot milk as a light frazzle of rain dances over the metal roof.

★

Early morning comes round in an instant and I make a cup of coffee, shoulder blades tensed against the chilly stillness. I'm wide awake with the cold and yet it is still not light. I think about winter work, rising in the darkness to load the van with flowers, setting off an hour before the dawn. I remember a time when I was in Exeter, making a radio programme about traditional Traveller work. I met up with four west country Romany women and a friendly New Traveller couple who were stopping on Haldon Hill. It was late in the autumn, and as we sat in a circle cradling cups of tea in our hands, the conversation turned to the lengthening nights and the falling leaves. It was at this time of year, said the women, that each of them started to think about making holly wreaths for Christmas. Most had grown up making them, and the wreaths were present in their earliest memories: the smells of the leaves and moss must have lain on the air that they breathed whilst asleep in their prams as babies.

They remembered collecting mistletoe, too, for selling in bulk or singly in wishbone-shaped lovers' sprigs. All of them except me had collected and sold mistletoe at some point, and there was unanimous rage about how its harvesting was banned now-adays, in spite of the fact that its careful collection does no real harm to the host tree. As one of them talked about climbing trees with her brothers on frosty days when the fields were the colour of peppermint, gathering mistletoe, I saw how the others' eyes started to widen, their gazes dipping down to the floor, seer-like.

Some had sold Christmas trees too, like I had as a boy. I remembered taking £20 notes in my mitten-clad hands from middle-aged men with estate cars. They were baffled to see that a nine-year-old boy had been left in charge of a lucrative family business. I became adept at grabbing the thin trunks of the trees through the branches, grasping one hand halfway up the tree, the other one down at the bottom to give it support. The waxy scent of the resin and needles announced that Christmas was here, and it smelt like money. I was earning my keep and learning to add up and get used to handling wads of cash, but the apparent trust and independence were only a part of the story. My family were watching me from the orangey warmth of indoors, making sure I was doing my job, and getting ready to come out when required, which was usually when the customers started to struggle and battle to get a tree into their car.

As we talked on it became clear that all our families had seen Christmas as a time to harvest money as well as spend it, taking advantage of the loosened purse strings of the general public. One of the women had married into a wreath-making family, and celebrated her first wedded Christmas by working night and day with her husband, making around six hundred wreaths. She remembered learning the awkward and prickly trade as she went, mastering the dexterity needed, persuading the still-alive sinews of the stubbornest plant in Britain to follow the skeletal curve of a thin wire rim, making it look as if that was where it belonged. It was work that at least one person in each of these women's families had always done, and which some of them still did now. Certain habits and trends emerged over the years, growing into quasi-superstitions. Some relations would only use berried holly; some used fruitless branches with 'berries' made out of small balls of red-coloured wax, rolled between their fingertips.

Other plants bore the name holly, too. Some Travellers, including Nan's brothers, gathered knee-holly, also called 'knee-holm' or 'butcher's broom'. A shrub that grows in squat bushes, its small leaves bear a single prickle at the tip. It was often easy to find and had the effect of holly in miniature, though its red fruits tended to grow after spring at the wrong time of the year. Others would use the eryngium plant, known as 'sea holly'. Unrelated to the holly tree, this tough and spiky maritime plant is a member of the carrot family and has a chilly, distinctive appearance. Its prickly, pastel-blueish green leaves are fringed with a creamy white, and are the most visible part of the plant when its thistle-like flowers have all died off for the winter.

The work of wreath-making always had two distinct purposes. The obvious one was to make a few quid before Christmas, selling the wreaths in batches to florists, or direct to the public from driveways or off a stall by the side of the road. The less obvious reason was to take wreaths to rest upon the family graves at Christmas, reminding the living and the dead that we hadn't forgotten about them. Some Travellers have a religious motivation for this, but for others it's simpler and subtler. 'They may be dead and gone now,' said one of the women in Exeter, 'but without them we wouldn't be here, and their story is part of our story. So it's important that we remember them, but especially at Christmas time.'

I've sketched out a map of the West Country, plotting my course back eastward using Rosie's list as a guide. I tape the note to my dashboard and it flaps about in the breeze. Until now I have been tracing old family haunts, but I am an outsider here, deep in other families' territory. There are two places I want to visit that aren't on the list: Land's End, and the village of Boscastle where I hope I might find some information about Cornwall's Gypsy witches.

On the road to Penzance there are snowdrops out on some of the roadside verges, on a day that looks as though there's always about to be a rainbow. There are slanted rain showers, then suddenly simultaneous sun, then just rain, then the sun again. In a dark moment once I remember asking Nan where the sun had gone, and her replying, 'Gone to find the daughter,' then both of us chuckling. I carry on down the main road before peeling off just ahead of Redruth. This is the neighbourhood of Illogan Highway, which is named after an ancient Cornish saint about whom little is known, his name carried into the future like a weathered figurehead.

The whole area is overlooked by the tan and dark green slopes of Carn Brea Hill. On its top is a village where 8,000 people make their homes alongside Iron Age and Neolithic settlements. The hill has been inhabited for almost six millennia, and as I glance up at it through the van window, Romany culture – and for that matter, Englishness – seem like recent flashes in the pan.

I arrive at my destination: the car park of a Morrisons supermarket, just to the north of a big industrial estate in Pool. I head for the quietest corner to set up my stove and cook my *hobben*. This used to be the site of an entertainment venue called the Flamingo Ballroom. Demolished now to make way for the shop, in its heyday it was one of the largest venues of its kind in the south-west of England. It seated 1,300 people, and hosted boxing matches, professional wrestling, and occasionally the Bournemouth Symphony Orchestra. The Travellers used to stop nearby, and maybe some still do. *You can knock a place down*, I think to myself, *but you can't knock down the outdoors.* I get out my stove and pan and with my little knife start to chop onions into a pot for a 'Joey Grey', a staple dinner of Nan's. I often try to recreate it but somehow it's never quite right.

'Joey Grey' is a name that Romanies use for their traditional soup, but no two families of Travellers seem to agree as to exactly what should go in it. We make ours by frying chopped streaky bacon with onions, then adding water and a tin of tomatoes, sliced potatoes and mushrooms, simmered with a bit of salt and pepper and served with fresh white buttered crusty bread. I once saw two Gypsy women, old friends, turn icy cold when one of them said she put steak in her

Joey Grey instead of the more typical options of bacon or minced beef. When I tried to calm them down by saying that back east in Sussex we make ours with a tin of tomatoes, they forgot their mutual quarrel and looked at me instead, with even harder stares.

As I eat my stew I watch black-backed gulls swoop around and then up to the top of a nearby chimney, the remains of an eighteenth-century mine. It looks as though grass is growing from crevices high up in the brickwork. I walk over and see that it's not grass at all, but spikes, put there to discourage climbers or birds. It doesn't seem to work for the latter. I watch as a starling, a blur of shiny brown, lands gracefully amongst the points and settles for a rest.

Cornwall is peppered with buildings like this. Mining in the area began during the Bronze Age: there are tunnels here that were dug four thousand years ago, before the siege of Troy. Some of the old mines have been abandoned for centuries, their cold and roofless wall tops softened to roundness by the weather, overhung with rugs of moss and haphazard spurts of grass. Below ground, the interlinking of vertical shafts with tunnels dipping just off the horizontal had a geometry something like a skyline full of cranes, but the buildings themselves have a sad and austere beauty, the ruined monasteries of a delving culture. Until recently the working mines provided a tangible link to the national past: the nearby South Crofty mine was opened during the reign of Queen Elizabeth I. It closed in 1998, the epoch of the Spice Girls and Tony Blair.

★

By nine o'clock the next morning I've had my breakfast, packed everything neatly away in the back, and spent half an hour picking up obscure words found in my box of old Romani dictionaries and grammars. Scholars of Romany culture have often scoffed at Gypsies who look to books as a way of improving their language, which always struck me as both hypocritical and absurd. At boarding school I was given a 'word book', in which to write down the definitions of words I didn't know. With English, this was seen as studious and commendable, but learning the Gypsy tongue from books is seen as inauthentic. There is also a common belief that the Romani language has never been written down, which I think about whilst staring at a Romani letter written, in florid Victorian copperplate hand, by Wester 'Dictionary' Boswell in 1874.

I wedge the dictionary back in the footwell and drive on, this time making for Land's End. I want to stand at the edge of the earth and stare out westward across the sea, and think about the motives of the Romanichals and other Travellers who accompanied their compatriots over the water towards the New World. The Americas now host some of the largest Romani populations to be found anywhere, with estimates of over a million in the United States, including large communities in New York, New Jersey, Arkansas and Texas; 800,000 or more in Brazil; and still more living in Canada, Argentina, Colombia and elsewhere. But when I arrive I see there's a big brown visitor centre blocking the way to the sea, with a massive pay-and-display car park that's almost completely deserted. I baulk at the idea of paying to visit Land's End. The shore, with its permanently shifting boundary between dry land and the deep, is nature's rebuttal of the human attempt to enclose everything in perimeters. The tide line cannot be fixed on a map because it never stays still. You can't charge people to visit a place that doesn't really exist.

I drive away, past the biggest solar farm I have ever seen. It seems exotic: an outgrowth of a different local economy, like a Spanish salt farm or a vineyard, and it makes me wonder how far it makes sense to call this place England at all. Recent genetic research has shown that, until modern times, Corns – the ethnic Cornish – hardly mingled with the nearby Devonshire folk, never mind the Norse and Germanic peoples off in the distant east. Science affords us a dangerous chance to remake our myths of belonging in the intelligent-sounding and seemingly neutral language of haplotypes and DNA sequencing. Ineradicable fluoride isotopes are trapped in the honeycomb centres of our bones, carrying the secret of our origins to the grave. The fluoride remains in the skeleton after death, surviving long after our flesh has melted away. Analysis of these chemicals in a clutch of sheep bones found at Stonehenge proves that they had been brought there, most likely alive, by people who had travelled all the way to southern England from the Orkney islands. Whether these people made the journey on land after crossing the Pentland Firth, or sailed round Scotland and down through the Irish Sea and past Wales, or by some other route, we cannot know; but the fact that they must have known about Stonehenge and felt confident enough to set out on such a long and perilous journey seems marvellous and significant. These ancient humans tender proof of an old nomadic streak in the British Isles, one that survived the onset of sedentary living, and one that to this day resurfaces every time someone sets out on a cross-country adventure.

I am here tracking Traveller roots along roads, but the sea is constantly nearby and always wild. Pictures of Celts in delicate coracles scuffing the salty surf are aligning with my habitual visions of wagons down country lanes. Gypsy history must be seen in the context of nomadism as the norm of human life until recent times. In his book *The Isles*, the historian Norman Davies writes that:

> The history of mankind on the peninsula which we now call 'Europe' has lasted for some seven hundred or eight hundred thousand years. For over 99 per cent of that vast expanse of time, man lived in the Stone Age ... Though various convenient caves and open sites were occupied, abandoned, and reoccupied over long periods, there was little permanent settlement as the human troops followed the herds across the ever-changing seasons and feeding grounds.

The Romanies' tenacious grip on their culture – keeping up old ways connected to motion, even long after you've stopped – has frequently been blamed on their far-flung Indian roots: on an inescapable foreignness that survives the passage of time. But what if this clinging to the trappings of nomadism simply mirrors one of the oldest facets of all of human culture: prioritising survival, and moving about accordingly, rather than grimly staying put until whatever end? I think of sea captains going down with their ships, or the Norse colonisers of Greenland starving and freezing to death in the dark: bleak fates which only a half-mad culture could romanticise.

I remember reading Tennyson's 'Charge of the Light Brigade' in a cold boarding-school classroom, mesmerised by this exotic perspective that seemed to suggest a charge could be utterly stupid and, at the same time, desperately brave. The Gypsy way to fight is to train, fight hard, and win; but even if you lose, to survive and live to fight – or not – on another day. And yet the cultures mingle and overlap. The Gypsy John Cunningham won the Victoria Cross at the age of nineteen, after he single-handedly stormed a German trench at the Battle of the Somme, fighting and killing ten enemies on his own. Cunningham survived and came back to England, but did not make old bones. He was buried in Hull twenty-five years later, in front of hundreds of Travellers and with full British military honours.

A small flight of lapwings interrupts my thought: they cross the path of the van, then ribbon off over a field to the west, skimming the breeze that moves inland off the sea.

Further on, about ten miles south of Bodmin, I pull up in a long lay-by well suited to lorries. I make breakfast – yesterday's Joey Grey, reheated. A path runs alongside the lay-by and I unfold my chair on it, then sit down to eat, facing into the sun. But there's a cold draught behind: a permanent link back to the darkness and to my own shadow, the other me that I cannot escape from at night; the me that is starting to struggle with the long and chilly and lonely stretches of darkness. Beside me, everything seems to be rushing and whirring and ticking: the road, the economy, axles and grease; pollution; the late and the on time; the retired; the stupid; the young and the new.

I am startled by a sudden tangle of motion, as a band of five little long-tailed tits fleck themselves at high speed onto the hedge of brambles behind me. I am surprised to see an odd number of them as they generally seem to go about in pairs. I know their tiny bodies are black and white, but as I look at them now they seem to flutter into a pale gold blur. I catch glimpses of their cute little faces as they flick and ping their way over the tangled brambles. They are meticulous workers, leapfrogging each other, gleaning for precious pieces of freeze-dried blackberry.

Suddenly, a huge twin-rotor helicopter swoops in overhead with a menacing, dark warble. The massive pulses of sound it generates go straight through my skin and my ribcage, seeming to threaten the regularity of my heartbeat. It is like the intervention of a terrible alarm clock, and it strikes me as a signal that I should move on.

On the road to Boscastle the trees become scary apparitions. They speak of winter and endless wind, like the hands of giant skeletons reaching up through the crust of the earth. At high points they are bent over steeply, fixed in a permanent backward bow to the raging of the Atlantic. Out of the wind in the dips and valleys, the trees are entirely different: where the air is stiller, their branches are draped with lichens, giving them the appearance of giant spectral antlers. I hug the wending spiral of thin road down into the village. It is like driving into the heart of a snail shell.

Boscastle is freezing and half deserted when I pull up. A sharp, wicked shard of sea wind shoots up into the place like a knife through its narrow valley. I walk to the bank of the cold river Jordan and watch as a lonely jet-black cormorant flap-foots down to the water's edge and calmly immerses itself in the freezing stream. The dark windows of holiday rental cottages stare out glumly into the streets. Behind the panes of glass, little carved wooden fish are stranded on painted windowsills. They seem to gasp in the bone-dry central-heated air, beached among desiccated stones and calcified scallop shells.

I walk round to the entrance of the Witchcraft Museum to enquire about Romany witches, but it is shut fast against me. Out from its heavy mahogany door stare faces in carved relief, solid and charismatic, fixed like charms against the winter. A sign explains that the museum is only open from Easter to Halloween, and closed for the darker half of the year. I have visited it before, and I stand and gaze through the window into the dingy entrance corridor, trying to remember details of my last trip. Photographs of the early Wiccans – English eccentrics like Gerald Gardner, Doreen Valiente and Alex Sanders – adorned the walls, and some of their personal effects were on display. There were various wands and robes, cauldrons and athames – ritual daggers – and models of the horned god that looked like props from a *Hammer Horror* film.

The museum had acquired several 'Books of Shadows' belonging to Wiccan priests and priestesses. These are handwritten records of rituals, some of them beautiful to look at, which form the liturgies of the modern 'craft'. To provide some historical context there was also a full-size diorama of a cunning woman working in her cottage, with jars of herbs and sprigs of dried plants hanging from the rafters, and – if I remember rightly – a taxidermy cat with green glass eyes. One particular object gave me an unpleasant shiver: a big black statue of Baphomet, Satan in his animal shape, that seemed to be made from a real stuffed goat with enormous horns. It looked as though it might actually have lived once, walked on its hind legs, even talked. I get a fresh chill remembering all this and decide to plod back up the hill to the van.

One of the few shops that's open is a crystal-and-gemstone parlour, so I go in to kill some time. On the counter are big glass jars containing magic wands of beech, ash and birch wood, all 'handmade in the West Country' and supplied with numbered explanatory certificates. On one wall, covering several shelves, is a comprehensive range of crystal balls, the smallest the size of a ping-pong ball. The largest, a dark sphere of smoky quartz, looks as though there is a whole galaxy frozen inside it. As I stare at it, it feels as though the line between aesthetic awe and superstition is starting to crumble a bit.

The shopkeeper ambles peacefully over, and asks in a strong Italian accent if I might need some help. Loose sleeves hang from her wrists, and her dark eyes almost match the jet-black hair that runs in sleek trickles from her shoulders. I ask how much the huge crystal ball is.

'Two and a half thousand,' she says. 'No discounts. You are interested in these?'

'I suppose I am. They are very beautiful.'

'You know about this, scrying? When you look into the ball?'

'Not really, no.'

'People associate with Gypsies, no? But in reality, is older.'

'Really?'

'Yes, really, really! The Romans wrote about it, you know.'

I ask her about the museum, and she is well acquainted with its contents. She tells me the story of Granny Boswell, who is mentioned in a display. A Romany woman reputed to have supernatural powers, she had been born in Ireland around 1817 before marrying an English Gypsy, Ephraim Boswell, and settling in the Cornish village of Helston. Granny Boswell is supposed to have once cursed the motor car of a Tory councillor whom she disliked, causing the axles of the car to collapse and leaving its owner stranded in the road.

'Did she use a crystal ball to do that?'

'No,' she says. 'You don't need equipment for this. Only the tongue!'

I thank her for her advice and leave the shop, wondering how the association of crystal balls with Gypsies became so entrenched. In my first year at boarding school, I was walking to lessons with a group of other boys and one of our teachers. Puncturing the silence, the teacher asked us why Gypsies walked funny. I felt myself blench, and the other kids' faces went blank. The teacher breathed deeply and then called out, 'Because they've got crystal balls!' A few nervous chuckles broke out. I felt shattered, a feeling that quickly gave way to shame. I didn't understand how a bad joke could hurt me so much.

Later, I look up the shopkeeper's reference to the Romans and crystal balls. In book 37 of his *Natural History*, Pliny the Elder wrote that it was:

> stated by medical men that the very best cautery for the human body is a ball of crystal acted upon by the rays of the sun. This substance, too, has been made the object of a mania … Crystal, when broken, cannot by any possibility be mended.

I get back to the van, and use the remainder of my paid-for parking time to tidy up, eat dinner and wash. Keeping my washing stuff safely away from the food and cooking utensils is hard in this tiny space, but I manage. The need to avoid being *mokkadi* is ingrained and very strong. It wins out every time over more convenient ways of doing all this, like having one bowl for everything, something I'd only be able to let myself do in the direst of straits. I get out the saucepan and stove to heat up some water, a litre and a half from a crumpled plastic bottle. I look at the three-quarters empty container and think that I've been a bit frivolous, but then I remember all the times

I've had a bath in a hundred times that amount of water and hardly thought anything of it.

Refreshed and clean, I open the door and step back out into the cold afternoon as steam rises off my damp hair. I climb the curling road back out of the village and drive south down the A39, then along the back road down to Bodmin, the B3266, which vaguely follows the southward route of the River Camel. I'm drawn on by the memory of a news story from a couple of years ago. Some Travellers stopped on a road in Bodmin called Midway Lane, which starts outside the town before arcing directly into its centre. There were the usual reports in the local news, replete with complaints of rubbish and noisy, unruly Traveller children. I'm tired and I decide it's my place for the night, reasoning that if whole families have pulled in there recently then there must be enough room for me.

I arrive, and the road is wide, lined by factories on one side, and a ramshackle scrub line of trees on the other, bent into sickles by cold winds rolling down off the lonely moor. There's a gate a few yards ahead of me. It separates the public part of the road from a private residential bit, and bears a warning sign saying that it gets locked overnight. A pink child's balloon is caught in a tree and I watch as it struggles vainly on the wind. The street lamps wash the road with an amber light that in my current mood reminds me of nothing but piss. I get in the back of the van, light my lanterns and half-heartedly warm up some beans.

A car passes by every now and then, until I hear the telltale slow rasp of tyres on gravel and realise that one has pulled up and stopped beside me. My door is slightly ajar and the light of my candles is flickering inside, so they will know that the van is occupied. Someone gets out of the car and I hear them walk up to the gate, faff about with some keys, and then padlock it shut. I get up, whilst preparing responses to typical questions: 'What you doing here?' 'Got permission?' and so forth. But whoever it is gets straight back in their car and drives off. I'm alone again, and for the first time I almost wish they had knocked on the door and asked me the questions I used not to want to be asked. Sometimes a rude person is better than no one at all.

The loneliness is getting to me, and it worsens whenever I pull up near a town. When I'm out in the wild, windy places it's different. I'm able to fully convince myself that I'm there on a meaningful quest: tracking memories, ghosts and a lost way of life. I can tell myself that my being alone is a wished-for and necessary state, a requirement of the journey I've undertaken. Out there, my reference points are explorers and hermits, voluntary exiles and half-lost adventurers, imaginary friends. But as soon as I get near a hamlet or village or, worst of all, a suburb or an actual town, it all changes. I am troubled by the presence of people I don't know, who stand in this middle distance between me and everywhere else. It reminds me that while I may not be alone, I am lonely.

It is Friday night. I am thirty years old, alone on a fake-fur blanket in the back of a cold Transit van. Most of my generation are out there in pubs, or indoors by the telly, canoodling, arguing or cooking, or going across to the thermostat to turn the heating up. I'm parked on a Cornish industrial estate with no warmth bar my own and the tiny wavering plume of heat that rises out of my lantern. This place is so lonesome that even the doggers, boy racers and stoners have spurned it. It's all mine for the night, a little domain of clogged gutters and flickering street lamps. I feel vulnerable and my hands search around for a weapon. I reach down the side of my bed for the jack-handle, looking for reassurance from its cold, hard, certain steel. Then I realise no one will attack me, because I probably look like exactly the sort of weirdo that people go out of their way to avoid. I curse myself silently. You're not a Traveller, my mate, you're a *div*. What sort of Traveller would come and sleep here on their own? I am missing a vital ingredient. I'm missing some company.

The phone rings. It is my mum's brother. His voice crackles, welcome as heat.

'Danes?'

'Alright.'

'Where you at?'

'Cornwall.'

'What you doing down there?'

'I'm in the van.'

'What, at this time of year?'

'Yeah.'

'Bit cold, ain't it?'

'Yep.'

'What you doing down there?'

'Going round some of the old stopping places.'

'Is there any there, then?'

'Course there are. They're everywhere.'

'No, I meant, is there any down there to do with us?'

'Well ... No, I mean ... Someone gave me a list ... '

'What, one of our lot?'

'No. A Travelling woman from over this way.'

'*Dordi.* Well, good luck.'

'What do you mean?'

'Don't matter. You know what you're doing.'

'No, what were you gonna say?'

'Well, if you go to every stopping place in the country you'll be doing it for a hundred and fifty years, won't you?'

'I'm not trying to see them all ... Just a few, you know ...'

'Oh, well, don't matter. How long you gonna be there for?'

'Couple of weeks.'

'Okay, mate, see you when you get back. Look after yourself.'

He puts the phone down. Troubled, I get into bed.

The next few days seem to run into each other: I meander back eastward, stopping at some of the places on Rosie's list. I spend a night in St Germans, a village just west of Plymouth that scabbards a straight central road. I open my eyes in the morning to find that ice has formed on the ceiling of the van. On one side it is a glimmering fan of twinkling, frozen feathers; on the other, a complex asymmetrical grid-like pattern made from thin lines of ice. It reminds me of diagrams of the old Cornish tin-mine shafts that stretch out under the sea. Then

I cough with the cold and the whole ceiling is obscured by billowing clouds of my breath. I check my little thermometer. It is minus 2 degrees centigrade: not polar-cold, but cold enough to make me get dressed in a rush and jump outside to try and warm up. At half past six in the morning the village appears completely deserted. The freezing night has covered it with a dusting of sparkling blue-white frost, and a red postbox keeps a silent vigil beside the bright green doors of a primary school next to the van. A cock crows in the near distance, and when I turn my head in its general direction I see a thin grey plume of steam rising straight upwards before twisting and turning like treacle.

I only stop once in Devon, at the top of the large and partly forested Haldon Hill, another place on Rosie's list. It's a natural waypoint and halting site after the long clamber up to the summit. This was especially true if you'd driven a horse – or horses – all the way up to the top, more so if one of them had just pulled a wagon up there. There's a service station at the top of the hill where I fill up with diesel and rest for a while. I doze off. When I wake up I drive around to a spot on the edge of some tall coniferous woodland. I know an encampment of New Travellers has been situated there for years, and I get the idea that I might drop in on the couple I met back in Exeter when we were talking about the holly wreaths and mistletoe harvesting. But the road is blocked off for roadworks, with diversion signs and big orange plastic blockades.

I sit there for a moment with the engine idling, staring down the road, then pick up my camera and take a couple of pictures of the road block. I am about to turn around and go when an old green Land Rover pulls up beside me. A heavyset, balding man in a cream-and-green checked shirt leans out of the window. He has a shiny face with red cheeks and grins at me without showing his teeth.

'Alright?' he says.

'Yeah, you?'

'Can't go down there, pal. She's all blocked off.'

'I can see that.'

'What you waiting for, then?'

'Nothing much.'

'Well, you look a little bit suspicious if you ask me.'

'I didn't ask you.'

'What was you doing with that camera?' He nods gravely at it.

'Taking pictures.'

'Oh, yeah? Of what?'

'What's it got to do with you?'

'I got land round here.'

'Well, you don't own this road.'

'Looked like you was zooming in. Stuff has gone missing round here. I've had machinery taken. So's other people.'

'I'm sorry to hear that.'

'People see unmarked vans, they tend to get suspicious.'

'Not much I can do about that, really, is there?'

'No. Don't suppose there is.'

He stares the van up and down for a few seconds.

'What you got in there?'

'That's none of your business.'

'Sound like you've got something to hide.'

'Look, mate, I came here to get diesel. I'm just passing through and I like to take photographs. I'm sorry your stuff's been nicked. But you're not the police and you're not looking in my van.'

'No need to be like that. Just making sure you're alright.'

'I am alright.'

'Can't be too careful. Lot of Travellers come round here.'

'So I've heard. See you later.'

I back away from his Land Rover, then turn in the road and drive off. I look back in the mirror. He stays where he is until I'm gone.

On the way back eastward I pull over by a frosty verge. I lie down on the green-white grass that is crispy and stiff with the frost, and take a photo of my pallid face, a keepsake of winter.

There is a reason, besides the season and Candis's absence, why the last few weeks have dragged. My uncle's troubling words have been playing on my mind: that if I visited every *atchin tan* in the country, I'd be at it for a hundred and fifty years. His Traveller's exaggeration masks a truth I have been suppressing. I cannot be systematic on this journey. There are too many stopping places. How can I hope to stay over at all the ones I'm told about, never mind every significant one in the country? It is impossible. I feel deflated as my limits start to crystallise before me. Spring and summer lie ahead. I need to work out where I'm going, and why.

Crossing back into Hampshire, I pull up at the Copper Kettle, the last place written down on Rosie's little list. The inn and camping fields that used to attract the Travellers here are gone, replaced by a small residential development with the feel of a private estate. The copper kettle the inn was named for still hangs from the whitewashed outer wall. I look up at it, a sign that worked as well for the illiterate as for anybody else.

I get the van ready to spend the night here and it dawns on me that this is a crossroads of my journey. The places Rosie told me about were genuine *atchin tans*, but for all the time I spent in them, I bought little in return. These campsites lacked a direct link to my family, or to me; and if they had a message, then my senses couldn't read it. I realise now that it isn't enough for a place to be connected to the Gypsies. We are all individuals, and there must be a link from each of us to the places we end up: something beyond a word; some concrete grounds for pitching camp, whether it's in the earth, or in ourselves.

The Bones

Bridie's Tan, Latton Common, Marshland St James

In 2006, a team of archaeologists working in Norwich city centre unearthed a human skeleton, buried in an Anglo-Saxon churchyard during the eleventh century AD. Its bones were carefully exhumed, brushed clean of earth, and sent away to laboratories for routine scientific analysis.

When the results came back, the team were astonished. Preserved in the skeleton's teeth was a rare gene: a gene which has only ever been found in the descendants of Romany people. Prior to this discovery, it was believed that the earliest Romanies had arrived in Britain as many as five hundred years later, towards the end of the fifteenth century.

I sit in the cab and wonder what this isolated specimen of Gypsy DNA might, or might not, mean. I try to argue myself out of overestimating its significance. It is hubris to think we can know where everyone was in the distant past. People sailed the seas, they came and went: why should anyone be surprised to find out that these fragile remains, plucked from the dark earth of an older England, had Romany roots? Besides, the skeleton was so old that it might not even be reasonable to refer to it as 'Romany', an ethnic identity that probably took many years to coalesce on the long road out of India into the west.

But I can't get it out of my mind. A lone south Asian figure, buried according to Christian law; enveloped in Anglo-Saxon ground a thousand years ago. I think I know where I am going. I start the van up and head east.

I stop for the night in Harlow, the first town in Britain to take out a district-wide injunction against unauthorised encampments by Travellers. Anyone who breaches the ban could be found guilty of contempt of court and fined or imprisoned. The council leader has told journalists that 'this is not and never has been about persecuting a particular group of people or their way of life'.

I pull into the town and approach Latton Common. It was once the site of the Harlow Bush Fair, a favourite haunt of the Gypsies in the eighteenth and nineteenth centuries. The fairs have always been dangerous places to get into a fight. In 1832, a Romany man called Elijah Buckley was mortally wounded here after an argument at the fair. He left behind a wife, Elizabeth, and two children, George and Leviathan. The common is empty now, and silent but for the susurration of the trees on its far side. I park in a gravelled space by the roadside and make dinner: new potatoes and cabbage flavoured with bacon. Not many people come past – a few drivers, one or two dog walkers. The sun sets out of sight behind the clouds.

The distant treeline of the common bleeds up into the falling night. I roll a fag and whistle a bit of 'The Star of the County Down'. Nobody comes to enforce the injunction. The night is quiet and cool. Despite my fear of transgressing an actual law, the darkness passes without incident.

Next morning I head east out of Harlow, then north on the M11, stopping at Birchanger services for a shower. I park opposite a spotless Transit truck. It has a shiny black towbar, chrome detailing around the lights and door handles, and wraparound vinyl stickers which advertise a small pressure-washing business. There are BEFORE and AFTER pictures of a block-paved drive, the first blackened with mildew and grime, the second transformed into pristine blood-red brick.

I get out some clean clothes, my washbag and towel and go into the services. Inside there is piped-in pop music, the crazy ting-pings of the fruit-machine area, and demented beeping melodies coming from grab-a-soft-toy machines.

I shower and shave, then walk back through the services, funnelled past a McDonalds and a tall cabinet full of brightly coloured doughnuts. My hair is wet and my towel and clothes are folded up under my arm. A teenage girl with a golden afro looks at me and says to her friend, 'Oh my God, are there showers in here?'

As I go to get back in the van, a man I assume to be the driver of the Transit truck walks past me, towel and washbag in hand. His tight curly red hair is gelled on the top and shaved close at the sides, and he's wearing a spotless Ralph Lauren shirt.

I give him the Traveller's nod, a slight dip of the head and a serious, unsmiling stare from just under the brow, neither aggressive nor too friendly. He slams his door shut and walks over.

'Alright, mate?' I say.

'Yeah, not bad, yourself?'

He's Irish. Softly spoken.

'Yeah, pulled up for a shower.'

He chuckles. 'You know, don't ya. Stoppin' round here?'

'On my way up to East Anglia. Working.'

'I'm on me way back from there now, I am. Down to London, you know?' He emphasises 'London' as though there's a good chance I've never heard of it.

'Yeah, I lived up there for a few year.'

'Did you so?'

'Yeah, I did.'

'How'd you find it?'

'Alright.'

'It's no place for a Travelling man.'

'You won't be hanging about down there, then?'

'No, I fucking won't.'

He gets out a packet of fags and puts one in his mouth.

'What you going up that way for, then?' he asks.

I'm hesitant about mentioning a skeleton from the Dark Ages.

'Visiting graves.'

'Ah, family up there, like?'

'Sort of.'

'Life's fuckin' short.'

'Yes, it is.'

He knocks his hand twice on the side of my van. Then he points at me with an outstretched finger, like Elvis indicating one of his fans.

'Be lucky, won't ya, my friend?'

'You too, mate' I reply.

He turns and walks quickly away, lighting his cigarette in cupped hands as he goes.

I spend the night in a lay-by somewhere in an out-of-the-way bit of Hertfordshire. Just before I pull over, I think I see a small wild boar run off the road and over a ditch into the darkness.

At seven o' clock, a narrow shaft of the sun sneaks in through a gap in my makeshift curtains and flashes in my eyes. Dawn is getting earlier every day, but I only really register the change when the morning sky is clear and free from clouds. I'm more sensitive to changes in temperature and the amount of moisture in the air, and life is getting better on both these fronts.

Instantly awake from the light, I don't bother with coffee or food, just pack up and move straight on, following signs for Cambridge until I pass it by in the distance, heading steep north-east for the Fens. They arrive with powder-blue skies, reed beds, pale light, and grass that glints with the nickel tone of cool water.

I pull up in a lay-by near Chatteris for porridge, a cigarette and a cup of tea. Chatteris Fen was a well-known stopping place for the Travellers who brought in the Cambridgeshire crops from these wide fields, vast and flat with scant cover from the wind. As I wait for the kettle to boil I see the hares are up and chasing each other between and over the low ploughed rows of seedlings. I look more carefully and see there are others, sitting bolt upright and perfectly still, and wonder how many more there must be, crouching out of sight and waiting out the daylight hours. I count six running and three sitting, nine hares. For Travellers who are into hare coursing, Cambridgeshire is spoken of like a sort of English El Dorado but also somewhere that's 'red hot', meaning the police are on constant high alert for the poacher's infractions; a place where irate farmers have been known to spray deadly white-hot potshots at fleeing estate cars full of skinny saluki-cross running dogs and young men in greasy wax coats. I imagine the great-grandfathers of both farmers and poachers, in an age of moustaches and hungrier guts, and picture a musket or blunderbuss taking aim at the Gypsies' backs as they flee across fields, an old scenario that occasionally flares back to life. I also wonder if many of the 'coursing men' eat the hares they catch. I have never been coursing in my life, and though I take no pleasure in the pursuit of frightened animals, it is emasculating to say the only hare meat I have eaten was bought from the game counter of a Budgens super-market in Finsbury Park.

The porridge is disappointing, but I'm grateful to have a full belly and am ready to move. As I wash up, a boy racer's toad-green hatchback slows down to a crawl on the road, and someone leans out of the window, points at me and shouts,

'He's fucking washing up!' Maniacal laughter and fag smoke spill from the car as it speeds back up and disappears down the road. I notice that I find it amusing, where in the past I would have been crushed to be laughed at in this way. Somewhere within me, the long slow gears of change are on the move. The world and all its habits are starting to wash over me, like the wind gliding over the van.

Travellers I knew from the east had 'lived rough' deep into the recent past, still working the farms right into the 1990s. By then it had been the best part of fifty years since anyone in my family had depended on that kind of work. So it came as a shock to meet Travellers younger than me who had grown up picking turnips in January. They described reaching down with a gloved hand and grabbing hold of the big leafy tops, an action that would sometimes send a plug of ice shooting upwards into the air.

I soon find myself cruising along raised banks, the engineered hems of the fens, eerily straight roads reclaimed from reluctant earth. They often run in unbending lines for a mile, two miles, sometimes more. Out here I've got no real idea how long or wide anything is. All things seem washed in a mixture of water and sky, petering out in a single horizon without a visible end.

From out of my left blind spot, a line of lapwings swoops into view, flickering black and white. It's the first time I have seen these birds since Cornwall and we're riding the wind together. I forget why I am moving and I laugh, happy in a moment of purposelessness.

Mesmerised by the birds, I almost fail to notice a sudden right turn. I brake hard and wrench the steering wheel round, only just keeping to the road, my left wheels carving through mud. I skid to a halt, hold on to my breath, yank the handbrake up, then slump back into the driver's seat. I start to hyperventilate. I am alive.

I look in the passenger-side wing mirror and see something marking the corner I almost missed. It is a roadside memorial, plastic flowers and a simple cross made from dark wood, with a colourful smear in the cross's centre, a photograph of the deceased.

I have been warned.

I stop in a village called Marshland St James. It is stretched out along a single, straight and seemingly endless road. I walk over to a small cemetery and my eyes scan the graves. Several of them are covered with tall marble vases full of multicoloured carnations, and the headstones are particularly large. This combination is usually a dead giveaway of a Traveller's resting place, so I step out of the van to take a look.

I stand opposite one of the graves that is smothered in flowers. They look fresh, as if those who brought them have only just left. Inscribed on the headstone in gilded italics is a verse I have seen on many Gypsy memorials:

> *They say memories are golden*
> *Well maybe that is true*
> *But we never wanted memories*
> *We only wanted you.*

These simple, unpretentious lines hold a double-sided message. Traveller culture, preoccupied though it can be with bygone times, has always preferred the tangible: today's bread, the here and the now. As Nan says, 'You can only eat one meal at a time.' In the past, writers took this as evidence that Gypsies inhabited a 'heroic present', lacking a sense of history and living so sharply in the moment that concepts like deferred gratification were lost on them. I have always dismissed such ideas as inherently dangerous: they are liable to slide into essentialism, and the belief that races have irreconcilable differences.

But maybe in turning so sharply away from a lie, I lost sight of a truth: that the present holds a finer promise than the past with its shadows and dust. In an inversion of the obvious, perhaps even the Traveller obsession with cemetery maintenance itself supports this view. After all, isn't the act of placing flowers on a tomb a gesture of bringing a little life back to the dead?

I reach out and gently touch the monuments of these people I did not know, and reconsider what I have been doing in recent months. Since Cand and I went to the fair at Horsmonden, I've largely avoided gatherings of people. Whilst I don't regret spending so much time in empty stopping places, or visiting forlorn churches and well-kept graves, it is dawning on me that there's only so much I can learn from this. Another of Nan's catchphrases comes to me: 'There are no pockets in shrouds.' Perhaps this saying, a caution against overzealous pursuit of riches, masks a second meaning as well. There is a poverty to death; a limit to how much a skeleton can teach you about a life it no longer knows.

When I return to the van I realise how sparsely furnished it is. Its naked pale blue surfaces stare at me like sheets of ice. I have been travelling with what I thought were the bare essentials – bed, stove, wash gear, clothes and so forth. But there were other trappings of Romany life, when it was lived most richly: beautiful furnishings, gilded surfaces, portable pictures, talismans and silks. I've been missing a trick: the means by which a difficult life was rendered liveable and even, at times, enviable.

I had thought about going to the spot where the skeleton with Romany genes was dug up. But it's not where I need to go. I need to make a change. So I turn back south.

On the way home I decide to try my luck stopping at one of the only 'transit sites' I know – a converted lay-by called Bridie's Tan, just off the A27 east of the town of Lewes. Before it was renovated by the council and reopened as an official stopping place, the lay-by had already been in use for decades, conveniently situated between the two southern Romany heartlands of Hampshire and Kent. As government-sanctioned, authorised *atchin tans*, transit sites are few and far between. They are usually full and often have an established clientele: if someone is pulling off, they'll give family members a ring to see if anyone is heading that way and might want the space before it gets snapped up by somebody else. What's more, I'm alone, because Candis has gone to look after her nan for a few days. Travellers don't tend to like lone men turning up when there are women and kids about, particularly during the day when most of the men are out at work. The more I think about it, the less it seems like a great idea.

As I slow down for the entrance to Bridie's Tan, I peep through the hedge and notice a lot of cars and a few big trailers. It looks as though the site might be full. A trailer door is half open, and an arm pokes out from around its corner and flicks the ash off a cigarette. There are cars, a couple of small drop-sided lorries and a few tourer trailers. I can't see if there's any room. The road is busy but moving fast as I indicate left and slow down into the entrance. After I cut the engine I can hear the small birds singing in amidst the budding bushes as the background whoosh of passing traffic pitches and falls like the sea seven miles to the south.

By the entrance stand five wheelie bins, recently emptied. There is a row of lockable bollards, a set of steel gates, and a sign that says entrance to the site is 'BY PRIOR ARRANGEMENT ONLY'. There are two phone numbers. I call one. The rings come through fuzzy and loud out of the speakers of the van. It rings and rings until I am about to put the phone down and try somewhere else.

A voice answers. A man, maybe forty or fifty.

'Hello?'

'Oh, yes, hello, I was calling about the Bridie's Tan Traveller site off the A27.'

'Yes?'

'Sorry, I was just wondering if there's any room on there at the minute?'

'Well, what's your situation?'

'I'm round this way working. I'm by myself, I haven't got a trailer with me, I'm just in the van. And I wondered if there might be a pitch going on there.'

'There isn't, I'm afraid, it's full at the moment.'

'Oh. Okay. Well, I suppose that's that.'

'Yes. I'm sorry.'

'Thanks.'

I go to put the phone down, but he has more to say.

'Yes, it is just a matter of calling up and seeing if there is any availability.'

'Right.'

'We don't take prior bookings or anything like that.'

'Okay.'

'Yes, you can stay on there for up to twelve weeks.'

'Really? I was only after one night ... '

'Ah, okay.'

'Well listen, never mind, mate. Thanks for trying to help me.'

'Okay. Best of luck.'

He beats me to putting the phone down.

As the conversation finishes, a Transit van comes scudding up off the road in a cloud of dust and stops right next to me, scouring deep tracks in the dirt. Two men about my age jump out and come running over in my direction. I'm briefly panicked, wondering what they are doing. One of them is saying, 'Fucking hell fucking hell fucking hell,' and I notice that he is holding onto his crotch. The two men part ways, running round either side of my van like fishes avoiding a rock in a stream. They skid to a halt by the tall, dense brambles that run round the edge of the site, and let out loud sighs of relief as they piss up against the hedge. Then they jog back towards their vehicle, laughing their heads off, and hit the road.

They are gone in the nick of time: seconds later, a black Volkswagen Golf hoves out of the site and takes their place. It pulls up next to me, slow as a crocodile, blacked-out windows whirring down with a low robotic buzz. Two teenage boys stare up at me with inflexible expressions. I put my thumb up to show I mean no harm but their faces do not change: instead, they simply stare at me a little while longer before turning to face forward again. They wind the windows back up before revving off up the dual carriageway.

I've never felt this conspicuous, and I can't stop myself from wanting to leave. As I roll a cigarette in preparation for taking off, I look to my right and notice that a man is standing about twenty yards away and staring at me: must be the site warden, I think, for he's on the threshold of a little house-like building by the road that goes down to the site. Like the boys in the Golf, he stares at me a little while longer, then goes into the house and shuts the door. I put the van in gear and drive on, feeling deflated. Were the Gypsy camps of England always this shut-fast and forbidding? Nan raised us with tales of Travellers who would share the last of their tea and sugar with another in need. Are those times gone, abandoned for secrecy, money and padlocked gates?

Half a mile up the road I notice a small white shape which seems to be working its way up the carriageway verge, heading in the opposite direction to me. It stands out against the green of the grass and glows bright in the westering sun. As I come closer I see it's a short man or possibly a woman – I can't quite tell which because of their loose clothes – with something large attached to their back, bound in colourful silks.

I turn around at the next roundabout and get alongside the figure. The large silk-wrapped object is a guitar, and its bearer has jet-black, slicked-back hair and a contented-looking dark face. He is a young man, wearing a garment that is somewhere between a long coat and a North African jalabiya. I look back to the road and then at him again as I pass by. He looks like a *Rom* from abroad. I can hardly believe what I'm seeing.

There's a five-bar gate up ahead with about thirty square yards of grass in front of it. I hastily indicate left and pull in, reversing the van and churning up the still water-sodden spring turf. I get out and throw open the doors, and a waft of wind from a speeding truck blows through the van, setting my silks and curtains fluttering as if I am camped on the steppes. I make sure everything is tidy and set about fixing myself a cup of tea. I sit down to drink it, trying to look nonchalant.

A few moments later, the man with the guitar on his back comes walking slowly along. He is in no hurry whatsoever but he is clearly coming towards me. I wonder if it is obvious that I've pulled up here because I saw him and wanted to talk. I gingerly sip my tea, stone-faced, and try to look uninterested in him. He comes up to me and stops and I see that he has a friendly look, hazel eyes streaked with piercing green staring out from his lightly bearded gold-brown face.

'Hello,' he says.

'Hello,' I say back.

'Please. You have water?' I can't place his accent.

'Of course. Here, sit down. Please.' I hand him a folding stool and he sits on it, exhaling with relief as the weight leaves his feet.

I pour him a glass of water, taking care to keep the spout of my water jack clear of the rim of the glass in case he keeps a conservative version of the *Romanipen*.

'Thank you,' he says, and takes a big gulp of the water. 'Are you sleeping in this?' He gestures towards the van with the glass in his outstretched hand.

'Yes.'

'It's good, yes?'

'It's okay. Cold in the winter.' He nods. Drinks some more water.

I decide to break the ice. '*Rom san?*' – You are Roma?

His calm face breaks into a smile. He doesn't answer, but nods in reply. '*Tu san Rom?*' – Are you one?

I tell him yes, and he starts to talk quickly in a form of Romani I can hardly understand. Every other word seems to end in the syllable *oy*, which throws me as it is not usually a common sound in the language. I nod along, smiling, but turn my palms upwards to show I'm not really following what he says. Finally I hear a phrase I understand, *Katar avilan* – where are you from – to which he adds a final customary *oy*. I point to the ground and tell him, 'England,' to which he responds '*Czech-oy? Ongar-oy?*', believing I must have some Central or East European roots. I shake my head and laugh and tell him again I'm from England. He seems to find this absolutely hilarious and starts to laugh with me and shake his head. The laughter is contagious and self-propagating, and we have to fight through it and catch our breath in order to swap names. '*Miro anav si o Damian*,' I say – my name is Damian. He shakes my hand with a slow, soft handshake and then says simply, 'Pauli.'

Code-switching between Romani, English and tourist's hand gestures, I offer Pauli a cup of tea and some food, but he waves the suggestions away with his hand, and just asks for another cup of water. He drinks slowly but steadily, finishing cup after cup. Eventually he has had enough and I wash his glass and my teacup and offer him a lift. He only wants to go as far as the 'next town', wherever that happens to be.

We take off in the van and I ask him '*Yek gili pe amaro drom*' – to play me one song for the road. Pauli obliges, unwrapping his guitar with great care from its colourful silks. He eases into picking the strings with the grace of someone who's been playing since they first learned to walk. He starts off with a bit of '*Nuages*' by the great Manouche (French Romany) jazz guitarist, Django Reinhardt, before breaking into a faster paced rumba tune that I don't recognise. He sings along in a language I can't understand at all. I slap my thigh, trying to keep tight rhythm, and he smiles, either because I'm staying in time or because my timing is so bad it deserves his pity. He stops and I shout out, '*Whupa!*' – the Eastern European equivalent of the better-known Flamenco *olé* of approval – and he stops playing, wraps his guitar up in its fabric, and smiles. He asks me once again where I am from, and when I tell him for a third time that I am from England, he asks about my family, who I say are from England as well. He chuckles and just keeps on shaking his head, as if I have told him I come from the moon. I ask him where he is from and he says, 'Katar Ongar' – from Hungary. I tell him I once spent a week in the town of Nagykőrös and he nearly chokes himself laughing at my inept pronunciation of the name, before repeatedly saying it in what sounds to me like exactly the same way.

A few miles later Pauli starts to get fidgety. We've been driving for less than fifteen minutes and I can see he has already had his fill of the journey I've been on for months. He doesn't seem like a fifty-mile-an-hour man. Perhaps this is why he wasn't thumbing for a lift when I saw him. He would rather just walk.

He keeps asking me how far it is to the town, until we get to a roundabout a little way north of Eastbourne. At this point he gestures to get out and I tell him I might as well take him all the way, but he's not having any of it. He wants out and he moves to open the door. On the left an extremely long lay-by rises into view, full of camper vans and trucks, and I swing into it, then ask Pauli if I can take a photo of us by the van because I'm scared nobody will believe this has happened. He obliges, and when I look at the picture, we're both pulling a similar face: bemused smiles.

Pauli says thanks and shakes my hand, then swings his silk-wrapped guitar back up onto his back and sets off along the road at his slow, steady pace. I watch him until he is out of sight, disproportionately sad that I will probably never see him again, this man I have known for less than half an hour.

It occurs to me that our sense of connectedness springs as much from the feeling that we are connected, as from the fact that we actually are. The Gypsies are descended from common stock, but so ultimately is all of humanity. Perhaps the difference is not whether you're part of a tribe, but whether you care to notice that you are.

There's a nice little pull-in between two skinny oaks and I decide to stop there for the night without over-thinking it. I play the spoons and sing for a bit as the sky turns peachy, then blue.

When I wake up the next morning I pack my bedding away and tidy the van up fast, noticing how I do these things with ever increasing speed. I clean out the cab and living quarters, each sweep of the brush a tentative gesture of beckoning to the sun.

When the clouds break, I move the van up onto a high grass verge. The sun streams in through the windows, intensified by the glass, and I sit and relish it for a while, the fiercest light I have felt on my face in months. When it gets too hot I throw open the doors to air the back, and I get out my old pair of spoons. Grasping them either side of my right fore-finger, I tap out metallic rhythms between my left palm and right thigh. Occasionally I run a trill of beats along the stiffly outstretched fingers of my left hand, a flourish Nan showed me how to do when I was little. I can only play the spoons in an English style, and I stick to the well-worn hornpipes and jigs that Travellers prefer to sing, dance and *diddle* along to. (*Diddling* means chanting well-timed but nonsensical syllables based on words from the Romani language, an old Traveller musical form that is dying out now – *dai-dum-pa-diddly-ump-a-diddly-ump-a-dai, diddly-ump-a-deedle-ump-a-du-dai-dai*.) Because the spoons were often used to provide percussive backing for step-dancers and accompaniment for singing, a consistent rhythm is favoured: the aim is to 'show time' and keep your speed regimented and reliable, unlike the constantly shifting rhythms associated with some other forms of Gypsy music. 'Tune me up, sister,' a dancer will say, expecting their backer to keep to the beaten track.

But this morning, Continental Romani lines are drifting into the mix. It must be because of Pauli. I keep to the same old rhythms, but bring into them the verses of '*Nane Tsokha*' ('I Have no Shoes'), a well-worn lament from Eastern Europe, and the words of '*Nash Balamo*' ('Run, Outsider'), a famed rebellious Greek-Gypsy song. It's the first time I've sung the foreign Romani songs whilst playing my great-grandmother's traditional instrument. Something about this simple act seems to suture a divide in my mind; to narrow the English Channel and beckon me south.

Once all my chores are done, I ring my mum. She has a collection of fabrics, silks and tapestries stored in a rented shipping container a few miles out of town. I'll have to raid these stocks, and need her keen aesthetic eye, if I am to bring about the sort of miraculous change the van so badly needs.

I arrange to meet Mum at the storage container and when I get there she looks happy, as if pleased that I've finally grasped the meaning of life. She unlocks the padlock and I pull open the huge green metal doors as daylight floods into the inside of the container, a cave of wonders out of place in these austere British surroundings. We walk inside and Mum goes straight for a see-through plastic box full to bursting with embroidered fabrics of every colour and texture. She pulls out a pile of cloths and sorts through them, handing me two. 'I think that one's Persian, I don't know where the other one's from,' she says. I take the cloths, one dark blue riven with pink and gold, the other a rich gold colour with stitched red patterns of tendrils, vines and leaves. I place them in the back of the van while Mum searches intently through the many boxes. She knows what's there, which keeps her calm amongst the teetering piles of stacked materials. I don't quite share her serenity. Seeing masses of stuff in storage makes me panicky and short of breath, perhaps because they symbolise the freight of life that ties us to a place. But in spite of this, the fact that Mum keeps all this is going to help me as I move, setting me up for spring and summer on the road. It is like visiting an oasis of good morale.

I would have been content with these few bits, but moments later Mum emerges from the container carrying a tall pile of folded materials in her arms. There is an Islamic purple velvet hanging, edged with golden stitching and arranged in a pattern of teardrops, that makes me think of Muslim Romani friends of mine from Kosovo. Next in the pile are matching Bedouin horse-cloths, given to Mum by a friend who was in turn given them, somewhere in the Maghreb. The larger of the two sits across the horse's back, and the other, I presume, goes over the neck. They are constructed out of navy blue and orange-coloured diamond shapes of fabric, stitched together to form a chessboard of gaps and squares that flanks a central rectangle of cloth, with little braids of horsehair fixed to the edges at various points. Lastly, there are another three brightly coloured Indian tapestry cloths: two square ones, and one in the shape of an arch. They shout in bright yellows and blues and greens and pinks, with tiny mirrors stitched into them alongside little embroidered birds, stars, flowers, chakra wheels and Hindu swastikas. Flags emblazoned with this symbol – tilted at a crooked angle – flew above the Gypsy camp at Auschwitz, where Romany people of Indian descent were slaughtered in their droves; an irony that speaks from amidst the heartening colours of these fabrics, that seem to glow and course with the captured energy of the sun.

I thank Mum profusely, which she brushes off with the nonchalance of someone whose life is spent amongst things as beautiful as these. Then I drive the van back to the yard and decorate it, clipping the cloths to the plywood lining with bulldog clips and larger, stronger, rubber-tipped market grips. The hardest part is hanging the Bedouin horse-cloth. I drape it from the ceiling, and suddenly the van simulates the experience of being inside a tent. After re-hanging my lanterns, I step back to absorb and admire the change.

I can't wait for Cand to see this. The van is completely transformed. Its contents come together into a nomadic aesthetic
all of its own; ramshackle, yet somehow making happy sense
as a whole. The bed with its floral-patterned blankets is
typical of the sofas in a modern Traveller's trailer; likewise,
the stainless water jack and electric heater symbolise the prag-
matism of contemporary Gypsies on the road. But the tiny
mirrors and lanterns hearken back to different transports, a
different time: a wagon that travelled the Silk Road during
the long Mongolian peace. But there's also a Honda petrol
generator, a Roberts world radio and a military stove, and all
these things are encased in a shell manufactured in twenty-first-
century Hampshire. The icy blue of the van's metal panelling
is barely visible now – I have put flesh on its bones. It feels
alive.

I am still standing there, as the breeze flows through the van
and the sunlight washes over all the fabrics, when my gran
and grandad – Mum's parents – wander over to see what I've
been doing. They seem stunned, but in a good way: 'Looks
like an old *vardo*,' Grandad says, and Gran remarks that the way
I've hung the cloths reminds her of the inside of the Travellers'
square tents back when she was a little girl. Their approval
comes as a relief. If any of the family had walked over and
taken the mickey, I would have classed it as a *gub*: a sprinkling
of bad luck; an inauspicious start to thousands of miles on the
road in this new incarnation of my home.

I am getting ready to leave when Gran walks over, and tells
me I can borrow the red cushions with gold tassels that used

to be in her old Carlight trailer, as well as her little 'Black Sarah' figure, a replica of the holy statue of St Sara-la-Kali – a Romany 'Black Madonna' and a patron saint of the Gypsies – which she brought back from the Camargue. I place the cushions on the bed and stow the statue carefully with my radio, my incense box and books. Having the statue there has introduced a pull towards the pilgrimage of St Sara, which takes place every May in the south of France: if not this year, then soon at least. Having her effigy in the van brings about a tightening of my allegiance to this little-known saint, who calls to me in the cold chalk hills of Sussex from her home in a crypt by the Mediterranean Sea. I close the van doors, high on the blessings I have received for the next phase of my *dinlo* quest.

8

The End

Aigues - Mortes,

Les Saintes-Maries-de-la-Mer

Candis returns from Kent for a few nights and we stay in the trailer. My old mate Anouar comes round for a drink and we sit outside on the step, toasting our relief at the coming of spring. Anouar grew up mostly in Sussex but his roots are Tamazight, from the Atlas Mountains of Morocco. We watch videos of his people singing and playing goatskin drums in the hills, a situation that seems to compare favourably with the winter he has just endured in sodden West Sussex. I show him the revamped van and the statue of Sara-la-Kali that Gran gave me, and float the possibility of heading down to Les Saintes-Maries-de-la-Mer to see the great Romany pilgrimage. Anouar is instantly energised by the idea and tells me his foster parents have a place not far from there, which we could use as a base if I drove down in the van. We keep talking and the drinks keep flowing until a drunken pact is made, to go down to the Camargue in a few weeks' time. I briefly protest that this will interfere with my pre-planned journey around Britain, but Anouar smiles a wicked smile and tells me I know in my heart of hearts I'll see things and get insights about my people down there that I cannot get here, which will put a new – and sunlit – spin on the journey.

I have been to France to see French Gypsies once before. Six years ago, I drove down to the small town of Barr near Strasbourg with Jake Bowers, where we met the Manouche virtuoso guitarist Engé Helmstetter and his family. The Germanic surname is not unusual amongst their people: not only because in this instance the family comes from Alsace, with its long history of being fought over by the French and Germans, but because many French Gypsies are Sinti, meaning they come from the same stock as the Romany people of Germany and the Low Countries. The ever-changing land borders of nations are often scant impediment to the movement of the Gypsies, and the same Sinti names crop up everywhere from the former Austria-Hungary to the foothills of the Pyrenees: Rosenberg, Schneeberger, Weiss and Steinbach, and the best-known of them all: Reinhardt. None of these families escaped unscathed from the war years, and the memorial wall of the Sinti and Roma Cultural Institute in Heidelberg lists thousands of Sinti murdered by the Nazis and their accomplices, not just in the concentration camps but in mass shootings from the near parts of Russia to the southern tip of Italy. The origins of the name 'Sinti' itself are disputed. A common notion, popular among the Sinti but disputed by some academics, is that the name has been carried by its bearers all the way from their origins in the ancient land of Sindh, which lies along Rajasthan's western border as the second-most populous province of modern Pakistan.

Jake and I filmed Engé as part of an effort to make Romany culture more visible throughout the European Union. He drove us in his black Audi through miles and miles of stereotypically green countryside and vineyards. We stopped occasionally to eat garlic snails and beef steaks beaten thin, before arriving at the Helmstetter household, its tall front entrance somewhere between a stable door and a drawbridge. Inside, the family were assembled in a central courtyard overlooked by three storeys of living quarters that rose up on both sides. Engé and his sister Tchatchi – the feminine form of the Romani for the adjective 'true' – were smiley and welcoming hosts, but I also remember their mother, who was in her seventies or eighties and very dark-skinned, sitting on a low stone wall leaning on a walking stick and throwing us a generous helping of hard, suspicious looks. It was obvious she didn't believe that Jake and I, with our sandy-blonde hair and light eyes, could possibly be Gypsies, an iron assessment in which Jake's charming Romani speech put hardly a visible dent.

We interviewed Engé, who spoke eloquently about his musical apprenticeship with the likes of Biréli Lagrène, and his thoughts about the position of Gypsies in contemporary France. At the time, President Nicolas Sarkozy was trying to win electoral points by cracking down on encampments of immigrant Roma and deporting them to back to Bulgaria and Romania. This in turn was having a huge impact on the lives of the Manouches, who have been a minority in France for the last six hundred years, and many of whom are often highly visible in big roadside encampments. Engé was a highly respected recording artist working in the tradition of Django Reinhardt and the Gypsy jazz and swing that he made famous around the world. He was sad about all this, but also sanguine, with an analytical, worked-at wisdom.

Being a Manouche is a private, personal matter, he said; he is a Frenchman, with roots in Alsace that go back centuries, and no government has the right to segregate the Gypsies along racial lines. He also said he was lucky; that (even though his jet-black hair and dark eyes gave him the look, to me at least, of a typical western European Gypsy) he could 'pass' as an ordinary Frenchman if things got bad, and as a result he had suffered less open prejudice in his life. For his parents, both of them darker-skinned, life had not been so sweet. In a rare reversion to type, Engé did state a belief that the different mentality of the *paysan* – the farmer tied by fate and family to a particular patch of ground – would always be fundamentally at odds with the Romany belief that the earth belongs, at the end of the day, to all of us, and therefore also to no one. As the interview finished he played us some Django tunes and a lovely, long piece of improvised jazz that ebbed and dipped and flowed with the seamless and yet unpredictable rhythmic changes typical of so many kinds of Romany music. Lastly, his young daughter came out and sang 'Nane Tsokha' as he played the guitar. She had the huge blue eyes of a cartoon child from a Japanese Manga comic book, and hair the same pale straw colour as mine when I was a child her age. It made me wonder whether the reason her grandmother didn't rate me and Jake as Gypsies had less to do with our pigmentation, and more to do with the general fact there was so much about us that was alien to the Gypsy life they knew: our Englishness, our body language, perhaps. When we left I wondered whether we might have delved a bit further into her view of the world if we'd had more time. We could have made headway with the aid of props. I wished I'd brought some family photos, and that Jake had brought his guitar.

I pick Cand up from her nan's place on the way down to Dover. The drive down to the Eurotunnel terminal goes by fast, as does the crossing. It's because I know we've got more than seven hundred miles to drive on the other side: nothing makes the first part of a journey go by quickly quite like knowing it will be followed by an arduous, much longer second leg. We emerge slowly off the rumbling vehicle racks into bright sunshine and a couple of miles of access roads that ease me into driving on the right. In less than twenty minutes we are out of Calais and onto the *autoroute*, and I put my foot down, resolved to bypass as much of France as I can before night falls. It would be nice to take in the country more slowly, by winding ways and in long, slow draughts, but I'm eager to reach the Camargue while the pilgrimage is in full swing.

The van doesn't want to be driven too fast, and I'm wary of engaging the turbo and burning through tankfuls of diesel faster than needs be. Consequently we trundle along, as a steady whoosh-whizz of saloons and estate cars goes purring by, sometimes at more than double our speed. I realise that my rehabilitation into a chilled nomadic state is incomplete: I am jealous of these fast cars and the way they eat up the road. We stop more times than I'd like, and I chide myself for my impatience. I just want to get down there, to the sea, but the road stretches on through the day.

At regular intervals on the French toll roads are the *airs* – large rest areas with toilets and picnic tables, sheltered from the thrum of the *autoroute* by plenty of trees. They don't seem to be policed and I reckon you could spend a week at one of these without anyone caring, or even noticing. But we need to refuel, and we decide it's probably safer to spend the night at a large services just north of Lyon: the *airs* are often deserted, and the thought of robbers trying their luck in the night – long as the odds might be – puts us off. We will sleep where larger numbers of people come and go, and the noise they make will surely be outweighed by the sleep-inducing calm of feeling safe.

We make dinner next to a massive lorry: I smile and raise my teacup in a gesture of 'cheers' to its driver, who puts his thumb up to me with a kindly, squint-eyed moustachioed smile, a face that speaks of a cordial understanding between roadside sleepers. I roll a cigarette and go for a walk around the services as if I own the place. It's better than any I've seen in England: nicely landscaped, with a variety of good-looking trees. And while the familiar black-and-white wagtails are walking around looking for food, which makes me feel at home, I see no sign of a mouse, nor of the Gypsy's dreaded 'long-tail'. The reason I don't often stay overnight at services in Britain is because they are so prone to rats.

In the morning we go into the services to take advantage of sinks and running water. We dodge and weave through hordes of teenagers on some sort of school trip, all of them wearing identical yellow T-shirts and hollering loudly as bleary-eyed teachers stand in their midst like outposts of moroseness: they look as though they have been immunised against the power of caffeine.

Back on the road, it takes ages to get past Lyon, the way through which is a congested marble run of rising and falling loops through tunnels, over bridges and alongside the wide river Rhône. South of Lyon, the A7 is called *l'Autoroute du Soleil* – the Motorway of the Sun – an appropriate name for the road that leads us south into ever more arid terrain. The number of palm trees, poking out of the watery heat haze, steadily increases. It is as though, in less than an hour, we've crossed into a totally different climatic zone, complete with the constant high-note whirr of grasshoppers and old men sitting inexplicably on short stone walls a hundred yards from the road. I stop to fill the van with diesel and look up the road we're on. A couple of websites say the A7 in Marseille was built by the Nazis, which makes me pleased we'll be peeling off from that direction north of Avignon, and heading towards Montpellier down to the west.

When I pop open the bonnet of the van to check the oil and water, I see to my dismay that oil has spattered everywhere, because the cap is missing. I must have forgotten to screw it back on properly last time. Whilst I get to work kicking tyres and shouting at myself for being a *div*, Candis is busy folding up a sheet of tinfoil and looking for hair ties in her make-up bag, with which she suggests I might be able to do a temporary repair. The foil makes a reasonably snug seal over the oil intake, and the hairbands keep it nice and tight. She was right and I'm lucky she's here. It reminds me of other family tales of emergency mechanical work: Nan once used a pair of her tights as a replacement fan belt on her older brother's truck, and Dad tied up the dragging exhaust on Nandad's little blue van with a piece of string he'd *munged* from a nearby pub.

We get to Anouar's foster parents' house around midday. It's in the town of Aigues-Mortes, the centre of which is a mediaeval walled city whose well-preserved fortifications glow in colours from cream to honey and amber in the various shades of the sometimes searing sun. It sits on a broad swathe of salt marshes, through which flamingos slowly mooch with the swooping focus of metal-detecting enthusiasts. The town's name comes from the Occitan phrase for 'dead waters', and salt has been mined and farmed here for thousands of years. It seems absurd that we've managed to get to a place like this in under two days, when a few hundred years ago, coming here would have likely meant weeks of travel, on horseback or foot. Anouar will be out to join us later in the week, on a two-hour flight from London to Montpellier.

By now we are proficient at getting by on the road for extended spells, particularly when it's warm and dry, but having a house at our disposal is a generous privilege that I have no intention of passing up. Nine months in the van have diluted my need to maintain the purity of a caustic experience for its own sake, and I am always grateful for running water, for bathrooms, for shelter from the black midnight cold and the beating noonday sun. That said, it only takes half an hour of being away from the van before I have an inclination to go back to it. I can almost feel it physically, like the tug of a fish-hook embedded within my chest. Partly I just want to check it's alright, that it hasn't been broken into, and make sure I haven't missed an oil or water leak or a slow puncture. But I also have the urge to sit amongst fabrics and my talismans of the road.

I'm calm in that little environment I have created with help from others. It is where the Romani words come easily, and where I can be less self-conscious singing or whistling, or playing the spoons. It's odd to think I have become joined at the hip to a van, but I still think it would be crass to refer to it as inanimate. It is full of objects that trigger comforting thoughts of the people who gave them to me. But more than this, I've spent so much time inside it, relying on it, that it is now my home, and I am prey to the same homeward tug towards it that other people get towards theirs. It may not be alive, but it breathes, not only with treacherous fumes from its exhaust, but with my struggles, aspirations, memories and dreams. Terrified that Travellers will take the piss, I've stopped myself giving the van a name – or rather, I've resisted giving it voice. I realise that in my head, the van's name is the two words I think every time I pat its dashboard at the beginning of each long stretch – *Kushti Bok*, the Romani for 'good luck'.

The legend of Sara-la-Kali states that she was a black Egyptian maid who accompanied the 'three Marys' – Mary the sister of Lazarus, Mary Salome and Mary Jacobe – on a voyage by boat from the Holy Land to the south of France. The story probably dates to mediaeval times, and its traction among the Romanies has doubtless been helped by their long-time association with Egypt, regardless of its origins in a deeply ingrained misnomer. Sara is also routinely referred to as an example of a 'Black Madonna', but the present-day Romany writer Ronald Lee is among many who have argued that the veneration of Sara has little to do with Christianity at all, and is in fact contiguous with the worship of Shakti – the feminine, empowering aspect of the godhead – in the Indian Hindu tradition. Sara herself, writes Lee, is 'a non-existent saint' who provides a canvas for the continuation of the ancient religious culture of the Roma: 'the worship of Kali/Durga/Sara has been transferred to a Christian figure'. From a distance, I have long wondered whether these three options are mutually exclusive: wouldn't the perennial mystique of St Sara, and the enduring popularity of the pilgrimage, be best explained by the interaction of all three?

We pick Anouar up from the airport and get ready to leave the next morning for Saintes-Maries-de-la-Mer. We're all decked out in our best, in a vaguely Mediterranean style that looks as though it would be equally at home in the context of an outdoor wedding, a nightclub or a church. Anouar and I gel our hair until is rock-hard and windproof, and Candis and I put on all of our gold, our necklaces, rings, cufflinks, the lot. It's not just to show off, nor even because of its genuine talismanic, emboldening value, but also because I was always taught that when you're travelling, the safest place for your jewellery is where you can feel it, next to your skin.

Aigues-Mortes is part of the 'Petit Camargue', less wild and marshy than the Camargue proper, which announces itself as we pass a humpbacked bridge over a river disguised by tall reeds. We are met on the other side by hundreds of small white horses, standing almost frozen in the whiteness of the sun. They look relaxed, slightly forlorn even, hardly walking, long practised at keeping still. The odd flamingo stands out like a pink question mark on the salt water, ringed by tall, stiff rushes. The light is intense and is everywhere, and the land wears a combination of colours I've never seen anywhere else: the pale blue of the sky and the pastel greens of the reeds; the pink-soda lakes fringed with silver crystals and crimped lime-green vineyards. It seems miraculous to have reached this land on my old four wheels. I pray that the bearings are alright after the long drive, listening carefully for any irregular noise, any faint sound of grinding or grating. I can't smell oil, which means Cand's repair must still be doing its job.

A few miles from the centre of town we catch sight of the first encampments of Gypsies. Their trailers gleam snow white in the sun, and are almost without exception immaculate. As we get closer I see that many are brand new, the best twin-axle living trailers made by the big Continental caravan brands. The current fashion is for black-and-chrome detailing, which gives some of them a streamlined, almost Space-Shuttle-like appearance, their front windows with the mean wind-turning look of a motorcycle helmet's visor. I can also see washing machines outside the trailers, apparently fully plumbed in: obviously you can get away with that in country as dry as this.

We drive slowly towards the seafront, and my attention is caught by the stoop-shouldered, unhurried walk of the women before I notice the colour of their hair, their skin or their eyes; the way they carry the babies astride their hips as though that's what hips are made for; the big hoop earrings or dangling ones made with coins, the hair pulled back all tight and neat; the unfussy stretchy tops and long skirts, jeans or simple trousers.

The sunlight is fierce and the Gypsy boys are in lairy mode, hair slicked back into frozen jet-black waves; some arrangements look like the glistening, curled-over fins of captive killer whales. Today, Saintes-Maries doubles for the Verona Beach of Baz Luhrmann's *Romeo and Juliet*. It is a light-bleached neo-Carthaginian seaside, flecked with the gold, red, neon and crystal-encrusted heels-and-jeans chic of the girls and the brash, loud style of the boys, which is somewhere between preppy yacht-owning brat and sun-loving Brazilian footballer. Every other Gypsy boy I see shares my love of hair gel and dark brown, gold-rimmed sunglasses. Divided by thousands of miles and hundreds of years, we cannot escape from our common love of the slick and the garish and the gold. Two boys catch sight of my grandad's saddle ring on my right ring finger, and they haggle imaginary prices they'd be willing to offer me for it. Everywhere I look there are Gypsies, relaxed, with no need to be tense or alert; Gypsies in superior numbers. A temporary nomadic seaside utopia.

There's a dead ringer here for every Traveller I've ever met, anywhere in the world from Jerusalem to Cumbria via Budapest, Alsace, Valencia. The palette of skin colours echoes humanity

– from south Asian browns to the pale Scandinavian tones I have always disliked in myself. Almost everyone is grinning or laughing or whistling; a couple of old men seem to be able to manage all three at once.

At the shore, the whistles reverberate through the masts and rigging of the yachts. We amble along by the tideline. A big family has taken their toddlers down to splash in the cool water. The dad has a baby in front of him, strapped in a carrier close to his chest: a rare sight amongst Traveller men.

We stop by for chips at a café run by Gypsies. I take mine and say, 'Merci beaucoup' to the mum with her no-messing aura of matriarch. '*Mais c'est moi qui doit dire merci*' – But it's I who should thank you, – she says, with a smile and a dip of the head. Saintes-Maries-de-la-Mer can add to its charms the most dignified *frites* seller in history. In the midst of pullulating music and technicolour culture, I've never felt so at home, not even at the horse fairs I've gone to since I was a baby. If there were a Gypsyland, it would be here in the sun, I think. Rain, beer, horses and mud – so often the order of the day at the English fairs – combine to make us surly and, over centuries, have drowned out some of our music and replaced it with money and madness. Not that many of the Gypsies here seem short of a euro or two.

There is one guitar player, a man in his fifties, that everyone seems to be looking at. He is Indian-dark with narrow, feline eyes and a tiny black pencil moustache. He strums with great energy, his brown forehead glassy with sweat. Coming to the end of a song, he slaps his guitar as someone shouts out, '*Allez,*

Jean!' at which he turns to the caller with a broad grin, throwing his arms out wide in a gangster's theatrical welcome. He holds court, semi-conducting guitarists in between gulps of beer, falling in and out of the bars and cracking jokes. The young men hold the fort, strumming on as Jean gets slowly pissed, though he never appears off balance as he pulls the strings of the party. Two big-eyed little girls sidle up to ask us if we want a CD: young pedlars, hawkers in training, continuing a trad-itional job that Gypsies have done since the outset of their documented history. '*Vingt chansons, dix euros*' – twenty songs for ten euros – a bargain ratio. They are shy and embarrassed and as cute as Disney princesses. With palms at their backs, their mother gently cajoles them to try and make a sale, encouraging them to lose the instinctive embarrassment that runs contrary to the entrepreneurial way. Echoing round my head I hear Grandad's catchphrase on this topic: 'There's no sweetness in nothing,' meaning money is required to make anything taste right. When Nan talks about a rich Traveller, she often says, 'He don't know what he's worth.'

Compared to smiling Jean with his cat-like eyes, the Eastern European Gypsies seem to be struggling for an audience. An old man with a yellow tie and a beer gut sits playing his violin on the steps of a fountain. He is a fine musician, smiling wanly as he produces delicate, mournful tones. Behind him, a tall, thin man with eye bags and a morose expression plucks sadly at his massive double bass. Anouar points out that the violinist must be self-taught, as his fingers are pressing so close to the ends of the strings. We stand for a while and applaud when there is a pause. I feel sorry for them: there are hundreds clapping to the rumba, and no one is here. 'They'll make money come night-time,' says Anouar. He's right: when we return later on, the pair are surrounded, their songs faster paced, urgent, as if all the money might suddenly vanish with sunset.

As we're watching them, a rank of tourists closes in on Candis: five middle-aged men and one woman, all with cameras. They are trying to catch her in the dipping sunlight. One comes in close, attempting to get a close-up of the pirate-lady tattoo on her back. It feels like an invasion of space and I move in, saying, 'Come on, mate. Jesus.' The man looks at me calmly as though I have no jurisdiction here, and motions at Cand, as if to say, 'I am taking a picture of her, not of you.'

As the sun sinks and floods the whole place with chrome tangerine light, we take a detour by a wide dusty area backing onto a canal and wide marshlands, the main stopping place for the Gypsies. There are at least a hundred flash trailers, Hobbys and custom built Tabberts and Fendts, each one next to a pristine white van. This being France, they're mostly Mercedes and Renaults. It's odd to see so many Travellers, and yet so few Transit vans.

We head back into town past three girls discussing which name they hope their future boyfriend might have – Michelangelo wins. Suddenly a priest in long cream robes is scampering across to the church as though there's some sort of problem. Crowds gather, the priests and one bishop are by the big doors, intoning liturgical phrases as people are magnetised inwards. The doors open. Singing and distant guitar are funnelled out into the main square as if through a tube: it sounds tinny and cooped up, so unlike the rest of the day. The church is packed but apparently festival numbers are decreasing year on year, as more hard-line Christian groups recruit Gypsies in their hundreds. They preach that the gaudy old cult of St Sara is unequivocally devilish. We struggle to tune in, then mooch off to find the van. Sun's down. It's time to turn in for the night. Tomorrow will be still more rambunctious: the day of the feast.

We drive across marshland by five-mile-long roads, perfectly straight like the ones I saw in East Anglia. The day's rhythms are strong: the shouting of the boys, the knowing 'Ahhhhhhs!' of the women; the ten slight variations on one reliable kind of rumba, the quick-fire tensions of strumming of strings and the shuttering slap of guitars; the hoarse, sandpapered laughter of old throats turned to bark by tobacco and tall tales and time. Occasionally, a dozen flamingos fly past, their bizarre silhouettes like unfurled paperclips. A single hawk follows alongside the van for a while, then peels off to the south over vineyards.

In the afterglow of dusk, a black boar is startled from his rest by the menacing roar of the van – a *déjà vu* of the time I thought I'd seen one on a misty night in Hertfordshire. He jerks into motion and gallops off down a row of short grapevines, and a final flock of flamingos jinks across the purple sky.

The next day the town is packed to the rafters, vans and trailers in absolutely every possible cranny of roadside space. Some are breaking parking rules but there are so many vehicles the police seem to have abandoned hope of bringing about any semblance of order: they stand about scratching their heads, half-heartedly asking the odd offender to go and park somewhere else. We do three or four circuits of Saintes-Maries before finding somewhere to park in a field of dry yellowish dust near the road into town. A young hippy couple from England are parked up next to us, smiling and playing the bongos and a guitar, their clothing slipshod, loose and free. But we are dressed for the occasion, and once we get into the town I'm glad about it.

The place is heaving with Gypsies and camera-wielding tourists, and other people who don't seem to be either and from whose serious demeanour I take to be Catholic pilgrims come to celebrate St Sara as a plain old Christian saint. We sit outside the same café as yesterday, but the place is more crowded and doesn't seem quite the same. As an accomplished guitarist, Anouar is beginning to tire of the endless, repetitive rumbas, and we walk around to the side of the church from where the more complicated strains of flamenco can be heard.

On a flight of steps, a huge mahogany-skinned man with long, poker-straight black hair and powerful arms is playing guitar to a rapidly gathering crowd; next to him, a man in his sixties or seventies in an Aran-pattern jumper and black leather pork-pie hat is singing along. He is a Gitano – a Spanish Rom – as his voice, gesticulations, demeanour and thin moustache all dictate, and he has severe vitiligo, his face a unique map of creams and pinks. The tempo of the playing increases, and those confident enough to do '*palmas*' – literally 'palms', or clapping – are keeping the *'compas'* – the complex beats and off-beats unique to flamenco music. Anouar smiles, elbows me and into my ear says a single word, *'Bulerías'*, a twelve-beat rhythm which is the most energetic and probably the most famous of all the *'compas'*; it is often used to end a performance on a note of high passion and energy. It might seem paradoxical that flamenco, so evocative of Mediterranean vitality, Gypsy spontaneity and musical fire, is one of the strictest, most regimented and difficult musical disciplines found on earth. But really there is no paradox, as throughout history, all of the typical symbols of Gypsy romance have required great craft and apprenticeship to execute well. From step-dancing and the violin, to wagon painting, fortune telling and the singing of a great store of songs, the roots of the famed heroic present are usually found in years of repetition, practice, rote.

People are filing down into the crypt beneath the church to pray to the statue of St Sara, many of them carrying special embroidered cloths that will be draped over her shoulders in layers of dozens, or hundreds, eventually turning the tiny sculpture into a caricature of royalty. By the time she is carried out later today at the head of the great procession, she will probably be the most overdressed female figure in all the world. I think about going into the crypt, but my claustrophobia gets the better of me; not only this, but now I am here it seems more important to absorb the living energy of my people, gathered here from all over the continent, than it does to form an orderly queue in the age-old Catholic way.

We need a drink but every bar is packed and heaving, until at last we come to one that, inexplicably, is completely empty. As we enter, the proprietor – a handsome, suntanned silver-haired woman in her fifties – is smiling but looks a little concerned, and asks us in English if we are sure we like the place. We all nod and reply in the affirmative, and I am still a little confused as I sit down, delighted to rest my legs. Then I realise why she asked us the question: the interior is overtly camp, all zebra-pattern throws, chrome fittings and pink-and-black leather decor, and the lady who showed us in is now standing behind the bar with her arm around a taller woman of a similar age. It's obviously a gay bar, and for the first time all day, I am sad: not just that this couple aren't getting the full benefit of the massive amount of passing trade, but, reading more deeply into the landlady's slightly worried expression, that they might have had some trouble from homophobes in the past. I stare at my shoes, hoping they haven't been given any grief by Romany people. The couple come over to us, and shower Candis with compliments – 'Beautiful, beautiful woman!' – with one hand gesturing upward in a supporting superlative.

As the afternoon wears on, the square in front of the church is becoming increasingly packed, and a change in the ambience of the town is detectable on the air: the vibe has shifted from raucous joy to excited anticipation. A service begins inside the church, and outside its great front doors, which are painted red and decorated with broad yellow ribbons and the anchors of the Camargue in enamelled black iron, the standard bearers are gathering with their various brightly coloured banners and flags, some bearing images of St Sara, some blazoned with Romany flags and blessings for the Gypsies. Two priests walk around energetically, making their final preparations: around their necks are draped wide, decorated cloths, and as we get closer, we see that they are embroidered with the symbols of Romany life: a campfire, a horseshoe, a wagon, a wheel and a hedgehog. It is evidence of a symbiosis of religious and ethnic minority life that is totally alien to the British Gypsy experience. I am momentarily jealous of the way this sacred festival is shared by the Manouches, the Catholic church, and the town.

Last to arrive before the statue of St Sara finally emerges are *les guardiens*, the local bull shepherds who, by proud, inherited tradition, escort the statue and the procession as it makes its way down to the sea. They are impeccably dressed in trousers, patterned long-sleeved shirts and wide-brimmed hats, and one in particular catches my eye: he is maybe seventy years old, but still lean and fit and tanned, with a neatly trimmed silver moustache and a spark of light in his narrow gaze. Some of the other *guardiens* make way for him as he joins the head of the procession, and I imagine that this is his thirtieth time in the saddle on the feast of Sara the Black, and that it was a job his grandfathers did before he was born.

After a wait that seems awkwardly long in the powerful, dipping sun, there is a sudden hush followed by a warm hubbub as the statue emerges at last, her tiny crowned head and shoulders piled high with cloths rising just enough above the ecstatic crowd for me to see that this is not just a veneration of a Black Madonna, but also the vaunting of the closest thing the European Romanies have to an actual Gypsy goddess. The procession gets moving, the *guardiens'* horses calm amidst the throng, the rainbow-coloured banners giving the whole thing a Mexican fiesta look. There are shouts of '*Vive la Sainte Sara!*' and a barrel-chested Gypsy man at the front of the procession theatrically gestures the crowd to stay back: he seems to love his role a bit too much, and Candis, Anouar and I exchange smiling winks. Like everyone else, we stand aside for the snaking column as it works its way out of the town and towards the bright, breezy openness of the beach. Upwind, the rigging of a thousand yachts is tinkling against their metal masts like a xylophone of the sky.

The procession passes a mock-up '*roulotte*', a plywood take on the traditional bow-top wagon of the French and German Romanies. At the top of its steps sits a pretty teenage girl who has dressed up to look like St Sara: her dark eyes glisten in the sun as she smiles for a chattering rank of long-lensed cameramen. By now, the statue is getting close to the edge of the sea, and the French Gypsies are working up to an emotional peak. Teenagers leap in the air to catch a glimpse. Middle-aged men are shouting and holding everyone back, making way for their ebony queen.

In a flash, I am struck by the thought that this might be the one chance I get to join in at close quarters with this extraordinary Gypsy custom. I tell Anouar and Cand, 'I might have to get in the sea.' They nod at me, understanding the urge, as I hurriedly take off my shoes and head down into the water with my camera. I want to be there when the statue is brought into the surf, re-enacting the arrival of St Sara at the French coast. The *guardiens* and their tall white mounts have formed a horseshoe shape facing the shore, and I manage to get just in front of them as the banners and statue are carried down the beach. The Mediterranean has barely warmed up from the winter, and its surface rises and falls like a cold lung, moving up and down my legs and torso as I try to keep my camera dry. The cold of the water stretches the moment and heightens my senses as the point of crescendo nears. The sand feels good between my toes, the water is up to my waist; the wind is at my back and the sun in my eyes: four elements combining, baptising us all together.

Up to their chests in a swelling sea, the horses seem transfixed, unnaturally calm, and as the priest begins to proclaim his bless-ings I am caught by the significance of all this: it suddenly seems to be a retrospective sanctifying of the coming of my ancestors to Europe, which thereafter would be their heartland, as well as the place of their greatest woes. The statue is held aloft to more cries of, *Vive les Saintes-Maries! Vive la Sainte Sara!* In spite of the order of the chants, it's clear that the day is all about the latter saint, this little black statue, so small amidst her mountain of regal robes and what she represents: that one of the world's most persecuted peoples still endures, and that whatever the rest of the world thinks, they still believe that dark skins can contain a pure, beautiful soul. Some boys are riding on people's shoulders now, waving and punching the air with the strength of pure joy. And after the last and loudest cry goes up, a new peace descends on the crowd and over the sea, as if some wrong has been righted, and the sun can finally set now, in peace.

St Sara is carried solemnly back to church. I stand alone now as the cold sea swirls around my legs and the hot sun beats upon my back. The camera that always felt heavy and wrong is suddenly light in my hands, as though for the first time I have every right to take pictures. I take no more, but linger longer than everyone else as they pass back onto the shore: the massive crowd subsiding, the banner- and statue-bearers now silent and slow. The energy of the place has vanished like the sudden dissolving of clouds, the music off and the lights back on in the club. I am watching the Gypsies pass into the world, ambling into the midst of the *gadje*, surfing the changing tides of their falling and rising histories, blended fates.

9

The Border

Kingsmeadow, Bala Lake

Spring is turning to early summer in England. The last outcrops of daffodils have become a darker, golden yellow, nodding like jazz-band trumpeters in the bucking and buffeting wind. Winter is thousands of miles behind me, slipping away like cold silk onto the other side of the world. The juvenile rabbits are running and jumping, I'm planning a trip to Wales, and I feel fresh and free.

'*Dik akai at the shushis a-prasterin,*' I say to Candis. '*The kam 'n the bavval's abri.*' – Look here at the rabbits running. The sun and the wind are out. She says, 'I wish you spoke Romani more.' I wish I did too, and since we got back from France I am a bit more bullish about *rokkerin'*. But it isn't a case of simply wanting to: I have to be in the mood. The speech must originate in the core, or the words come out stilted, staccato and stupid, bent arrows shot wide of the mark. On sunlit, happy days like this the old words run out of me, spinning as free as my wheels. Other times I will not speak a word for a week, maybe longer. But I am thinking about the language more than usual today, and that's because Wales is in the itinerary.

For anyone interested in the Romani tongue, Wales, particularly north Wales, has a unique significance: it is seen as the last redoubt of the oldest form of British Romani. Wales was where the Irishman John Sampson (1862–1931) conducted most of his researches into the language. Though less famous than his predecessor George Borrow, Sampson was probably the greater scholar of Romani. He is chiefly remembered for two contributions to the study of Gypsy culture. The first of these is his magnum opus, *The Dialect of the Gypsies of Wales*, a hefty and detailed dictionary of *Romimus*, a variety of Romani spoken by a few related families who lived in rural north Wales. Sampson's second legacy, which springs directly from the first, is the belief that because the Romani dialect spoken in north Wales was grammatically conservative, it was purer (and therefore better) than the crumbling, corrupted tongue of the English Gypsies. Ever since his dictionary was published in 1926, Sampson and his successors have drawn a stark line between the Gypsies of England and Wales. It is even believed that a firm ethnic border exists between the English *Romanichals* – a rough breed, their language and lineage tainted by too much mingling with non-Romany travelling folk – and the *Kålē* of Snowdonia and its surrounds, a small and racially purer caste with a sonorous Romani speech. This seemed to be corroborated by the way the Welsh Gypsies spoke about their English counterparts: they called them the *bengeske hachiwichi* – the diabolical hedgehogs.

But can it really be as simple as that? Romany people had lived in England and Scotland for over two hundred years by the dawn of the eighteenth century, so it seems unlikely that none would have resided in Wales until that point; nonetheless, it is widely believed that the first Gypsy to live permanently in the principality was Abram Wood, a moustachioed fiddler who travelled there around the year 1730. This was before the 'wagon time' and Abram and his family journeyed with donkeys and mules, their possessions stowed in saddlebags and packs. Abram was described by his great-granddaughter Saiforella as a dark-skinned man, tall and thin with rose-red cheeks, wearing a three-cocked hat, gold rings, and a pocket watch and chain. Although he played the violin, his descendants would later adopt the Welsh harp, becoming some of the instrument's most celebrated players.

On a council site in Surrey I once met a Welsh Gypsy man, who clearly believed his people were of a superior caste to the polluted Romany bloodlines of a hybridised and over-populous England. He had a smooth and shiny face, and a moustache clipped into two distinct black halves which hardly moved as he pontificated on the wonders of his folk. 'There was never many of 'em … But they were proud, see, very proud: true-bred, proud to be *tatcho*, like, to be proper Gypsies. And they was dark, they'd look down on the fair ones, half-breed Travellers, like,' he told me, pausing as he leaned out of the window of his truck to look down at me. 'If someone asked them if they were Gypsies, they'd go, "Nah, nah,"' he said, waving his hand in front of his face as if to discourage a fly from settling down. 'They knew there was no point telling people, see ... They wouldn't understand so there was no point telling 'em. And they didn't call theirself Gypsies. Amongst theirself, they'd say, "We're *Kålē, Kålē*, you know, and that means 'blacks.'"'

The fact that the Welsh Gypsies referred to themselves as *Kålē* only added to the mystique: this seemed to place them in a category with the Gypsies of Spain and Finland (who used the same name for their own tribe) and therefore further, it seemed, from their English cousins, the *Romanichals*. There seemed to be a purity here that had been lost almost everywhere else. Although Sampson himself documented copious uses of English and Welsh terms in the north Welsh Romani dialect (the speakers of which were mostly trilingual, being fluent in English and Welsh as well as Romani), he never doubted that it was the best form of the language extant in Britain. The oldest, the most conservative, the least flexible, it seemed resistant to the rust of change. It was also spoken by a tiny number of people: coincidentally (or not), this meant it was a form to which he and his confidants could control access. It was a tongue they could guard and keep to themselves.

It's hard not to be seduced by Sampson's take on his favourite subjects. In his preface to *The Dialect of the Gypsies of Wales*, he invites us to share his view of the Gypsies and their language in unashamedly romantic terms. The third paragraph of the preface is famous in the world of Romani Studies and deserves to be quoted in full:

For several decades before the period when my own Gypsy studies began, Anglo-Romanī, through the gradual loss of most of its inflections and a great part of its original vocabulary, had sunk to the level of a semi-jargon, while the so-called 'deep Gypsy' possessed by a few aged pundits of the tribe exhibited little more than the débris of a once stately and beautifully constructed language. It was therefore with sensations which will be readily understood by those who have indulged in dreams of treasure trove that in the summer of 1894, while on a caravan tour through North Wales, I chanced upon a Welsh Gypsy harper at Bala, and made the discovery that the ancient Romanī tongue, so long extinct in England and Scotland, had been miraculously preserved by the Gypsies of the Principality. As I listened to Edward Wood unconcernedly discoursing in a dialect hardly less pure than that of Paspati's Tchinghianés, I felt almost with a sense of awe that Borrow's dream was fulfilled in my own person, and that this was the very speech of two hundred years ago. For our Welsh *Kâlē* are the descendants of an eponymous ancestor Abram Wood, reputed King of the Gypsies, who was born before the close of the seventeenth century, and the dialect so religiously kept intact in the fastnesses of

Cambria is thus a survival of the oldest and purest form of British Romanī.

Treasure troves, tours and discovery; purity, fastnesses, deepness; survival and dreams. Sampson brought to dour linguistics the bright atmosphere of intrepid exploration. He had ventured into 'deep Gypsy' like a linguist in a submersible, sounding in a mysterious ocean trench.

Yet Sampson, like many of his successors, wrote about my own Romani dialect in very different terms. 'Sunk', 'débris', a 'semi-jargon': these words connote seabed detritus, not the living, long-suffering speech of a tenacious and harried culture. Perhaps I'm just bitter that my family did not inherit the florid, fantastical language found in Sampson's dictionary: our dialect, composed of shards of Romani studded into the mortar of rural English, is a disappointment to the romantic soul. While Sampson was jotting down the mellifluous proclamations of ringlet-haired Welsh harpers, Nan's dad was probably knocking another man's teeth out somewhere down a Hampshire back road, an act hard to transcribe.

On the other hand, there is clearly a double standard when it comes to how intellectuals have tended to write about English – always in terms of evolution and improvement – and how they have tended to write about Romani, in terms of degradation and decay. John Sampson's opinions about the Romani language are the exact opposite of those which the Elizabethan antiquary Richard Carew, for example, expressed about English. The traditional strengths of English

– adaptability; tendency to absorb new stores of vocabulary; ability to shed superfluous or cumbersome grammar – are nearly always seen as tragic flaws in the Gypsy speech. In his famous *Epistle on the Excellency of the English Tongue*, Carew writes that in English:

> the long words that we borrow, being intermingled with the short of our own store, make up a perfect harmony, by culling from out which mixture (with judgement) you may frame your speech according to the matter you must work on, majestical, pleasant, delicate, or manly, more or less, in what sort you please.

More than four hundred years later, the broadcaster Melvyn Bragg expressed similar sentiments in his book *The Adventure of English*. In it, he called the evolution of English from 'a few tribal and local Germanic dialects spoken by a hundred and fifty thousand people' into a global language fit for all purposes:

> a tremendous adventure ... English, like a living organism, was seeded in this country over fifteen hundred years ago ... From the beginning it was exposed to rivalries, dangers and threats: there was an escape from extinction, the survival of an attempt at suffocation, there was looting, great boldness, chances taken and missed; there were and there are casualties ... This book is about where the English language came from and how it achieved the feat of

transforming itself so successfully … It continues to rein-
vent new Englishes wherever it goes and shows no sign
at all of slowing down.

Romani rarely elicits such proud triumphalism. It is typically
seen as diminished and threatened by change; staggering along
the road to its own demise.

I was once standing in the yard with my uncles and cousins. I
would have been about seven or eight years old. There was a
small dog running around in circles, chasing its tail, spun into
a canine frenzy. I laughed, pointed at it, and said the phrase,
'*Dikka the juk*,' meaning 'Look at the dog.' Someone tutted
loudly and mimicked my words in a stupid accent, then
compared me to an old Travelling man of whom he was not
that fond. The message of this was abundantly clear: I did not
have the right to use the old language.

But no one who knows these words can avoid using them
for long. The language is too useful, especially for making
sure other people around you can't understand what you
mean. And it's flexible, clay-like, elastic; somehow seems to
lend itself to the on-the-spot formation of names for things
you don't already have a word for. Nine times out of ten
these are either recent inventions or contraptions that wouldn't
have been familiar to our ancestors, for whatever reason. And
the names must, of course, be comprehensible to the Gypsy
you're talking to, as they somehow always, magically, seem to
be. I'm proud of my ability to come up with words for things,

on the spot, that make sense to the person I'm speaking to: *ratti-peever* (blood drinker) for 'vampire'; *jinnin-mukta* (thinking box) for 'computer', and the like.

Almost everyone who has studied the Romani language in Britain has remarked on how adept its speakers are at coming up with names for things. In some ways, talking *Romanes* means having to be constantly inventive and alert, both in terms of creating words and also interpreting the new ones that get spun off the cuff and thrown into daily Traveller conversation. There is no stigma attached to inventing words, as there so often is in English; nor are new words looked down upon as annoying neologisms we'd be better off without. Invented words are more likely to be smiled upon or chuckled at as evidence of a witty, intelligent mind; one with a good and flexible grasp of the ancient Travellers' tongue.

Besides, if Romani is to retain one of the functions which has kept it alive thus far – and which it has in common with almost all minority languages – namely, to stop 'outsiders' knowing what you are on about, then it will always be necessary to invent new ways of saying things. The meaning of old reliable words becomes too widely known, their cover blown by the winds of time and funnelled into the pricked-up ears of power. According to a Belarussian Romany man I once met, a word is no longer a truly 'Romani' word once its meaning becomes known amongst the *gadzhe* – it's useless, dead, and best left where it is. This is an extreme opinion, but it points to a common anxiety: that the language will lose its power if it becomes too widely known. Yet words come and go as they please, like mood and temper; traded by friends, explained by lovers, and hurled across the fray. Every Gypsy who 'gives away' the Romani language risks the accusation of treason, as though they were the first, which they never are.

Many police officers will know at least one of the terms by which Travellers refer to them, but I bet there aren't many who know all seven words that I was taught for an agent of the law, and still fewer who could conjure a brand new Romani word for themselves on the spot, and have it be understood by someone else. Having said that, there is now a Gypsy Roma and Traveller Police Association, which has over a hundred paid-up members across the modern UK, all of them serving police officers from different Romany and Traveller backgrounds. I've met several GRTPA members at conferences and meetings and was honoured to shake their hands. Every single one of them has a charmingly stoic attitude to what people perceive as the inherent irony of having a Gypsy policeman, and a brilliant, bright impatience with the idea that there are certain jobs we simply cannot do.

On the way up to Bala I take a detour at short notice to do a day's filming work. I meet up with some Welsh Traveller friends who live in a remote part of the historic county of Sîr Frycheiniog – Brecknockshire – long ago a small, independent Welsh kingdom. It has now been absorbed into the Welsh super-county of Powys, which covers a huge tract of eastern Wales bordering England. Their home is a Gypsy's paradise, tucked right down the end of a country lane which narrows and narrows until you eventually think you might get stuck and never escape. The place is invisible at first, then you get within a hundred-odd yards and see a few aerials poking over the line of the hedgerow. You could live two miles up the road all your life and never set eyes on this place.

It takes a bit of manoeuvring to get my van round the tight corner and into the drive, but once I do I come face to face with a home where I could happily end my days. There's an old farmhouse surrounded by an assortment of four-wheel-drive vehicles, various trailers and bewildered, grit-pecking chickens strolling about. It's a lung of a homestead, one that seems built to expand and contract in accordance with fluctuating family needs. Travellers' places always make me think we'd do relatively well in the event of the apocalypse or a zombie invasion. Whether ramshackle and scrapyard-esque, or obsessively neat with a privet hedge and jet-black wet-look tarmac, there is always a whiff of survivalism about them. It is a tentative stillness: settled, but always on tenterhooks. Gas bottles, proximate livestock, a truck for all seasons. There is a preparedness that their owners can't hide. If we were Americans, I'm afraid we would probably be a rock-solid Republican vote-bloc.

We drive to the brand new site at Kingsmeadow, built as a result of progressive Welsh government policy which requires local councils to provide 'pitches' for Travellers. It's the first site of its kind to be built in Wales since the 1990s and is overlooked by the long blue misty ridge of the Brecon Beacons.

I'm warned in advance that the main man there is 'old-fashioned' and that 'he don't suffer fools', euphemisms that let me know I will be on my most respectful and deferential behaviour. I'm thirty now, but warnings like this turn me straight back into a little boy in my heart. I can hear my grandad saying, 'Don't act the goat or you soon might regret it.' I run through the things I will do: call him 'uncle'; not speak until I am spoken to; stand to attention with both hands behind my back, at least until we have settled into a comfortable conversation. For a supposedly 'free and easy' tribe we are rich in behavioural shibboleths. Chief amongst these is to be 'disbelieving': to openly question the truth of somebody's story. Centuries of being presumed to be born liars has made us intolerant of this accusation. In company, I do my best to forget the line between raconteur-ship and exaggeration; the border between a recollection and what sounds more like a tall tale. It isn't wise to start playing the amateur barrister when you're listening to a Gypsy man spinning a yarn. If he told me he'd just done the guttering round the roof of Buckingham Palace, I'd nod politely, and say, 'Cor, you're doing alright, *mush*.'

Nor do I forget that Travellers will be Travellers, which means the man I am hoping to meet might not even be there when we arrive. Last-minute rejigging of diaries is common practice, and isn't always announced. If something more important has come up at the last minute, it may well cause him to forget all previous plans; and if this is the case, I wouldn't expect him to make a big deal out of apologising to me for not turning up. In the age of mobile phones, Travellers are more likely to call or text to let you know they won't be able to honour a meeting, but there's no stigma attached to failing to do so if you're caught up with something important. This basic difference from accepted Western standards of manners is the curse of many people who work with Travellers, and one source of the idea that they are fundamentally, irredeemably feckless. A Traveller sees it differently, wondering where the virtue is in prioritising something that is no longer your priority. A Romany man from the Isle of Sheppey once told me this is precisely the sort of nonsense morality that he worries a *gorjer* school will drum into his sons. 'If my boys are too *trashed* to make hard decisions 'cause someone thinks they're being rude, how ever are they gonna be able to run their own business? Politeness don't buy bread.'

The Kingsmeadow site has been carefully designed to nestle in a natural cup of the land, and it is difficult to see from any of the surrounding roads. All that is visible is a handful of little pitched roofs, made in the deep dark grey of heavy Welsh slate. These are the roofs of the 'dayrooms', little buildings the size of large sheds that the Travellers use for washing and daily chores, returning to their trailers to sleep at night. The way the site has been concealed leads me to a double-edged question. Is this a good bit of sensitive landscape management, or are they trying to hide the Gypsies away from view? I decide that the two aren't mutually exclusive, and anyway, the fact that it's been built at all is a miracle in twenty-first-century Britain.

I pull up near the entrance, careful not to block anyone's way in or out. We amble up to the main man's pitch and he eventually strolls out, in no great hurry to meet us. Wearing leather boots, plain grey trousers, and a short-sleeved white shirt unbuttoned to halfway and showing his big hairy chest, he moves like an exiled emperor who has only partly given in to his quieter state. His garb is the uniform of the old Travelling men, and combined with his heavy build he reminds me of how Nan's brothers looked back when I was a boy. His hands are enormous, and the same thought I have had a thousand times drifts into my mind: is there some gene that codes for the old Travellers' huge hands, or is it the fact that they've grafted and shovelled and built and been injured and scarred and punched their way into this massiveness? Their size seems somehow in proportion to the way their owners have often dragged themselves out of poverty, into the present.

My thoughts are torn between nervousness and a feeling of being at home, even though I'm two hundred miles away from where I grew up and have never clapped eyes on this man before in my life. His suntanned poker face betrays no emotion as he walks up and comes to a halt.

'Alright?'

'Not too bad, uncle, you?'

'I been worse, boy. I been worse.'

There's still no change to his flinty expression, but under his words I detect a still pool of contentment.

'Where you stoppin' at?' he asks.

'I'm in Hereford, working up this way, you know. But I'm from the south coast, Brighton way.'

'Brighton ... Oh, yeah, I've heard of Brighton. Meant to be alright down there, ain't it?'

'It's alright, uncle, you know, there's good bits and bad.'

'Same as anywhere, ahh?'

'Same as anywhere, yeah.'

He's got an accent I have heard before in this part of the world, from Herefordshire into the near part of central Wales. It lilts along like a Welsh accent, but in between, traces of West Country English are there in the vowels. There's a pause, and now I can see him sizing me up. He cuts to the chase:

'What you after, then?'

I was there to do some filming of the site, to help other councils understand that Traveller sites can be well managed and have their place in a community. I tell him all this. It was all supposed to have been set up in advance, but if someone had failed to make things clear then this might not go as smoothly as I had hoped. There was another pause, then he said:

'Ohhh, yeah, so-and-so said about that. Yeah, do what you like. But I would say don't get filming right into people's places. You best point that thing you got over that way.'

He motions at my camera, and then toward the line of the distant blue mountains, across the site's central green, and out through its currently uninhabited edge.

By now, though, I'd become less interested in the filming I'd come here to do: I thought he had something important to

say, and so was pleased when he sparked up the conversation
once again.

'Hereford, you said you're stoppin' at?'

'Mm.'

'Hereford, see, that's where my people is from.'

'Oh, yeah?'

'Yeah. All round Hereford. I grew up round there, mostly. I
did.'

He reels off the surnames in his family line, one of which
belonged to my great-grandad. I tell him. 'His people could
have come from up this way, then, I expect,' he says.

'I should think so, if you went back far enough.'

'All Travellers is related at the end of the day though, ain't
we.' His voice is warmer now. He's alright with me. So I bring
the conversation back to the business at hand. 'It's a good job
they're still building sites over here, ain't it.'

'Yeah.' He pauses. 'Yeah, it is.'

'Unlike the ones on the other side of the border.'

'The thing is, you say the border,' he says. 'But let me tell you
something. I'm living here now, and I've lived over there, and
my people is all here and there. And let me tell you something
about that border. That ain't no border to us, boy. And never
has been. I am a Travelling man, that's what I am. And ain't no
border stopped my people making their way.'

Whether he knows it or not, he's just struck a heavy blow
against my lifelong need to know if I'm one thing or another.
Certainty's borders begin to dissolve. At the edge of the early
summer sky drift tiny white clouds, high on the wind.

★

After I've finished filming, Cand joins me and we head north again, zigzagging up the A470 towards Bala. We arrive just before sunset and stop in a lay-by I've used before: small and square, it stands at the lake's edge like a little pier.

A visitor's plaque informs us that Bala Lake was once Wales's largest body of fresh water, until Thomas Telford raised its level to boost the never-to-be-completed Ellesmere Canal. The lake is home to the gwyniad, a fish endemic to Bala and found nowhere else. When the Ice Age ended it was stranded in the lake, beginning an isolation that would last ten thousand years. It is now listed as critically endangered, a fact which lends a prophetic air to its wide-eyed and permanently frightened expression. Naturalists believe its young and eggs are preyed on by the ruffe, a hardier fish introduced to the lake a few decades ago. Concerned that a dark cloud hangs over the gwyniad's future, conservationists have introduced a few into the nearby Llyn Arenig Fawr. This means, if the species' luck does not improve, there is still the chance a daughter clan might outlive the dwindling lot of Bala Lake. We wonder about the fate of these fish: an endangered species, like the old Welsh Romani speakers who lived nearby. Perhaps, somewhere within sight of the lake, a few of them still do.

The air shimmers with reflected light. A haze of flying insects dances about above the whispering waterline, and I am glad to see they have returned. They are a sign of summer.

Cand and I take turns to wash in the back of the van; while she is washing, I mooch off down to the shore in my jacket and cap. A cool breeze blows in off the lake and I sing 'The

Cross of Spancil Hill'. As I look up towards the van I see Cand has emerged from her wash with a towel wrapped around her head. I shout up for her to take a picture of me, in which I look tiny next to the massive, majestic greyness of the lake. When I get to the end of the song, it occurs to me how many Romany people with crabbily anti-Irish views have spent their lives learning gutfuls of sad Irish songs.

We spend the rest of the morning reading in silence: Cand is engrossed in an Anne Rice vampire novel, and I've got Sampson's dictionary out. Sitting here at sunlit leisure, smoking a roll-up and poring over the work of a monocle-wearing Gypsylorist, I can feel something else shifting. Maybe it is the boundary between myself and the scholars of Romany culture. I am inside and outside at once. I have ended up on neither side of the border.

Nobody drops by to see what we're doing, not even the fishing patrol man. I'm not even sure anybody is aware that we're here. By the time the sun's getting high I notice some dark and wispy-topped clouds coming up towards the lake from the south-east. We stare at them for a few seconds and instinctively close our books and pack everything up, tensioning our bungee cords around our possessions before we move again.

10

The Money

Blackpool Sands, Appleby, Barnard Castle

Until the 1940s, Nan and her family walked along with the wagon and horse at the only speed that was possible, and therefore the only speed that made sense: the speed of the hoof, the foot and the trundling wooden wheel. Over time, the horse's pulsing heart of grass-fuelled flesh and blood was replaced by the engine with its black blood, pistons and wheels. It was a move that brought great fortune – wealth and choices never before dreamed of; the potential for striking out into new territories, colonising unseen kinds of lives. But contained in every blessing was the shadow of a curse – the joining of the rushing shoals of everybody else. In old times, Romany Travellers referred to their breed as the *kaulo ratti*, 'the black blood'. Abetting their transition from the old life to the new was the internal combustion engine: hard and cold as the old Gypsy life, and dripping with the blackest blood of all, it provides a strange memento of the times it helped bring to a close.

I have more or less stopped using my sat nav, preferring to come up with silly mnemonics for the numbers of motorway exits and the bald, alphanumeric titles of roads. For the A494, I picture a gigantic ace of spades playing card – the A – on which the four Beatles are playing to an audience of the nine ringwraiths from *The Lord of the Rings*, lit by four gigantic floodlights. The more ridiculous the image, the better you remember it, and with a bit of practice it starts to be second nature. I am happy in the absence of oppressive digital predictions of how long the journey will take. It is always tempting to try to compete with them, and I no longer want to rush. It's still over a week until Appleby Fair, and Candis and I don't want to get there too early – we might end up wanting to leave before the fair gets going.

Eventually, we come at Blackpool by a long, straight road, the M55: a simpler mnemonic, my mum waving with both hands. The bulk of Lancashire that we left behind had been all familiar England: fields and copses, blue-signed circular roads, and the warehouse-peppered, fraying edges of towns. There had been ripples and undulations in the earth. Blackpool, at the end of a miles-long highway fit for a mad cop chase, is nothing like that. It is broad and flat and it seems to syphon you in as it gears itself up to the point where it meets with the sea. And the sea is a good place to aim for. Our journey's end is land's last stand in the face of the waves: Blackpool's south shore, which in tales told to me was called Blackpool Sands. It sounded like a crumblier and more liminal bit of ground than almost any other in Britain. A belt of desert that is somehow able to survive in one of the wettest places in Europe, snaking and stretching its way alongside a shoreline famed for electric lights and the industries of fun.

Blackpool Sands is a place jogged over by dogs and kids during the day, but by nightfall it is emptied of human life. Whoever chose to live here, on the uncertain and shifting earth, was doing so in defiance of the biblical principle that a fool builds his house on sand.

When I first mentioned Blackpool Sands to Candis, she already knew about the place. She had visited the Romany archives at Liverpool University, where there is a series of black-and-white photographs illustrating the life of the south shore in years long past. In one of them, a family stands by the sides of their proud, six-foot-high 'rod tent'. It is a pumpkin-shaped structure of curved wooden rods with a thick dark cover, made of what look like blankets. Some of the blankets are furled right up to the top at the front to provide a door. It is an ancient sort of home, a simple design. But this rod tent has been perfectly put together, sprung and proportioned so properly that it looks as though it's pushing its chest out, swollen with pride, showing the world what rod tents can and should be. And the people standing to either side are dressed in the finery of a bygone age. Girls of twenty-odd stare off to the sides of the camera, their nonchalant, relaxed but unsmiling faces failing to dampen their obvious beauty. They are wearing long dresses with corsets beneath that give them the elegant look of upturned champagne glasses. With them are young men in dark three-piece suits, handkerchiefs peeping from pockets, with glinting watch chains and immaculate greased-down hair. They peer almost snobbishly into the camera, looking unsure if they're happy it's there, even though they have got all dressed up especially for the picture. Or so we presume they have.

Another picture shows a tent that slopes down to its back, making it look like the entrance to a tunnel, or a mysterious mine that stretches into the earth beneath the sands. Above it is a wooden sign, white letters on a dark background. It proclaims that this is the way 'TO GIPSY BRITANNIA', a fortune teller from a clairvoyant lineage of renown. A young man in a flat cap stares into the tent's dark mouth, but we can't see a figure inside. Round and about, other tents and wagons are cupped in dips of sand, including that of MADAME CURL – PALMIST and FORESEER.

A 'Gypsiness' nobody speaks of these days seems to emanate out from these pictures: a silent and austere-faced haughtiness. A manner of dressing both dapper and solemn, funereal almost.

In between the eyes that stare out from these pictures, and ours as we try to look into the past, there seem to be two barriers: the impassable one, which is time, and something else that is not always there in other old photographs. It is a steadfastness in the deep pride of their race; an absolute lack of desire to be anyone else. And race is what it was: an irreducible difference from other people; a difference nobody ever had questioned, neither them, nor their enemies. They were Romany Gypsies, the true-bred Travellers of England. Envious of no one, monied by mysterious means, and kings of this thin strip of sand with its defiant bursts of grass.

Back in the present, I stare at the weird and pitted lilting sandscape. It seems so un-British. I've seen similar places at

Camber in Sussex, and Holkham on the north Norfolk coast, but they always seem magically different from everywhere else. They are geared towards aridness, weird outposts of desert, colonies of sand exiled from where they should be. I allow myself to wonder whether some dream of their past had led these Victorian Gypsies to stop here; whether some half-memory of their far-off roots had convinced them to pose in this way: to show a rare moment's deference to posterity. 'Yes, look at us now ... Look how far we have come ...' Yet even in wealth and relative comfort, they seemed to have come almost full circle to where they'd begun: dressed to the nines, encamped on golden sand, clearly posing yet simultaneously disdainful of onlookers. They had done alright, and in this case it gave them the look of Gypsies who'd ended up, bizarrely, on the same sort of desiccated terrain the Gypsies had started off from, a thousand years before.

The road by the sands is a wide boulevard and the traffic comes and goes in long pulses. Biological metaphors always suggest themselves: we speak of transport arteries; of bypasses built to relieve the overwrought heart of a village. We wait for a break in the flow, which coincides with a quiet space in between my thoughts, and pull up the van by the Sands, resting two wheels up on the kerb. We are parked parallel to the old stopping place. I cut the engine, open the doors, tease out the folded legs of the stove, and with hardly a thought my hands go for water, matches, flame. The actions are now fully habitual: it all takes thirty seconds or less, a wordless ritual. As I light the stove Cand holds the pan, silently standing there like an ancient priestess, waiting to pour out a precious libation of wine. We sit down again and wait for the water to boil. The idea of trying to do anything else before the tea has been made is unthinkable. A routine has set in. Perhaps we are living this now: no longer pretending.

A herring gull swoops in and lands on the bottom corner of a bungalow's pitched roof. Flapping her wings in strong, slow strokes, she powers up the hip of the roof, arriving at the top with a final flash of beating wings. She folds them in with a bustling flourish of white and silver and grey, and scans the world with a sideways swing of her elongated head.

With the tea brewed, I decide to jump up on the roof of the van, to get a better look at the scene and give my boots a polish. It crosses my mind that this might look like an attention-seeking gesture; that I want to flag up the fact that I haven't come here for the same reasons as everybody else. Like the gull, I am also after a vantage point. And something else has changed. I'm not worried about being noticed. The fear of looking bolshy or like a show-off matters less to me now, because for the first time, I'm certain we're not showing off.

As I daub polish onto my boots, enjoying the rising sweet petroleum smell, a long blue articulated lorry pulls to the side of the road in front of us, its air brakes making a big, deep hiss like the blowhole exhalation of a whale. Its driver gets out, has a stretch, and then starts to walk slowly down the tarmac path towards us. He's a black guy, about five foot ten with bright eyes and a cheerful face. He shouts up to me, 'I could smell that boot polish from right down the road, pal!' His Lancashire accent is literally broad, its warm vowels seeming to spread out like the sand dunes in front of us. 'Ain't a bad smell, is it, mate?' I reply. 'It is not, aye,' he says with a chuckle, then carries on down the path.

Staring at my brightening boots, and thinking about the Sands' former dapper inhabitants, my mind wanders back to Nan, sitting at home in her bungalow where the seagulls also call. All my life she has been immaculately turned out. Her typical get-up consists of a pair of small golden earrings, a pressed blouse, a navy skirt or smart pair of trousers, and a pair of tiny Italian leather slippers bought from the only place in the county that sells them. The overall look is respectable, spotlessly clean, with a little touch of flash in the form of jewellery or gold buttons on a quilted jacket, but nothing anywhere near as ostentatious as a popular imagining of a Romany woman. When I was little Nan would dress up a bit more for a trip to the seafront fair in July, with gold chains and little American gold dollar earrings that flashed in the sun against her wavy black hair as she laughed. My mind goes back to the Gypsies in the Blackpool pictures again. Everyone wants nice things if they can get them. The yearning for a spartan life sometimes comes to a culture later, when the wolf of poverty no longer scratches at the door.

Our family took special pride in being well turned out, revelling in their ability to buy Italian suits, Swiss watches and hand-made Northampton boots, because within living memory things hadn't always been so rosy. The families that lived on Blackpool Sands at the dawn of photography might have been rich, but the majority of Britain's Travellers were not, as many still aren't. Nan's mother and father had ten children to keep, in a way of life centuries old, and without electricity; without many certainties at all, except the seasons. When times were rough they would sometimes get their clothes 'out the rags', but they always did their best to look neat. 'We was never sent home from school for being dirty, not once,' says Nan. 'Me dear old Mum always made sure we was clean, and they never sent us home for having nits or nothing like that.' Her brothers wore suit jackets or chequered sports jackets whenever they could, and followed their father's habit of never failing to shave in the morning, come sunshine or snow, rain or gale. Nan's dad would sharpen his cut-throat razor on the reins of his horse. He died decades before I was born, but I think of this image every time I shave, the blade of the razor sweeping forward and back in a practised functional motion. The blade relied for its sharpness on the very device its owner used to steer his horse and his life; to maintain the viability of everything, at the weathered rural edge of civilisation, in a way of life he imagined would last for ever.

As people seldom of fixed abode, Gypsies were latecomers to bank accounts. A Romany woman descended from some of the oldest Gypsy lineages of Devon and Cornwall once told me that in years past, her family had buried their money in the raised earth under a hedge at one of their regular stopping places: a literal interpretation of 'putting it into the bank'. Credit cards and commercial debt took longer to catch on, and are looked upon by many Gypsies not merely as bad ideas, but as shameful. It's similar to the situation in working-class circles, except Travellers have generally been even slower to adjust to the whole-scale embracing of personal debt. In an age of cheap credit and American-style car finance deals, buying something 'on the drip' or 'on tick' is seen as a sign that your wealth is a sham: it's 'a show-up', a *ladge-up*, an embarrassment that is avoided where possible. And so lies get told about how things have been paid for; and as with all lies, sometimes the lies are found out. 'Look what think's he's a big concern in the new Merc, strapped right up, that is. I couldn't *kur* it *chavi*, driving a motor about what you can't afford.' The avoidance of debt is a red line for Nan, one she has crossed only once: to buy her first cottage with Nandad. She hasn't borrowed another shilling in sixty-five years.

In the old days, there was another rule in Nan's family when it came to clothing: nobody was allowed to wear anything green. Nan had a younger sister who was born with an incurable illness. What exactly the illness was is a mystery now, perhaps because it had mystified the visiting doctor, or maybe because it had a scientific name that the family struggled to remember. Instead all Nan has to tell is that 'there was something wrong with her, you know ... The doctors said that she wouldn't live to get a great age.' Nan's father had done well at work one week and bought her little sister a green velvet dress. He brought it back to the camp and put it to one side: the girl was asleep in the tent. He went into the woods to collect some wood for the fire; while he was there he was approached by a big black dog, which he took for an omen. He hurried back to the camp and asked Nan's mother to check on his girl, but they were too late, and found her lying as if still asleep, the life gone out of her. She never got to wear the green velvet dress, and so Nan's father cursed it and defied his remaining ten children to ever wear anything green in his presence again. And so the colour of the woods, of vegetation – life at the primary level – was banished from their dress while he lived.

I go for a walk on the sand dunes, where green is also banned by geological decree. What does dwell here keeps close to the ground, and I kneel to get a better look at the lowly little life forms, spying out tiny pink flowers on short stems that bob and bounce about in the stuttering breeze. The grass sprouts up in windblown tufts like the crests of waves, caught magically in time. A family jogs past, smiling with their dogs. The children are playing 'it', laughing and trying to catch each other, stumbling across the higgledy landscape of tuffets and tiny channels hollowed out by small animals. They pass across the dunes to the beach – their destination, one step further on than mine – but I stay put, wondering what attraction this place has lost; the reason the Gypsies abandoned it, and why the crowds of visitors are thinning by the year. An iridescent blue-green beetle, shining in the sun like petrol on water, creeps around the face of a bright yellow flower. The beetles have stayed, defying the ban on green. They must have somewhere to hide when the storm comes in, as it always must in the end.

The sun beats down, but I can't escape my habit of trying to picture what the place must be like in winter; weighing up if I'll get blown back this way when the days are short and cold. Yes, storms would hove in off the sea from time to time, but the shore remains less likely to freeze than places further inland. Amongst the Romanies, the Showpeople – our mutually suspicious cousin group – are known for running amusement arcades in Britain's seaside resorts, ensuring a trickle of money remains when the fairgrounds are muddy and closed, and the rides all packed away for the darkest months. But sometimes even the arcades shut when footfall reaches close to nil at midwinter. The poet Don Paterson describes such a scene in his poem 'The Sea at Brighton', in which non-Gypsy imaginings of Gypsies echo the Romany stereotype of the Showmen, collecting bags of jangling change in a land of lonely gulls:

> The bird heads for the Palace, then skites over
> its blank flags, whitewashed domes and campaniles,
> vanishes. Below, the shies and stalls
> are locked, the gypsies off to bank the silver;
>
> the ghosts have left the ghost train, and are gone
> from every pebble, beach-hut, dog and kite
> in the blanket absolution of the light
> of a November forenoon.

I imagine a year when November never returns. Maybe this might be that year: it won't, but I let myself believe it might.

233

The lengthening days are stretching out beneath my wearing wheels, pliable, idle and long as I want them to be. On days when we stay put in one place, a trippy sense of endlessness seeps in. We are cheating the regular pace of human life. In the van, an idle hour can seem days long, spilling out like an ink stain over a dozing daylit mind. The sun moves just perceptibly, casting lens flares over the seats like the translucent shadows of ocean plankton drifting by, caught between the measurelessness of daylight and the depths. They move with a dreamy slowness across the steering wheel, my chest, my resting hand, and over the pulsing luminous red of the insides of my eyelids. In these moments I am in some world I carry with me inside the van, a bubble of placelessness where the stopping place doesn't matter so much. I am at the roadside, miles from anyone I know, and yet still in my place, inside my home, my own little world. I feel a mounting dislocation from the constant need for an end point, eyes on the clattering announcement board before rushing to make that train. The phrase 'it gets me from A to B' feels slightly sinister now, an indictment of our tendency to curtail our endless horizons.

The ruling classes have always sensed a danger in the footloose and the Gypsies: what were once called 'freebooters' or 'masterless men'. Calm by abandoned sands, I can feel a brief upwelling of the strength they were afraid of. How do you stoke the patriotic embers in a person who regards a place as neither here, nor there: as *land*, not 'ours' or 'theirs'? Most people fantasise, at some point in their lives, about a move, and almost always to a certain place: 'What if we went to Yorkshire, France,

Australia, the Bulgarian countryside?' But Travellers are alone, perhaps, in visualising a destination which has no proper name; knowing that if needs be, they could go back to living nowhere. 'Back on the road.' 'Roadside again.' Back to wherever we end up, each hedge or lay-by only so different from the next; and so on.

For Travellers, it is the money that intervenes, that same battery of ties to a local life that roots each settled person to a certain place. So my family had been connected to Petersfield, tethered by the fragile flower trade to those who wanted what we had. For others there is the land, the house, the eyes that know you in the local pub; the ever-evolving credit ratings of rumour, knowledge and memory; all things that seep from the fact of being a face in a community of others. The very phrase 'a certain place' betrays the slippery goal of steadiness amid uncaring tides. Perhaps that's what we're looking for: a certain and reliable place to stand, far from the shifting sands that whisper of the vanity of human things. I realise I am attempting to pull off a trick: to conjure the genuine sense of home in no particular place. My van may have its wheels, but I cling to the familiar neighbourhood of its inner space.

It is early June now. The longest days are approaching, and since we go to bed early in the van, we hardly ever see true night. On the way up to Cumbria we stop in the Lake District after driving around for a while at random, enjoying the way the narrowness and the constant sloping curves of the roads appear to brake all things to a calmer pace. Just after the sun has snuck behind the mountains to the west, we happen across a bedraggled but clean lay-by, sheltering behind a row of grass-topped shoulders of stone. It is a perfect place to hunker down, out of sight from most directions, and just before darkness falls a young German couple spots it too, pulling up beside us in a smart, expensive camper van. We exchange polite half-smiles and waves before retreating out of sight behind the Transit to get the lanterns out and cook the tea. A sheep walks over. Its bright white legs and fixed expression poke out of its blue-black fleece, a puff of charcoal dust. It stares at us for a moment, chewing the cud, looking bored as if by an inane advert, then wanders back into the purple gloaming, out of sight.

By the time we wake up, the young Germans have gone. Today will be our first day at the fair, so we get dressed up to the nines, do our hair with extra care and fuss and – for the first time since the festival of St Sara in the Camargue – we deck ourselves out in all our family gold.

The Austrian Romany artist and Holocaust survivor Čeija Stojka was once filmed at her dressing table, putting on her necklace of gold talismans and coins. As she delicately fingered every item on her chain, she explained which member of her family had given it to her, or whom it represented in her heart. For this reason, she said, her jewels were physical yet psychical protectors, charms against bad luck, the evil eye or wicked intent. People may think the Gypsies crass for adorning themselves in this way, but for Stojka, it was a serious, almost religious act, reminding her who she was; a ritual of self-armouring before crossing the threshold of that other world, outside. I wear the chain Nan gave me for my sixteenth birthday, when it felt too heavy for my skinny neck, and my grandad's saddle ring and hand-made solid gold horseshoe cufflinks, each one enclosing an old half-sovereign coin. Cand wears two chains, both bearing things my gran once wore: a Victorian sovereign, and a miniature wagon that used to be on her jangling bracelet of charms. We give off a differ-ent aura now, and at the services a man elbows his wife and says, 'Look, Travellers.' I smile when I hear it, wondering whether I really have earned the name – although as Dad used to say, 'You earned it by being born' – and also, maybe, that I no longer mind whether people use it in an ethnic or functional sense, or even if they have no real idea what it means at all.

I have been to Appleby four or five times before, but this time it is different. The old and heavy senses of decorum, of having to be on my best behaviour, seem to have dissipated, or at least become diffuse and indistinct, their edges blunt against the soft parts of my soul. The old desire to prove that I belong is also weakening, its roots receding away. I wonder if this is the onset of the peacefulness of age, or a direct result of having spent so long on the road. I think I smell a paradox. Living on the road can change you, make you less afraid of hardship or the unreliable currents of daily life; yet it also slowly induces a sense that keeping on the move is not as essential to life as you might once have thought. None of this matters all that much, I think, as long as there's light and air. Perhaps

I can only see past the road because I am looking outwards from it now.

And then, as the old van rises out of a dale and past a gap between oak trees, we see a thousand caravans a-glint with light reflecting off the sun. Everything around us pulses with the greens and dancing grass of June. I'm moved again. My people, here another year, in spite of everything; drawn to a gathering whose central purpose is to happen once again. Somehow they are still being them, still thwarting explanations or attempts to sum up Gypsiness in words. I look across to Cand and see she is smiling too, the fast fresh air of Cumbria tumbling in across her face and hair like freedom.

The common conviction is that Appleby Fair was founded by a Royal Charter of James II in 1685, but many books and websites revel in the debunking of this belief. James did grant a Royal Charter to Appleby itself – which is still referred to on several street signs as a 'Royal Burgh' – but the charter was never properly enrolled, and in any case, it had nothing to do with the fair. There was an old meet-up in Appleby that took place at Whitsuntide and possibly dated to the early modern period, but the 'Appleby New Fair', which gravitates around the hills just outside town and is associated primarily with Gypsies, seems to have started in 1775 as a drovers' and sheep sellers' event. Since it offered precious chances to trade, and an opportunity to pitch tents for a while, Gypsies and Travellers would naturally have been attracted to it, and so the now centuries-old association of Appleby with my people began. Nevertheless, many Travellers continue to claim a Royal warrant for the fair – after the fashion of their distant ancestors who bore papers of safe conduct from the Pope – as a symbolic argument that it should not and cannot be shut down. In the 1970s the fair was halted for a short while, with locals claiming – as they later would in Horsmonden, Kent – that it had outgrown the town. Sylvester Gordon Boswell, elder statesman of the English Gypsies and grandson of Wester 'Dictionary' Boswell, led protests and had the New Fair swiftly reinstated. The unlikely but pompous symbolism of a Royal connection has its gothic counterpoint in another symbol of the fair: one of the hills it takes place on is known as Gallows Hill. It was once the spot where executions took place, back in the time when it was a hanging offence to be, or to associate with, Gypsies.

It's a few days until the footfall peaks at the fair, and there is little traffic as we drive into Appleby. I am shocked at not having to queue, even slightly disappointed: a slow entrance gives you a chance to take things in, where much will pass you by at even thirty miles an hour. Every other time I've come it's been on one of the main fair days, when progress is slow, and huge, higgledy-piggledy lines of flash cars, wagons, flat carts, horse-boxes, big pickups, vans and *gavvers'* motors snake into the town. Today there's none of this: people are speckled everywhere, but there's no real bustle yet. All the same, I look towards the hills and see that space looks tight up there. If we want a place, we'd better get a move on.

We head for one of the two main hills that are used as stopping places during the fair, picking the southernmost of the two, which from a distance looks less crowded. A pair of muddy tracks lead up to it, guarded by three people in high-vis jackets, two women and a man. They have money bags strapped to their waists like the ones we used to wear on the market, and are collecting tenners and twenty-pound notes from people who want to park.

'How much is it?' I ask.

'Are you staying on here?' the man asks. It's a stupid question. Of course I'm staying on here. The two women by his sides stare at me through sunglasses, hard, stony faces; accusatory.

'What do you mean? How long do I want?'

'I mean, will you be camping on the hill overnight?'

'I don't know, mate.' I don't know what it will be like up there, and I'm not paying until I've had a look round and gauged whether there's likely to be any trouble.

'Alright,' he says, 'just give us a tenner for now.'

I fumble around in my pocket for the note, in a light red mist of frustration at the seemingly arbitrary pricing. Meanwhile, behind me, an eagle-eyed and less scrupulous person has spotted an opening. Seeing that the three high-vis vest people are preoccupied with me, he takes immediate advantage, keeping his pickup in first gear and screaming past on my left in a flurry of dust and fumes, his twenty-two-foot trailer bumping over knuckled ground and away from the queues. The attendants stare at this, then back at me, looking shocked and impotent, and I can't resist a subtle smirk as I hand over the cash.

We trundle up over the high ground, from where you can see the green, maroon and gold of the bow-top wagons lined up along the side of Flashing Lane, the famous narrow tarmac road where the horses trot at breakneck speed below. The grass is short, the earth is dry and we find a nice, flat spot on its own, with no other trailers or vehicles within twenty feet of us on any side.

I can't believe my luck – I've been warned more than once about trying to park up on the hills at Appleby. Families have ancestral spots reserved by habit of the passing years, arriving weeks in advance to plant the invisible standards of their family name. It's not wise to upset the easy rhythm of such unspoken, small traditions, especially with certain families known to be 'fighting breeds' of hard and fearless men, not to mention women who will stand and have a fight if it's required. It dawns on me that of all the places I've stopped in England, Wales and France, I've never been so anxious as I was pulling onto here. Of all the possible sources of attention and malaise – the police, the civil authorities, French *gendarmes* or skulking figures of the night, nothing worries me more than a confrontation with my own, the Travellers of England. But since I've pulled up and made it clear we've arrived, and nobody's approached or said a word, I think we'll be alright. And so we lock the van and walk off down the sunlit hill towards the fair as it basks in the afternoon.

I have never seen the fair like this before. Yes, there are people milling around, busying themselves with stalls of wares and summer foals unsteady on their feet. But the atmosphere is less like a day at the races, more like a town on market day, a town where 90 per cent of the population are Gypsies and Travellers.

This casts over Appleby the illusion that a Traveller micro-state has sprung up in the early summer air, and I wonder how odd this must be for the people who live here during the other fifty-one weeks of the year, when the town reverts to a sleepy, ancient, isolated burgh.

We stroll around the town for a bit, and sit down next to the Eden for a few minutes to watch the bravest boys and girls ride their horses in and out of the river, stopping in between on the gravel beach to rub soap into their animals' slick wet coats, a baptism across the line of species. On the bridge overlooking the water, a couple of photographers with telephoto lenses are snapping the scene, trying to get close to the Gypsy life from a distance. I take a couple of pictures on my phone to send to Mum, mostly just to let her know we're here.

Outside the Grapes, one of the only pubs that stays open all the way through fair week, crowds of bare-chested men of all ages are counting out £20 and £50 bets on the toss of a coin. Tiny shimmers of metal fly upwards, eight or ten feet in the air, and the men's gazes jerk after them as if they hope to witness an apparition. On the surface of it, it's a simple game of luck, but there are travelling men who have practised the art of the coin spin all their lives, regulating the number of turns with precision, until this archetype of chance is bent into a skill. A man in Sussex is known for being able to throw heads nine times out of ten.

Today all the gamblers are half-cut with beer, foreheads and necks a brassy sheen of sweat. Some hold horsewhips; a custom-made catapult carved from a piece of antler juts out of a skin-tight back jeans pocket. Everyone is holding a pint of beer – there isn't a single bottle or small glass to be seen – and some men have a drink in each hand, which reminds me of Dad and makes me laugh as I point it out to Cand. I've heard the Grapes takes more money in fair week than it does in the other fifty-one weeks of the year combined.

We walk back towards the hill as a green Lamborghini full of young men, hair slicked back as though they've just emerged from the river themselves, drives past as slowly as possible, bowls-club speed. Suntanned arms hang out of its windows, some of them heavy with thick gold bracelets. Inside, I can make out grinning white smiles and the lacquer black of sunglasses fixed in a beady arc above them, as the lyrics and synthetic beats of a pop song pulse and pound out 'I Need a Dollar' at incredible volume. We pass under the old road bridge as it echoes with the clip-clop sound of occasional passing horses. Six men sit on a traditionally painted and gilded flat cart as it manoeuvres past the Lamborghini, legs in grey slacks and immaculate boots dangling off the edges, their soles almost skimming the road. I try not to notice a posse of girls aged from their teens to their thirties as they strut past on enormous heels, their busts and behinds trussed up in tight tops and miniskirts of bright and brash design. Behind them, a stately middle-aged woman with dark skin, wearing a colourful *diklo* scarf, her hair neatly piled up and pinned on top of her head, throws them a rapier glance of intergenerational disapproval. I think of Grandad telling me that years ago, you could spend a whole week here and not catch sight of a single naked knee: you'd be more likely to see all the women of a family sitting cross-legged in long skirts and dresses on a cloth stretched out before their wagon, sipping cups of tea or simply watching the rest of the fair go by. He also said that a man would have been ill-advised to go about bare-chested, as so many nowadays do. Taking your shirt off would risk being interpreted as a challenge to every single man on the hill, and you might have found yourself in trouble fast, if you were even still conscious to know it.

We bump into a relation from back home, walking along with his two young sons either side of him. They are all smartly dressed in short-sleeved shirts and trousers, and their hair is cut close but with just enough left on top to gel it back. Both the boys remind me of their dad, with the same round, friendly face and narrow eyes as if fixed in perpetual smiles; but the taller one is blonde-haired with fair skin and freckles, the younger one dark-haired with smooth and olivey skin. I greet the dad by his first name and the boys as 'boys', making eye contact with them as they nod at me seriously, saying nothing, the younger one jingling coins in his pocket, the older one fiddling with his catapult. I've heard he's a 'dead shot' and can shoot any bird from a tree at a reasonable distance, and I hope that he mostly sticks to stuff they might actually eat. But I think back to how the boys and I were back when I was his age, and to be honest with you, I doubt it.

We continue down the lane and as the number of horses grows I remember the words of an East Kent Romany man

I once interviewed for a film: 'There's no such thing as a good horse ... Any animal can turn,' and those of Billy from the New Forest: 'A horse is a very powerful animal, and really, he doesn't know his own strength.' I'm snapped out of this haze of quotes by a wild-eyed chestnut colt, who comes careering by in a hail of clips and clops on road. Riding him, and leaning back to show his full command and lack of fear, is a fit and topless suntanned teenage boy, who couldn't care less if everyone else is waiting for the weekend: the fair is here, and so is he, and everyone should know. His face is a satisfied half-smile of knowing he has hit the early summer of his life, and as he canters off, his heavy gold chain flits and dances off his shoulders with the lightness of a garland in the breeze.

We weave our way off the road and through a narrow gap in the fence towards the market, dodging the muddiest bits of ground and the rubbish strewn here and there. It makes me angry: even though it's no worse than any other festival or fairground, music gig or rural show I have attended in the past, it plays up to the image of the feckless, unclean Traveller, and I wish we could avoid it; keep ourselves above suspicion; parry sneers. Then I check my thoughts, and realise that doing anything to impress the *gorjies* is not the Gypsy way, and so I shouldn't be surprised at how these polystyrene cups and Coke cans sit amongst chip paper as it flutters in the wind. We may have different roots, but we are not a different species. We are people, this is England; this is not a poet's reverie of what these things should be.

I am on the lookout for a good wash-bowl and stand, made out of stainless steel, traditional essentials of the Traveller roadside life. Romanies used to call this stuff 'a *kushti* bit of flash', and it was always obvious why: it's never been cheap, so you had to have a few quid to buy it, but more than that, high-polished stainless steel literally flashes in the sun, and gives a Traveller's set-up a bright and blinding, spotless look. The black pot and kettle of the 'black-blooded' folk were traded in, old ways betrayed for pieces of false silver.

It's fitting that I want to buy these items now. We've got by without them for almost a year, and I mull this over as I roam the fair, eyes peeled for shiny metal. I realise it isn't a question of need; more a refinement of a well-worked routine, a way of making everything a little easier and more glamorous. A wash-stand keeps a bowl high off the ground, especially important for the 'clean' bowl used for washing-up and doing dishcloths and muslins, and it has a metal platform at its base, on which a small gas stove can burn to heat the water above. I also want my own water jack – the tall, kettle-like water jug beloved of the Travellers – to replace the one of Grandad's I've had for a year on a generous long-term loan. He had it custom made up north many years ago, and it's of especially good quality, thick steel and strong, with his name hammered out on the neck like a steel tattoo. I want to give it back to him before it gets damaged or lost. And I need my own one now, as much for a symbol of the fact that I know how to live this way, as a highly functional object, a design that has never been topped, and a bit of 'flash'.

The etymology of the contemporary Romani word *chordi*, meaning 'stolen', is exactly the same as the root of the old Romani word *choradi*, meaning 'poverty stricken' or 'pitiable'. To steal was therefore literally synonymous with being in poverty: in Romani, if you steal something, you 'poor' it, an expression which is difficult to translate into English. The way the phrase is used – 'We used to *chore* the odd few taters and turnips out of his field' – implies that stealing out of necessity, for instance, to ward off starving in the winter, is less immoral than other kinds of stealing, which I think most people would agree to be correct. The problem is that this softened sense of the word *chore* compared to its English equivalent, 'steal', has in some cases survived the transition out of poverty, and brought along with it the sense that stealing is not something morally serious; rather, it only really matters if you get caught, and face the consequences. But this is an issue over which Gypsies and Travellers are bitterly divided. When I was five, I stole a pack of Askey's ice-cream wafers from a newsagent when I was out with Mum; I didn't really want them, I just wanted to see if I could get away with it. Mum was incensed and marched me back into the shop, making me hand over the wafers and apologise to the shopkeeper as tears of shame ran down my little cheeks. The boundaries had been made abundantly clear – stealing was wrong, and was punishable by horrendous penitential moments in the stocks. But for other Travellers I knew, the lines were far more subtly blurred, and I remember people declaring they'd *chored* things and being met not with riven frowns, but with cheeky laughs and smiles; with shakes of the head that said not, 'Boy, that is wrong,' but rather, 'Boys will be boys.'

After passing stall after stall that has already sold out of the kind of stainless-steel wares I am after, I find one that seems to have everything: a nice big oval wash-bowl on a stand; a smaller round steel bowl that'll come in handy for the lesser jobs; and a medium-sized water jack with a hammered chrome-like finish and a neat plug on a chain to stop the water spilling out when you move. The stall owner comes over, tapping the ash off a superking cigarette, then returning it to her mouth as she pulls her curly black hair back and ties it up.

'How can I help ya, now?' she says, in a husky Irish voice.

'I'm after one of the stands and bowls ...'

'A wash-stand and a bowl, you mean?'

'Er, yes, please, and a little bowl and one of those medium water jacks. If you've got clean ones.'

She throws me a dark look; as soon as I'd said the words, I realised they were poorly chosen, and could be seen to imply that she wasn't clean, something an Irish Traveller never wants to hear, especially from a man with an English accent.

'You know what I mean, ones what ain't been on display,' I say, defusing the silent bomb.

She walks over to the back of the van and motions to her daughter, who rushes to grab a new little bowl and water jack, still wrapped in clear plastic that rustles in the breeze.

They walk back over towards me, the woman carrying a large oval wash-bowl in one hand, and a large flat cardboard box in the other.

'You've a brand new stand in here,' she says. 'The last one in its box. They're the good ones, these. They sell out quick. They'll last you for donkey's years, they will.' She's shifted to speaking to Candis, who is presumed to be the one who cares most about the washing gear.

'What do you want for the lot?' I ask.

She names her price. I go in at just over half that, and she laughs, hands on her hips: 'You're joking now, I'll sell out of these all week at the price I've asked, and you know I will!' I laugh as well, and offer three quarters of the original amount.

She nods, 'Alright,' and I count out my notes, then take a last look in the box to check it's all there.

'There should be screws and everything as well ... ' the woman says, also looking in the box to see it's alright.

At this, a man comes over – her husband, I think – and says in a low, clear, certain voice, 'Everything your man needs is in there.' He's my height but broader chested, feet apart. He can handle himself.

'You're alright, mate,' I say. 'Just making sure, save coming back, know what I mean.'

'Alright,' he says. 'Me wife'll take your money.'

'Don't take Travellers' cheques, do you, mate?' I say. It's an old joke, but I just want to make sure there's no bad feeling between us – I don't want to remember a sour glance every time I look at this gear.

They both laugh at the crapness of the joke. 'Ah, good luck finding someone who'll take them here!' says the woman. I hand over the cash, and she pushes the notes down into the pocket of her skin-tight jeans.

Back at the van, we get ready for dinner, peeling potatoes and frying onions and bacon for a Joey Grey. The van is neat and tidy and our steel gear on display: it pulses in the sun like polished bits of armour, and I suppose it is a shield of sorts, keeping a clean life greaved against the dirt. Cand adds chopped mushrooms and a tin of tomatoes to the saucepan with a pleasant, bubbling sizzle, and I roll a cigarette and sit down on my old fold-up chair. I take a drag of smoke and watch the evening haze descending over the Eden Valley, marvelling at how I've landed on my feet once more, and found the ultimate *atchin tan*, hallowed on the Gypsies' holy hill. Mum's oriental fabrics blow in the gentle breeze behind me, tiny mirrors tapping with a tinkle on the metal of the van. Midsummer, and all is perfect. I have found a lasting peace amongst my scattered kin.

These thoughts are still crystallising in my head when a bloke my age comes walking over wearing a T-shirt, tracksuit bottoms, brand new trainers and a cold look in his eye. He stands about six feet from the van, facing me, chest ever so slightly pushed out, but still relaxed, as though he's got every right to come and be so close. I give him the benefit of the doubt – maybe he's had a couple of pints and wants to have a chat.

'Alright,' he says. He's got a southern accent. I reckon he grew up not too far from me.

'Alright, mate,' I reply. There is a short pause.

'How long you two been Travellers for, then?'

No, he isn't friendly. We are on the edge of trouble.

Asking how long we've been Travellers is a declaration that we aren't Gypsies. It means he thinks we're 'New Travellers' or 'wannabe Gypsies', tourists in his world. I've never been asked this question before – at least, not in this particular way – and I realise it's because of the way I've decorated the van. In the back of my mind, there's a dim recognition of the irony that having Indian items in my van makes me look like a counterfeit Romany: such is the aesthetic distance between the Gypsies' homeland and most English Gypsy lives. But I'm wearing a saddle ring and I'm immaculately dressed, and my wife is cooking a pot of English Traveller's soup at my side, so I think there's more to this than a simple mistake: I reckon he actually wants to have a row. I keep a tight lid on my anger, knowing he might be handy with his fists, and that he's probably got some backup loitering elsewhere on the hill. Trying to sound as though I haven't taken offence, I tell him how long I have been a Traveller:

'All my life, mate. You?'

He's surprised, but slightly amused, as if it might be fun to see what this idiot has to say.

'All your life, ay? Beat that.'

There's a very uncomfortable pause as he tries to figure out what I mean. Do I mean I'm a hippy and I've been travelling all my life, or do I actually mean I'm a Gypsy? He goes for the former option first, and asks me where I've been travelling.

'Just got back from the south of France,' I say. 'There's a Travellers' thing down there, Saintes-Maries-de-la-Mer, ever heard of that?' It draws a blank. 'We've been stopping in the van. Ain't got me towing licence and it's good enough for us, mate. Know what I mean?'

At this point his mate, or brother, or whoever he is comes walking over, finishing up between us to one side, the position the referee takes up before a boxing match.

'Alright, *pal*,' says the new bloke, immediately more friendly than the first. He's from the north, and seems slightly embarrassed about his aggressive friend. 'Just pulled on here, have ya?'

Bloke one answers for me. 'Yeah, he's just got back from the south of France. In that.' He nods disparagingly at the van.

'It's alright, though, ain't it?' says the friendlier bloke. 'Got everything you need in there, like.'

I take the opportunity to look over my shoulder and check if Candis is alright. She's wisely gone and sat in the cab of the van, and is reading her book, apparently without a care in the world, though I know she'll be taking every bit of this in.

'Does us alright, *mush*, know what I mean? There's only me and her, so it's all we need.'

I've done it now, I've used a Romany word. So bloke one smiles at last, and asks me the million-dollar question:

'Who's you one of, then?'

I tell him, reeling off the list of well-known surnames in my family tree, then half-sarcastically asking him if he's heard of any of them.

'I know a so-and-so from Guildford way,' he says. 'Anything to do with you?'

'I expect so, somewhere along the line,' I say. 'Guildford, ay, is that where you're from then?'

'Round that way, yeah,' he says, reluctant to be any more specific. I ask him if he knows my cousin's husband and his family, who are well known in the town. If he really is from there, their names will ring a bell.

'Nah, don't think I know them,' he says. I can see in his eyes that he knows exactly who I'm talking about, and at this point I become sure he's up to no good. On the other hand, he can't really admit he knows them, two minutes after he's come straight up to me out of the blue and called me a wannabe Gypsy to my face.

His mate has had enough. 'Nice talking to you, *pal*,' he says. 'Be lucky.'

'Be lucky, mate,' I say as he walks away.

There's another brief, awkward pause as the first bloke sways almost imperceptibly from side to side. I notice he's clenching his jaw and tensing the muscles around his eyes. I reckon there's more to him than a skinful of drink: he's on the coke.

'Thing is mate, people's got their places up here, you know what I mean?' he says. Beyond hope, he suddenly sounds as though he's being reasonable. 'Then you pull up, no one knows who you are ... You know what I'm saying, don't ya?'

'Look, mate, we don't want no trouble. I'd rather just pull up somewhere else.'

In his intoxicated eyes I see the first faint trace of remorse.

'I ain't got a problem with you being here,' he says. 'But you might find some of the neighbours aren't so friendly.'

He motions with his head towards three brand new top-of-the-range Tabbert trailers parked the other side of his.

If he reckons he's friendly compared to the neighbours, then I've got no intention of waiting to see what 'friendly' means to them.

'Each to their own though, bruv,' he says. 'No trouble, ay?'

'No trouble,' I say. He ambles off, and I sit down, trying to look unperturbed.

After he's well and truly gone, Cand gets out of the van and walks over to where I'm sitting.

'Once that dinner's cooked, we're eating it, nice and calm, like nothing's happened,' I say quietly. 'Then we're packing the gear up and we're getting the fuck out of here.'

'I agree,' says Cand.

I force myself to eat all the Joey Grey, mopping up the last of it with a buttered white crusty roll. It's tasty but I am angry – my guts are tight and my appetite is gone. I'm only eating to save face: a man who's really scared wouldn't be able to sit there calmly and finish a big pot of soup. To get up and leave without eating would be too much of a *ladge-up*.

Once the dinner's finished, we waste no time in packing up, but we do so smoothly, taking care not to look as though we're rushing. I roll and smoke a cigarette, another gesture trying to show I'm not running off with my tail between my legs. But

I'm not a fighting man, and stabbings have happened on this hill in previous years. I think back to Essex and the story of Elijah Buckley, lying there in his own blood at a horse fair in 1832. I flick away the end of the roll-up, jump back in the van, and off we roll, as the deep orange sunset starts to melt at the purple edge of the sky.

We agree we don't want to stop in the town tonight, so we drive off, intent on finding a stopping place somewhere outside. As we drive away from Appleby, the pointlessness of the whole encounter dawns on me like rain. I start to rage at the injustice I've just experienced. We've driven thousands and thousands of miles and stopped in *atchin tans* from here to the Mediterranean, with hardly a tale of trouble to be told. Yet it's here, at the English Gypsy's Mecca, a place where Dad, Grandad and Nandad have trod before me for fifty years, that a Travelling fella strolls up to put the mockers on my week. I put my foot down, revving the engine, then swear and punch the steering wheel with the underside of my fist, which beeps the horn and surprises a few pedestrians by the kerb. Cand reminds me that this won't help. 'You're right, it won't,' I say. But it feels like it has.

We drive for a while, and stop for an early break by the rugged, ruddy walls of Barnard Castle. I remember Grandad telling me about a horseman from this town whom my family still refer to as 'Yoke 'im up man', because he would always say those words as his horse was being readied for the trots. The thought of 'Yoke 'im up man' and his catchphrase, echoing down through Traveller time, brings me temporary relief. My mind is foaming and flickering over the encounter with the bloke on Appleby Hill, and I can't stop turning it over in my mind. 'There must be a meaning to this,' I tell myself. Every new thing I've experienced on the road has taught me something. Whether elemental – a gust of gale-force wind telling me to mind how I open the doors – or moral – a still-lit candle rolling along my carpet towards a petrol can and thereby warning me not to leave in haste – each fresh experience seems to have power to teach, and even if it doesn't, it's an axiom I have ended up believing. But the purpose of this last encounter seems to be eluding me. It wasn't supposed to be like this. I've just been pushed off one of the oldest Gypsy stopping places in England, and it wasn't by a *gavver*, a council man or an irate landowner with a gun. I was, in effect, 'moved on' by a Gypsy, one of my own. My mood turns bitter as I picture him back at his home, counting his money in a sterile yard full of featureless trailers and vans.

We use the loos in a friendly-looking pub before driving off. By the time we get out of Barnard Castle it's growing dark and I haven't any idea where we're going. I'm so busy thinking about the day's events that I don't look to see where the sun is setting, so I don't even know which compass direction we're heading in, or how far away from Appleby we've come: I'm just driving out of a lack of other plausible alternatives, and it shows. Cand asks me where we're headed in a voice low on volume but high on cutting edge. I haven't got an answer. I don't know. It's getting dark.

Suddenly the verges broaden out on either side of the road, and my attention is caught by two blue portable toilets that seem utterly out of place in this remote, unpeopled spot. My headlight beams are visible now, and cutting through the fading purple light, they illuminate a sign that has been hammered into the earth:

TEMPORARY STOPPING PLACE
PROVIDED FOR TRAVELLERS
TO APPLEBY FAIR

I read the words aloud to Candis. I've never seen a sign like this in my life, openly inviting Travellers to pull onto a verge; and it surely means Travellers with a capital T, because it's in relation to the most famous Gypsy horse fair in the country, maybe the world. I look across the road and there's another sign, exactly the same, sticking out from a patch of tall grass bending gently in the wind. There are dates on the signs: the right to stop on here expires tomorrow.

Not only has the council set out roadside pitches for Travelling people to use, a second miracle is that there isn't anyone using them. I pull the van onto a square of concrete set into the side of the wide verge on the left, leaving the engine running as if I think this might be some sort of trap. A car passes every thirty seconds or so, but other than that, there's nobody around. It's lonely here: a thin, straight lane runs off the main road, and a farmer has blocked a nearby gate with massive logs that would need machinery to move. I look at the sign again for reassurance, cut the engine, and get out of the van to take a look around.

There are a couple of wide tyre marks on the grass, but crossing over them, as if stepping over a threshold from the present into the past, I find a pair of narrow tracks running alongside, with timber offcuts – used to keep wheels in place – left behind at their sides. Nearby are a few straws of hay and some fresh manure. A horse-drawn wagon has stopped here, and by the look of the manure, it has only recently left. The only rubbish I can see is a few crisp packets, which I gather and put in a plastic bag to throw away later on. Considering there are no bins, the lack of litter means the Travellers stopping here were as rubbish-conscious as me, and I guess the crisp packets were probably dropped by their children. I walk a bit further, and under a hawthorn tree by the fence separating the verge from a pasture field, there is a fire scar that has been covered with fresh grass in the traditional Romany way. I brush the grass to one side and find that under the cold top layer of ash, there's warmth, and maybe embers glowing still. I realise I am living out a childhood fantasy – long nurtured by westerns, cowboy ballads and old relations' tales – of stumbling across a camp and looking for signs of who was there, and why; testing the temperature of ash to try and gauge the length of time since they departed. I never thought I'd actually be doing this, much less at a stopping place that had been used by Travellers with a proper wagon. I've been on the road for nearly a year, but this is a brand new experience. I'm stunned to have found an *atchin tan* like this.

I look behind me: Cand is boiling water for a final cup of tea. So, we are stopping here for the night. Of course we are: how can we look this gift-horse in the mouth? I walk around the verge picking up sticks for firewood; amazingly, at the foot of the fence lies one of the posts from the previous one, half sewn into the grass. I pluck it out, collect the offcuts from over by the wagon tracks, and take them all back to the ashes of the fire. All in all, there's enough wood for a *yog* to last an hour or so, and that is all I want: to stare at it and think on the day before night falls. I use a stick to poke at the ash and there are a few small embers where the fire has gone to sleep. I put some kindling on top, then look in my pockets for paper, and pull out a till receipt: holding it close to the embers and blowing them, I attempt to coax a flame into life, but the last of the fading orange light ebbs out before I can.

I pull out my matches and get the fire started – my fire, it turns out, since I have failed to rekindle the old one. I go back to the van and get my folding chair, then sit down on it by the fireside and roll a cigarette. Cand brings me my cup of tea and sits down next to me for a bit, but she returns to the van before long, registering that I might need a minute to commit the day's proceedings to the flames. At the last edge of the gloaming, a pair of lapwings reel overhead in their repeating pattern of straight-on flapping and sideways barrelling, then soaring, straightening up, and they repeat their squeaking call to each other as it seeps off into the distance. It is night now and peace is descending with the darkness. Another realisation: having a good place to stop is more important than having someone's blessing. You don't need people's approval – not even your own people's – as long as you've got your fire. The shadow of the drunk guy on the hill begins to pass.

A Transit pickup drives past beeping its horn, an arm stretched out of the window with a thumbs-up signifying we've been spotted by other Travellers. One of them bellows out cheerfully, 'Y'alright, *chavi*?'

I smile and put my thumb up. I'm alright.

The Beginning

Romannobridge, Stirling, Blairgowrie, Skye, the Tinkers' Heart of Argyll

There are few clouds, high and free in the blue, as we drive across the border into Scotland. I am relieved to cross the line, man-made as it is. The intensity of Appleby has taken it out of me, and Scotland promises long and narrow roads, and long, broad days. I have come here for a quiet resolution to my endless searching; to find my journey's end in the place where the people who inspired that journey had their old beginning.

Scotland is where the main progenitors of Britain's Romany Gypsies first set foot on British soil, on specific dates now lost to the vicissitudes of time, but probably at some point towards the end of the 1400s: we can't be more precise. Sir George Mackenzie wrote that during the reign of James II of Scotland, 'a Moor ... came in with some Saracens to infest Galloway', and it is conceivable that this refers to Romany people; the historian Donald Whyte suggests they may have been among the 'masterful beggars' described in a government Act of 1449. More concrete evidence is provided by the record of a payment of £20 made by the King of Scots to the 'King of Rowmais' in 1492. Ten years later, another royal bursary was made to a man claiming to be the 'Earl of Grece'. But according to Whyte, the first indisputable evidence of a Romany presence in Scotland is found in the *Accounts of the Lord High Treasurer* of the year 1505. A sum of £7 was paid 'to the Egyptians', and a royal letter of recommendation to the King of Denmark was made out to a man named Anthonius Gagino, who claimed to be making a pilgrimage across the Christian world. A leader of the Scottish Gypsies emerged, known as 'Johnnie Faa', 'faa' (or 'faw') possibly being derived from an Anglo-Saxon word for 'coloured'.

With the exception of 'oure lovit Johnne Faw', who continued to enjoy royal protection, the Romanies soon fell out of favour: there were reports of thefts by 'Egiptens' in Aberdeen in 1529, and in 1553, a warrant was issued by the privy council for the arrest of a Gypsy leader known as Sebastian Lalow, together with his criminal accomplices. In 1590, a Lady Foulis was tried for witchcraft, and accused of sending a servant 'to the Egiptianis, to haif knoawledge of thame how to poyson the Young Laird of Fowles and the Young Lady Balnagoune'. The Gypsies who refused to cease their wanderings and predations became known as 'that infamous societie'; a 'damned fraternitie' of rogues and thieves. From 1 August 1609, all 'vagabonds, sorners and common thieves called Egyptians' were banished from the kingdom of Scotland, never to return, on pain of death.

We drive past the Scottish border, announced by a massive sign astride the verge, blazoned with a saltire in a deliberately skewed perspective, and bilingual in English and Gaelic – 'Welcome to Scotland, Fàilte gu Alba'. The last three words on the sign are not welcomed by all. Apart from a tiny number of place names, including Innerleithen in Tweeddale and Kilbucho in Peeblesshire (respectively meaning 'meeting of the grey waters' and 'church of St Bega' – an Irish princess), there is little evidence that Gaelic was spoken much in this embattled part of Britain. Historically, the Old Welsh language of Cumbria and Strathclyde flourished in the western borders, and Old English, ancestor of modern English and Scots, predominated in the east. Thinking about these languages, inconstant as the paths of rivers and the sea-eaten lines of coast, I wonder what the first Romanies to come here in the late fifteenth century might have called this wind-whipped land.

Old dictionaries of the Romani language often contained Romani names for places. They are rarely heard today, but may still have been commonplace until around the end of the nineteenth century. They would have had an obvious utility, concealing information about escape routes and itineraries, useful both in business situations, and when facing off with sheriffs, lords and local keepers of the law. These secret toponyms usually consisted of the flexible words *gav* – village or town – and *tem*, meaning country, county or land, compounded with either straight translations of or puns on the local place names. Liverpool was *booko-pani-gav*, the 'liver-water-town';

Bedfordshire was *woodrus-gav-tem*, or 'bed-town-land'. No ancient Romani name for Scotland survives, so far as I am aware; but it is unlikely the mediaeval Gypsies would have called it *kaulo-tem*, or 'dark land', as this would have required knowledge of the Latin origins of the word 'Scot' (from *scotia*, 'darkness'). A speculative shortlist of possible names begins to form as we drive. *Shirilo-tem:* 'cold-land'. *Brishindesko-tem:* 'the land of constant rain'. Or perhaps, given they'd already been living in Northern Europe for a few years, the early British Romanies might have lighted on a less depressing moniker: *baro-veshengo-tem*, 'the land of the great forests', or something scarier: *ruvengo-tem*, 'the country of wolves'. Then it occurs to me that before long, they would probably have settled on the simplest name of all, and that would have been *kova-tem:* 'this land'.

In the distance I catch sight of a range of hills on which great blotches of gorse have broken into yellow flower like lichens on a rock. It calls to mind the time, before I went back on the road, when I heard the Scottish Traveller author Jess Smith singing 'The Yellow on the Broom' one rainy afternoon in Pollokshields, now home to one of the biggest communities of immigrant Roma in modern Britain. The gorse coming into flower is Nature beckoning Travellers back onto the roads after winter, and as Jess's trembling, almost ululating, voice rang off the white walls of a strip-lit Glasgow room, I felt the call myself. As far as I know, I have no family connection to Scotland whatsoever, but I was bursting with

the need to get out onto her roads, cooped up as I was like
the 'scaldies' in the song:

> *The scaldies cry us 'Tinker dirt'*
> *And sconce our bairns in school –*
> *Who cares what a scaldy thinks*
> *For a scaldy's but a fool*
> *He never heard the yarlin's song*
> *Nor seen the flax in bloom*
> *For they're a' cooped up in hooses*
> *When the yellow's on the broom*

'*Scaldy*' is a dialect word, both in Scotland and parts of Ireland,
meaning a fledgling bird confined to the nest, one not yet able
to take flight on its own: a bird that cannot fly, and therefore
is not free.

For all its flighty connotations, Gypsy culture can be stifling
in its demands for living in line with its hidden rules. Rock
stars employ the word 'Gypsy' to mean those who have escaped
from moral claustrophobia, but in reality, Gypsies are just as
likely to feel confined as anybody else. The same day I met
Jess, I watched as a troupe of little girls from the local Roma
community danced in brightly coloured dresses at a community event. They clicked their fingers on outstretched arms
and sang '*Ja tuke tuke*' to a furious klezmer beat. The audience
clapped and twirled, unaware of the lyrics' meaning: 'Get away
from me.'

In Scotland, as in England and Wales, the various groups of Travellers also have a long-standing tradition of mutual suspicion and harshly consonantal insult, and a main fault line runs along the divide between Celtic and Romany breeds. There are those who trace their lineage back to the oldest Romany families, including the famous line of Johnny Faa, and the Shaws and Blyths. Historians have tended to distinguish these 'Lowland Romany Gypsies' from those descended in the main from the Highlands – many of whose *Mac*-prefixed names would seem to speak of descent from the clans, and therefore, ultimately, Irish stock. But surnames make an unreliable guide to someone's honour, lineage or folk allegiance, especially over spans of time as long and deep as these. Increasingly, I have no interest in other people's attempts to divide the indivisible as they did in Apartheid South Africa, where an 'octoroon' – who had one black great-grandparent – was allowed to play golf with the whites, but a 'quadroon', who had more than one, was not.

When I've been in the company of Travellers from Scotland, I try to wear my southerner's naivety on my sleeve. I let people tell me what they make of all the above; whether they call their language Romany or Cant, or something else; and whence they ultimately deem their people came to Scottish shores. But as with their counterparts south of the border, the tongues of Scotland's Travellers seem to swear to anything but cultural purity. Words of Scots, Gaelic, Romani and uncertain origin jostle and throng together in lilting and listing proportions across the different forms of the Cant.

The Perthshire Cant described by the late academic Sheila Douglas is peppered with words that are alien to me, including 'shan' for 'bad', 'coul' for 'man', 'naiskil' for 'father' and 'kinchins' for children, as well as the evocative term 'wammilin coocavie' for a 'boiling kettle' ('coocavie' is a variant form of the Romani word *kekavi* for the same object). By contrast, the Scottish Traveller artist Shamus McPhee, whose family have lived in caravans at the Bobbin Mill site in Pitlochry for decades, speaks a dialect that at times hardly differs from the Romani I grew up with, studded with words like *pukker*, *vonger*, *monnishin* and *fam* – words we used for 'tell', 'money', 'woman' and 'hand'. In 2008, Shamus and his sister Roseanna gave evidence in court, including demonstrations of the descent of much of their language from Indic vocabulary – that helped lead to the official recognition of Scottish Gypsy Travellers as a national ethnic minority. It took until the twenty-first century for a judge to rule that a people who had been referenced in Scottish literature for half a millennium were a genuine 'people' at all.

As for the connection between Scotland's Travellers and the Highland Gaels of old – and as Jess Smith also told me – the devil himself associated the 'gypsies' of Scotland with those scattered members of the Highland clans who sought Canadian asylum in the 1780s, as Robert Burns has it in the 'Address of Beelzebub' (1786):

> Get out a horsewhip or a jowler,
> The langest thong, the fiercest growler,

An' gar' the tatter'd gypsies pack
Wi' a' their bastards on their back!

We've driven straight up from Cumbria, and by the time we get to Lockerbie we're knackered and on the lookout for a place to spend the night. As we take a random B-road round a small hill after dark, my headlights swing through the lattice-work of a low tree and light up the shape of what looks like a large tawny owl, its white-hot eyes like miniature moons. Two or three turnings later we find a reasonable stopping place down a long, straight, quiet road. I make no written record of where it is, but I keep hold of the memory of a shallow pull-in – barely half a lay-by – edged by thick black mud and leaf mould that smells strongly of damp woods, even though it has been a dry week. I don't know where we are – I check my phone but there is no signal at all and it can't place us on the map. During the night I hear just two vehicles pass, and when in the morning I ask Cand about it, she says that she only heard one, before falling asleep. We wake up late and it is still cold enough to see our breath, although the sun has lit up the far side of the green valley to the west of us. Off to the east, a steep-sided slope, hundreds of feet tall and bristling with conifers, completely blocks out the fine June weather from our position.

After a quick bowl of porridge we're keen to get out of the dank shadow of the hill. Our first stop is the village of Romannobridge in Peeblesshire, about fifty miles north.

On 1 October 1677, two Gypsy families quarrelled here and fought with blades, resulting in the death of a man and his pregnant wife, and the serious wounding of his brother. The incident shocked the Scotland of the day, and five men who had taken part in the fight were later hanged at Edinburgh. I draw a pair of cutlasses crossing the rough spot of Romanno on the map, a gesture that seems to bring my quest in line with the wider history of the island as a whole. In Britain, the sign of crossed swords on a map is an insignia of the land; a signet-seal that validates our status as a sceptred, storied isle. But the sight of Gypsy cutlasses crossing each other might not work this way. I fear it would be interpreted as a hallmark of our savagery, shorn of any bravery, *noblesse* or old romance.

I think back to when I was growing up. No one wanted to get into an argument with Travellers. Their reputation preceded them and that was the way many of them liked it: every Gypsy knew the police were institutionally racist, that you would get scant help from them in your hour of need, and so your best bet was to be able to 'have a *coar*' and, if possible, to make sure people knew that you could. There is no stigma attached to a fist fight between two people of the same gender, unless one of them is obviously sick or old, and to vanquish an attacker – especially one who is bigger than you – is in some Travellers' view the greatest thing you can achieve, aside from becoming a self-made millionaire.

Since most people didn't respect Gypsies as equals, fear was the closest thing to respect that a Traveller could usually engineer. Every now and then, when this fear might have started to wane, something spectacular always seemed to happen to make sure it was immediately replenished. On a Sunday, we would watch saloon brawls in John Wayne and Clint Eastwood westerns, enjoying the horsewhip cracks of fists on the jaws of their unlucky foes. And there was always a fighting chance that the men would re-enact these episodes before too long.

I remember an incident that happened during my early teens. My uncle got into difficulties in one of the local pubs. He had been drinking by himself, then started talking to a group of six stable lads who were doing a bit of work for a local horse trainer. After a few games of pool the atmosphere had turned sour and my uncle realised there might be a fight. The stable lads were blocking the exits and he knew if he tried to leave he would be vulnerable to a sucker punch, so instead, he went into the toilet and phoned my grandad for backup. Grandad answered simply, 'Wait there. I'm on my way.'

Grandad picked up my other uncle first, and they drove to the pub together in one of the vans. Our family had drunk in there for years, so they were familiar with the layout of the place. Knowing they were outnumbered, they decided to come in through the back and make the most of the element of surprise.

By the time they burst through the door to the bar the fight had already commenced, and my younger uncle was taking a beating from several men. The stable lads weren't fighting fair so my grandad and uncles had no intention of doing so either. Fists flew; pool balls were unpocketed; cues used as weapons on both sides. When it was over, my relations left the pub and returned to the yard, where Gran was waiting with a first-aid kit like a boxer's cornerman.

The next day, word spread quickly that our family had won a fight against 'a gang of fellas', and that the bar where it had happened 'looked like a war zone'. I spent the day hoping I would never get into a fight like that, but that if I did, I would be on the winning side. There was an atmosphere of unambiguous triumph. A moral lesson had been doled out to men who attacked 'team-handed'. Our reputation was flying high, and everyone walked with their shoulders back that day. It was like a beginning.

I wanted the name of Romannobridge to be connected to the word Romany, but the linguist Alan G. James traces it back to the Old Britonnic rǫd mönach, probably meaning something like 'monks' fort' or 'monks' enclosure'. Still, it seemed an odd coincidence that the most notorious encounter in the history of Scotland's Romany people took place in a village with a name that sounded like their own.

We cross the bridge and pull over near an elderberry bush to get our bearings. I look at various maps, including part of an old Ordnance Survey one I've got saved on my phone, and try to figure out exactly where the fight might have taken place. Meanwhile, the familiar routine: Cand throws open the van's side door to make some tea, and I roll a thin cigarette. The air is hazy with dappled sunlight. My mind is running its practised course of thinking about what this place will be like in the winter. I close my eyes and picture it in lashing rain and howling winds that blow for weeks on end. Then I open them again, and all is peaceful, but for the gentle breeze that blows our mirror-dotted Indian curtain against the van with a tinkling tune.

After our tea we set off in search of the location of the 1677 Gypsy fight. I am hoping to get as near to the actual spot as I possibly can. I've read an article about it by the Scottish historian Mark Jardine, which includes a picture of an ancient trackway, overgrown with grass and leading up a small hill, towards what looks like a narrow stand of wavering beech and ash trees on its crest. The picture is burned in my mind, and I look for the view as we walk up Dovecot Road. It takes its name from a structure that was built six years after the affray as a symbol of peace. The dovecot itself is no longer, but whilst it stood it bore the inscription:

> *The field of Gypsie blood which here you see*
> *A shelter for the harmless dove shall be*

There are smartly kept houses at the bottom of the road, with gardens full of blooms visited by butterflies and bees. But as we climb the road it narrows, turning into a rougher track with small rocks underfoot, and a sense of trepidation starts to build in me. I reckon Cand feels it too as she walks on carefully, silently, by my side.

Walking further up the track, we pass a small farm: nobody seems to be around, but there are some cows in a pen, who stare up at us mournfully without making a sound, increasing my sense of unease. There is a loud, pulsating buzzing noise. As we get closer we see, behind a sheet of corrugated iron propped against a wall, the rotting carcass of a sheep. Its legs poke rigidly out from its body, and hundreds of black flies swarm in and out of its burst rear end. We reach up our hands and cover our mouths as the smell of death enshrouds us, and we quietly say in unison, 'Oh, my God.'

Shaken by the gruesomeness of the sheep, we move warily on, until we can see what I think is the view I remember from the photograph. Either way, we cannot be far from the spot where the 'battle' took place. Alexander Pennecuik, who owned the Romanno estate in the years after the fight, wrote how:

Upon the first of October 1677, there happened at Romanno ... a memorable Polymachy betwixt two Clans of Gipsies, the Fawes and Shawes; who had come from Haddington fair, and were going to Harestanes to meet two other clans of those rogues, the Baillies and Browns, with a resolution to fight them.

They fell out at Romanno amongst themselves, about dividing the spoil they had got at Haddington, and fought it manfully. Of the Fawes there were four brethren and a brother's son; of the Shawes, the father with three sons; and several women on both sides. Old Sandie Faw, a bold and proper fellow, with his wife, then with child, were both killed dead upon the place; and his brother George, very dangerously wounded.

In February 1678, old Robin Shaw, the gipsie, and his three sons, were hanged at the Grass-Mercat for the above mentioned murder committed at Romanno; and John Faw was hanged the Wednesday following for another murder. Sir Archibald Primrose was justice general at the time; and Sir George McKenzie king's advocate.

The place is peaceful and bright in the sun, but I can't forget the pulsating corpse behind us, which seems to fix the murders of the past in sharp relief. My mind drifts back to that of Elijah Buckley in nineteenth-century Essex, and on to more recent stabbings and shootings on the Traveller sites of contemporary Britain. Of course, these are all isolated events, and of course, they happen all over the world, especially amongst people who live at the rough edge of civilisation, and who frequently arm themselves with sharp tools in response. But still, I am disturbed by this violent thread that runs through the tapestry of Gypsy and Traveller history. Worst of all, in this case, a clutch of lives had seemingly met their ends with the same old, hackneyed, ultimate explanation: a falling-out between families due to an argument over money. The idea that there was anything 'manful' about the fight is parried by the sickening fact that a pregnant woman was killed. It is true that many Gypsy women, then and now, will stand their ground and fight the same as men, and this incident might provide an awful example of the fact.

Cand and I take photographs of each other to mark the fact that we were here. But afterwards I regret it. I'm not so sure how glad I am to carry the memory of this eerie spot. This isn't a stopping place, it's a dying place, and there's no way I'm waiting around to taste its atmosphere by night.

We make towards Edinburgh; Cand is planning to get a train back south the next day. I don't want to darken the atmosphere between us before her journey, so I try to put a brave face on it, but I am disconsolate at the idea of spending the next few weeks by myself. On cue, as if to celebrate my impending solitude, the engine maintenance light pings on. And moments later, the heavens open.

I have never seen water like this: merciless, endless fat drops. There seems to be more rain than air. Hoping the dashboard light just means the van needs an oil change, we try our luck at a small garage. It is a relief to drive under the forecourt roof and out of the hammering deluge. The mechanic strides out with a harried look on his face: he is six foot four, with curly black close-cropped hair, his chest and arms covered in black oil and dull yellow grease. Clearly under the *cosh* with work, he has no great need for my custom, but still does his best to be polite and help. He says he can do it if he's got the right oil and runs back inside to check. We've been in Scotland for several days, yet his accent comes as a shock: apart from Cand, the last person I spoke to was the bloke who ruined our stay on the hill at Appleby, and he was from Surrey, a good four hundred miles south of here. The mechanic is out of oil but we thank him for trying to help, to which he replies, 'Okay, folks?' and quickly returns to his workshop. We get back on our way as the rain subsides.

We try another garage, where a short and happy man in his early twenties, wearing a pristine polo shirt buttoned to the top, quotes an eye-watering price. He grins and I interpret the hike as a spot-tax on my accent.

Eventually we get the job done at a big chain garage with fixed and decent prices. We collect the van just before the place closes, by which time the sun is westering and we want to turn in for the night. We go to a small car park in the village of Carlops. It lies on the A702 near one end of the old Thieves' Road, an ancient drovers' track that crosses the moors by the Pentland Hills, and would almost certainly have been used by Lowland Gypsies in the past. Adjacent to the car park are two large and craggy rock faces with a short gap in between them, known in Scots as *Carlins' Lowp* – the Witches' Leap. As the sun disappears a group of bats emerges, picking off flying insects with small dull pips. When the moon comes up, we can see the grey cat's-cradle shapes their flight paths make against the pale cream glow of the summer moon.

The next morning, Edinburgh and its environs are hit by an even worse downpour than yesterday's, the heaviest I've seen in years. It strikes as Cand is cooking pasta in the car park of a Tesco's in Penicuik. Inches deep in water, the tarmac seems to turn to colourless jelly, and after hurrying back into the van, we spend an hour penned in by a billion drumming bolts of rain. Cand meditatively shuffles a deck of tarot cards while I stare at the blurred kaleidoscope of the window, trying in vain to read sense out of the sky.

When the rain does finally stop, the water leaves trails of silver silt in its wake. They pattern the tarmac of the car park like the stripes of a giant zebra, cutting across its painted white lines with curved, organic shapes.

We have a final cup of tea together, then drive to Waverley station under the darkening cloud of my mood. After a frantic and rushed roadside goodbye I watch Candis disappear into halls of stone and glass. My mood is strangely lighter now. Perhaps it's because I'm no longer able to dread the fact that she's leaving.

I take a brief look at the map, then drive off westward towards Stirling, the first recorded stopping place of Romany people in Britain. I have no idea whereabouts in the city they stayed, but I know that they were welcomed at the time – by James IV, King of Scots, who made them a loan of £7. I hope I might find some kind of northern epiphany there, echoing my moment in the Mediterranean sea at Saintes-Maries-de-la-Mer: that in contemplating arrival, newness and opportunity, I might wish away the staid and stodgy consistency of the Gypsy vs *gorjie* tension that has been the norm ever since.

Not knowing where else to go, I make for Stirling Castle, driving up a steep and winding road that wends its way in a curl to the mighty defensive walls, from whose cracks and crevices peep the little purple flowers of campanula. The music of bagpipes lifts onto the evening air and down across the town. The melody seems to summon me to the castle platform itself. I drive up its cobbled approach as if arriving to spend the night by royal invitation. I realise too late that the bagpipers are part of a large procession, and that there will not be room for me to drive in and everyone else to march out. I am become the Gypsy stereotype, my vehicle a thorn in the side of the orderly running of civic pomp. Mortified, I back the Transit away from the castle ahead of the sound of the pipes, to the bemusement of the people who have gathered to take pictures of ancient pageantry.

I park up on a flat area of the road, and spend the evening playing the spoons and whistling the same old songs.

I wake early. I've rested but it seems Stirling is not to provide any great moment of insight. I head for the small town of Blairgowrie in Perth and Kinross, also known as 'the Berry Toon'. Blairgowrie was once famous for its textile mills, but the last of these closed in 1979; since the late nineteenth century, its main export has been soft fruit. The town may be best known for its raspberries, but the rich soil and mild climate in the area also make it perfect for growing redcurrants, strawberries, blueberries, gooseberries and aronia – also known, appetisingly, as 'chokeberries', because of the way their sour flavour makes you purse and pucker your mouth.

The huge quantities of fruit grown in the area could not be brought in by the town's labour alone: even today, there are fewer than 8,000 residents. Help was required from outside, and as with the hop harvest in Kent, a labour force mainly composed of Travellers and urban working-class people duly obliged. A local encampment of huts sprang up – 'Tin City' – with its own grocery shop and post office. The 'Berry Toon' was a central part of Scottish Traveller life: when the celebrated documentary director Philip Donnellan set out to make a film about Gypsies and Travellers in late 1960s Britain, he made it a priority to get to the fields of Blairgowrie in the growing season. It was the most obvious place in the country to meet with Travellers, who'd come from all over Scotland to gather in the fruit. The great Traveller singer and storyteller Belle Stewart, whose life was immortalised in her daughter Sheila's biography *Queen Amang the Heather*, wrote one of her most famous songs – 'The Berry Fields o' Blair' – about the bulging of Blairgowrie's population at harvest-time:

> *When berry time comes roond each year*
> *Blair's population swellin*
> *There's every kind o' picker there*
> *And every kind o' dwellin.*
> *There's tents and huts and caravans,*
> *There's bothies and there's bivvies*
> *And shelters made wi tattie-bags*
> *And dug-outs made wi divvies.*
>
> *There's corner boys fae Glesgae,*
> *Kettle boilers fae Lochee,*

There's miners fae the pits o Fife,
Mill-workers fae Dundee,
And fisherfowk fae Peterheid
And tramps fae everywhere,
Aa lookin fir a livin aff
The berry fields o' Blair.

There's travellers fae the Western Isles,
Fae Arran, Mull and Skye;
Fae Harris, Lewis and Kyles o' Bute,
They come their luck to try.
Fae Inverness and Aberdeen,
Fae Stornoway and Wick,
Aa flock to Blair at the berry time,
The straws and rasps to pick.

Sheila Stewart was born in 1935 in a building that had once been a stable. The Stewarts lived in Blairgowrie all the year round, and their genius as folk singers, musicians and raconteurs attracted luminaries from the world of folk music, including Ewan MacColl and Peggy Seeger. Sheila Stewart was also invited, by President Gerald Ford, to sing at the White House bicentennial celebrations in 1976. The Queen and Prince Philip were also in attendance: prior to the event itself, Prince Philip asked for an impromptu performance from Sheila, and when he was told that security wouldn't allow it, he replied, 'Fuck security.'

In 1982, Sheila sang live in front of 385,000 people gathered in Glasgow's Bellahouston Park for Pope John Paul II's official visit to Scotland. 'When they asked me to sing for the Pope, I says, I cannae do that, I'm not a Catholic,' she later recalled, 'and they said, Oh, the Pope won't bother.' A newspaper report of the event said that only two things had silenced the gigantic crowd: the Pope's arrival, and Sheila Stewart's singing. Her obituary in the *Daily Telegraph* stated that 'a notable charac-teristic of her style was the *conniach* – a hard-to-pin-down term suggesting a gift for conveying the emotional heft of a ballad – with which she imbued many of the oldest and most epic songs in the canon of Scottish folk song, including "The Twa Brothers" and "The Bonnie Hoose of Arlie".'

As the sun goes down I walk along the bottle-brown river Ericht, where the air is heavy with midges and the pungent smell of wild garlic. The river is famous for the salmon that fight their way through its waters to spawn, prolonging their ancient line, against the tide, against the odds. The sky is still pale with the gloaming of the sun when I go to bed, listening to Sheila Stewart's voice singing the ancient ballads of Scotland to me, out of a mobile phone made of brittle circuit boards and glass.

I wander north-westward for Skye, but take my time, progressing at an outdated pace. I camp somewhere along the A9 south of Dalwhinnie, and I am spooked when an entire day passes without my catching sight of a single bird.

I stop again by the A87 in Glen Shiel, site of the crushing defeat of a combined Jacobite and Spanish force by British government troops in 1719. The Catholics had held the high ground, and believed themselves to be safe, but the redcoats came with accurate mortars and managed to strike upwards successfully from the road, killing five times as many men as they lost themselves. Rob Roy fought on the Jacobite side and survived, but one hundred and twenty-one men died and hundreds more were gruesomely wounded. I remember the words of an old Irish Traveller man I met a couple of years ago, who at that time was living with his adult children in a disused works yard in York. 'Millions of pounds they spend, the country people, blowing each other up with guns and bombs. And they think the real problem is us lot parked on a verge. And you know what? It's always been the same.' 'Country people' means non-Travellers, but in this instance, it sounded like a term of reprimand for the follies of militarism and nation states. I couldn't decide if there was an essential difference between this kind of war and the violence I'd seen, and read about, involving Travellers. But there is always a vast disparity in scale, and that has to mean something.

In Glen Shiel I go for a dip in a freezing burn, frowning as I ignore Nan's warnings, audible in my head, about the dangers of pneumonia and how it irreparably damaged several of her brothers' eyesight. The bottom of the stream is covered in smooth round stones, blue in the water and soft underfoot with translucent skins of algae.

★

Skye. I have been living for four days in a lay-by on the A87 north of Sligachan. It is large enough for five or six vehicles, but in the time I have been here only one other has pulled up, and not for long. The lay-by is next to a shallow reed-edged burn brooded over by the grey pyramids of the Cuillin hills. I have just flicked through the photos on my phone to check how long I've been here. Lately, the edges of my days seem to be bleeding into each other, so I cannot trust my guesses as to how much time has passed. I wonder if this marks another development in myself: a quiet abandonment of the need to progress; to keep track of time and rate.

For a change of scene I go to Glen Brittle to cook my dinner whilst staring up at the jagged grey line of the Cuillins. They might call them hills up here, but to a southerner like me they are mountains, huge and forbidding. It is midsummer and there is still a faint trace of snow visible on the tallest Munros, in spite of the roasting heat down here in the glen.

After lunch I walk up to the Fairy Pools, a series of little waterfalls and plunge pools hollowed out over lifetimes by the cold appetite of the stream. The water they contain glows in otherworldly-looking spectra of gemstone blues and greens, water clearer than air, that makes the rocks at its bottom shimmer as though they've been kissed by a god. I press on up the trail until the rest of the tourists are a long way behind, eventually stopping a few hundred yards off the summit, a grey, scree-slope world of desiccated pyramidal stones. It is a world perpetually inclined at angles off at least 45 degrees and even with the sun beating down on my chest, the place seems to pulse with the threat of the mad storms that lash it for chunks of the year. There are one or two crows up here, squawking every minute or so, and at one point I think I see an eagle, but it is gone up and over the mountain before I can tell. I can see from their occasional scats that sheep sometimes venture up this far, and maybe they go even further, right up to the crest. Tiny white orchids freckled with purple spots grow from odd patches of earth. The wind sounds like water. I think about what I would need to survive up here for a year, what equipment, how deep into the mountainside I would have to bore a retreat.

Great black clefts in the mountain summon me onwards, and I have already climbed beyond safety before I realise that it is probably time to head back. I understand now why the Fairy Pools are so named – they beckon you further to places where old gods still live, and where mortals cannot, and unless you're snapped out of your daydream just in time, the pools will be the death of you.

I turn around and look back down the mountainside, which funnels my eye down to the spectacular expanse of Loch Brittle below, a silver swathe laid out naked for the immense delight of the sun. I sing the old Traveller song '*Mandi Went to Puv the Grai*' – 'I Went to Put the Horse to Graze'. It tells of the South: a distant land of five-bar gates; a surfeit of pubs by shady fields; of oak trees, and of hardly any wind. A note of homesickness creeps into my serenity. It's possible that this is the first time Romani words have echoed around this particular mountainside, a kind of tiny conquest. I have never been this high up in my life, and I'm a couple of miles from my base, without water, but reckon I could die up here in peace, and that nothing in my life matters enough to worry about. It also suddenly hits me that my interest in the old Gypsy ways and my fascination with British explorers are not so contradictory as they always seemed to me: people equipped to live out in all seasons, making fires and cups of tea to boost their tired morale. I put my hands behind my head and lie back in the sun.

My thoughts of death and peace turn out to be vainglorious and flimsy. Out of nowhere the horseflies start to court me, unnerving and menacing bruisers that soon have me scampering back down the hill like the foreigner I am. The resident crows, who must be the hardest and most stoical crows in Britain to live up here, mock my retreat with occasional cackles and caws.

On the way back down I stop to wash in a high pool, turquoise with the hue of the stones. A young couple, who I reckon from their accents are Swiss, pass by with expensive cameras and ask me if there are any more pools to take pictures of. I tell them yes, but that they've already passed the best ones and there's no point going further; plus, you'd need to be a professional rock climber to safely get to the top. They ignore me and carry on anyway, exactly as I would have done. I keep an eye out for them, tarrying and looking over my shoulder periodically for almost an hour and a half. When I can finally see they are back on flat ground, I relax, and return to the van.

★

I have stopped in a series of other lay-bys on the A87, the main road across Skye from the bridge to Uig, via Portree. The Highland Council reckons this is a seasonal stopping place so I've tried to have a guess at where Travellers would go. There are several pull-ins big enough for three trailers plus vans or trucks, so those are the ones I use. Nobody bothers you in the slightest – I've seen one squad car in eight days, and it was empty and parked outside the police station in Portree.

The island is full of camper vans, but I reckon I've seen a maximum of three Travellers in as many days. One pulled up alongside me, a young fella in his early twenties in a post-office-red Transit tipper, customised with a visor and chrome wing-mirror caps. He slowed from 60 to 10 mph to eyeball me with his elbow hanging over the wound-down window. I stared back and gave him the Traveller's nod. He didn't return it, but his eyes narrowed in a weird mixture of acknowledge-ment and confusion, as if his family were the only Travellers who came here, and he couldn't tell if I was a lonesome hippy or one of his own. I can't tell either.

I saw two other men I thought were Travellers one evening, as the sun glimmered off the Atlantic, making the cows in the fields look fuzzy with light. They had a pair of newish white Transit pickups, parked up on a wide triangular verge just south of Dunvegan. Two men in their forties sat in the cab of the one facing me, both with tanned faces and sandy-coloured swept-back hair. One was wearing a blue vest that showed his big arms as he stared down at his phone; the other, in a white shirt, stared out of the window in a moment of exhaustion or peace.

I didn't pull up, I never do. But being out here on a limb of the land, with the sun still up at 9 p.m., makes me think that maybe I should have, just this once. That they would have been happy to talk to someone from seven hundred miles to the south, too far away to be a rival. But weeks spent alone, or with no one but Candis, have rearranged the floor plan of my mind, and I don't want to talk to anyone. Words have become a finite resource, not to be parted with lightly. I'm afraid of rejoining society in the south, where the currency of language is devalued by overuse.

Time passes to another morning. It is 7 a.m. Thousands of midges are whirligigging around the outside of the van, which I have not left for nine hours because I don't want to let them in. A few dozen make it in anyway, navigating the labyrinth of tiny ventilation gaps in their efforts to get at my blood. I spray on some repellent and light a couple of incense sticks. The noxious mixture sends the midges into confused fits, and makes me cough and splutter like Doc Holliday. At least we're all in it together.

After four scorching days the grey skies have returned. My cues for movement are now mostly prompted by the weather or animals: the rain makes it hard to cook and clean so the time is better spent driving. I pack my gear up tight and head east, then south back down to Argyllshire, and the last stopping place on my list. Perhaps I should be sad about this, but I'm not. I no longer see my 'quest' as a penned-off phase of my life, neatly partitioned from everything else like a prison term or a cruise. If anything, it is more like a beginning, a fresh start with new capabilities. I know how to live like this now. The power is within me, like a new organ, a second heart.

I drive slowly around Loch Lomond and Loch Long, before finally coming to the spectacular lookout point of Rest and Be Thankful, named by the soldiers who paved this impossible pass. There is a freshly laid tarmac road just above it. I remember that I was trying to come this way last year and turned back because they were laying the road. It pleases me to think that here it is, this road I saw the birth – or at least the re-birth – of. I wish I could tell my younger self that at a future point, I would see that it had been worth the inconvenience of having to turn back then.

The road runs behind the glen towards another low point, I can't tell precisely where. I follow it. It goes down and down, further than I thought there was depth in the land. I see a grand total of two vehicles in a quarter of an hour: a big red tractor, also beetling downwards, which I overtake, and a silver hatchback thrashing its way as fast as it can up the hill. After a mile of steep decline I think I must surely be below sea level, in some subterranean part of Scotland where spirits tend to pool. But then the road opens out slightly just ahead of a junction, and all of a sudden, I recognise where I am.

From here I can see Loch Fyne below, and Ardkinglas, a remnant of old-growth beech wood just along the track. As I slow up, a wide lay-by opens to my left, perfect for my needs. Part of it has been scrappily tarmacked, almost as if by accident; the rest is covered in woodchips and other debris. A dozen-odd tree trunks are laid along one side, and great tractor tracks are impressed in both the tarmac and the mud.

I stop the van at the mouth of the pull-in, not yet ready to arrive. I get out and have a look around. The lay-by is shaped like a light bulb, opening out from its narrow mouth into a generous bowl like an alchemist's bottle. There are a few bits of rubbish – a lot, in fact, for a place so remote. It is the usual stuff – drinks bottles and faded crisp packets; a couple of mysterious rusted springs that could have been from a mattress, a long-dead vehicle, or something else. No contraceptives or evidence of ablutions, I observe, half-smiling. But there is also a pair of well-used forester's gloves that seem to go with the pile of tree trunks at the side. Both the trunks and the gloves wear a heavy patina of grime that seems to suggest they've been left here for a couple of years at least. So I won't be expecting company. I've already made up my mind: this is my stopping place for a while. I pull the van in, find a nice level bit with two wheels on the tarmac and two on a sturdy swathe of coarse, compacted grit. Dinner is a cup of tea and a cigarette. I want to light a fire, not so much for the heat as for something to do, but the light would be reflected off the bracken and might be seen by a farmer: I don't want to worry anybody. Instead I settle for rubbing my hands above the dancing bunsen flames of my stove.

In the morning I open the back doors to see fresh deer tracks, pairs of half-moons pressed into the dark brown mud.

I smile at the thought that I was asleep while these harmless animals browsed around the van, an alien in their world. I boil some water and shave using my wing mirror, stripped to the waist in the cool of the Highland breeze. Then I walk off down to the only *atchin tan* with National Monument status. I am at the Tinkers' Heart, also known as the Gypsy Wedding Place. Lying before me, in a field overlooking Loch Fyne, are a series of quartz stones set into a heart shape. It is a Traveller monument indeed, its position triangulated by a combination of mythical-sounding place names and alphanumeric route codes.

There is a small, unassuming, laminated plaque on the gate that leads to the monument, with a brief explanatory word about how the Travellers used to meet here and wed at the crossroads. I go through and walk to the Heart, which is now enclosed by a short black metal fence, hemmed in with wire like the residents of many of Britain's Traveller sites. The stones barely peep out above the surface of the ground. It seems fitting that a monument of the Travellers is so unobtrusive: it is the opposite of grandiose, rising hardly above the earth, the ghostly white quartz easy to miss unless you know it's there. Visitors have thrown coins down as if the Heart were an ancient sacred well, making whatever small prayers they will: for health, wealth, happiness; children, perhaps; or love. I rub a 50-pence piece between my fingertips and flick it up into the air; it lands on the Heart, but my mind stays empty, not knowing what to wish for at the end of so long a journey. I sit on the fence for a while and stare across the massive mirror of Loch Fyne, as patches of sun, pale gold as sovereigns, move across the deep green countryside, blessings of light from a star. There can be no more beautiful place to get married in all the world than this.

I walk down to Ardkinglas, its spectacular beeches – as Nan taught me – a sign of a good place to stop, because they prefer drier soil. I spend a while walking gently over the cushioned floor of thick moss and leaf mould, moving through the filtered beams of light that play on the trunks of the trees, vast and knotted necks of silver, patient in growth beyond the thoughts of creatures like me. Some would have been saplings when the first of the Travellers to marry here made their vows in the presence of water, earth and sky. I reach down to touch a tiny seedling that has sprouted up between two huge, python-like roots of a mighty beech, and carefully feel around its roots until it comes free from the soil. I'll take it back to Nan's garden to remind me of this day, and of my year in the van: something rooted and green to symbolise the end of the road, and of black-and-white certainties. I roll the stem of the seedling between finger and thumb. I am neither addicted to motion, nor itching to settle down. I flirt with the thought that I don't care if I'm a Gypsy or not any more. Somewhere along the way, the question seems to have lost its importance. After all, I have been a free man, at least for a while.

As I leave the wood, stepping carefully over its ancient, moss-clad wall, I see that a great beast has walked up to the Heart: a Highland cow, with two upturned horns and a bluff of matted fringe, just like the one that stared across at me from Shalden Green, the place where Nan was born. It looks at me, maintaining its gaze as I walk along the path, until I am back at the gate. I want to walk calmly away, but instead I turn and look across the Loch once more. I've lost the constant need to get somewhere. *We are all somewhere*, I tell myself. I go back to the van and put the key in the ignition, in no great hurry to hear the engine start.

Glossary
of Romani words used

These are from English Romani, unless otherwise stated

abri out, outside; second syllable *-bri* rhymes with English 'free'

akai here; '*gavvers akai*' – 'the police are here'; meaning is sometimes closer to 'just over there': 'he's in the *rooker* up *akai*' – 'he's in the copse just up there'

amaro our (continental Romani)

atch usually 'stop', as in *atchin tan*, 'stopping place', though it can also mean 'shut' as in '*atch your mui*' – shut your mouth; or as in the expression '*atch on*' – 'carry on' or 'ignore that'

atchin staying, stopping, camping

bar pound sterling

bavval wind

bengeske of the devil; diabolical

booko liver

bori big (*baro* in continental Romani)

brishindesko rainy

293

canni chicken

chavi child; used between adults, it can also mean 'mate', a bit like English 'kiddo': 'Alright, *chavi*?' 'Not bad, you?'

chokkers shoes, but especially connotes boots, as in *kushti chokkers*, 'nice boots'

choori knife

chordi stolen, as in 'stolen goods'

chore steal

coar to fight, box; 'he can have a *coar*' – 'he knows how to fight'

coggi swede (vegetable)

cosh wood – as in firewood – or a stick, especially one designed to beat someone with

del give; sometimes means 'hit'

diddakoi this word is often cited as meaning 'half-Gypsy' and is derived from the phrase *dik akai* 'look here', which half-Gypsies were supposedly unable to pronounce correctly; I have only ever heard it used by non-Gypsies as a term of abuse towards Travellers, and by some Romany people from East Anglia, as a term for Irish Travellers.

diddle sing rhythmic nonsense based on sounds from the Romani language

dik, dikka look

diklo silk scarf, traditionally worn by older Gypsy men and women

dinlo fool, or foolish (works as a noun and an adjective); sometimes pronounced '*dindler*' in the North

div a fool – from the Romani adjective *divio*, 'foolish'

dordi! an exclamation; somewhere between 'wow', 'blimey', 'no way' and 'oh, my God'

drom road

dui two

eddest biggest or best

fam hand

fauni ring (jewellery)

gadje non-Gypsies (continental Romani); variously spelled *gadzhe* and *gaje*

gadji non-Gypsy woman (continental Romani); variously spelled *gadzhi, gaji*

gadjo non-Gypsy man (continental Romani); variously spelled *gadzho* and *gajo*

gav village, town

gavver police officer; probably derived from *gavengro*, 'man from the town' *geero* unfamiliar man; 'who's that *geero vellin'* up *akai*?'

gorjie non-Gypsy; also pronounced *gorjer*

gilly sing; a song

grai horse; rhymes with English 'eye'

graimengro horseman

gub a curse; bad luck; also heard as *guv*

hachiwichi hedgehog; hedgehogs (Welsh Romani); usually just *hotchi* in England

hobben food

ja go (imperative, from continental Romani); *jel* in English Romani

jigger door

jin know

juk, jukel dog (*juk* rhymes with English 'took')

kam the sun; *kams* can also mean 'money', because gold coins look like little suns

katar from where (continental Romani)

katar avilan? where do you come from? (continental Romani)

kali black

kaulo black; also heard as *karlo* and *karli*

kekavi kettle

kekker/kakker similar in meaning to 'leave off' in English; can mean 'shut your mouth', but when telling a story, it sometimes means 'No, I'm serious' – '*Kekker,* this is all true'; can also work as a negative particle: '*mandi kekker jins*' – I don't know

kova this (continental Romani)

kris Romani court (continental Romani); a gathering of the community to resolve an internal dispute

kur multipurpose verb; usually translated as 'do' or 'make', it is similar to English 'do' in that it can also mean 'have sex with' or, in the passive, to be overpowered, as in '*mandi's kurred*' – I'm spent (i.e. in a fight); rhymes with English 'err'

kushti good; lovely; a multi-purpose positive adjective

ladged ashamed

ladge-up a shameful spectacle

lesko his (continental Romani)

lowvul money, a south coast pronunciation; in most of England it is pronounced 'loova', with a 'u' sound somewhere between English 'put' and English 'love'

loovni prostitute; 'u' sound as in English 'took'

mandi I, me

mass meat

-*mengri* -thing (nominalising suffix)

minge vagina

mingries police; from Romani *mengro* 'man'

miro anav si o ... my name is (continental Romani)

mobili car (continental Romani)

mokkadi dirty; of a place, it can mean it feels unlucky

mollisha woman; *monnishin* is also heard

mukta box; 'u' as in English 'put'

Muller-Mush from *muller* 'die' and *mush* 'man': child-stealing bogeyman used to frighten children into behaving

mullerdi deathly, spooky, haunted; 'u' as in English 'put'

mung beg; get something (or get money) for little in return; rhymes with 'sung'

mush man; rhymes with English 'push'

nane tsokha I have no shoes (continental Romani)

nash balamo run, outsider (Greek Romani)

needi a Traveller; derived from the Irish *daoine* 'people' and unrelated to the English word 'need'

pani water

peeve drink; alcohol

poggadi jib the 'broken tongue', a name for the Angloromani dialect, so called because its grammar has been largely replaced by English

pogger break, hit

posh half; may be the origin of the English word 'posh' via the Romani *posh-ori* for a half-crown coin: someone who had lots of these was rich, hence 'posh'

poshrat half-blood, specifically a mixed-blood Gypsy

praster run; run away

pukker tell; answer

putsel pocket; sometimes pronounced *putsi*

puv earth, field, ground; can be used as a verb i.e in '*puv* the *grai*' – 'put the horse out to graze'; 'u' as in English 'put'

puvvies potatoes; literally 'earth-ies'

radgey mad

rakli girl

ratti blood

rokker talk; in the phrase 'do you *rokker*?' it means 'do you speak Romani?'

Rom san? are you Romany? (continental Romani)

Romanes the Romani language; final syllable -*nes* pronounced as in 'Loch Ness'; variations include *Romanus, Rummanes, Rumnis*

Romanipen a collective noun for the battery of Romany customs around cleanliness and living habits

ruvengo of the wolves

shero head; rhymes with English 'hero'

shirilo cold

shok cabbage

shushi rabbit; the 'u' is roughly the same as in English 'push'

tan place, home; as in *atchin tan*, 'stopping place'

tatcho true; authentic (as in *'tatcho Romanichals'*)

tem county; country; land

trash frighten, scare; pronounced the same as English 'trash' but the meaning is unconnected

tu san you are (continental Romani)

tuke you (continental Romani)

vardo Romany wagon; sometimes also used for a modern caravan

veshengo of the forests

vonger money; apparently derived from the Romani word *angar* meaning 'coal'

waffadi sick, ill; can also mean generally bad, in the sense of bad weather *woodrus* bed

yek one

yog fire

yogger gun

Acknowledgements

I thank Candis for putting up with me.

I thank all my family, especially Nan, Mum and Dad († 9.12.2017), Gran and Grandad († 29.5.2017), Gordon and Josie, and Joey and Liza.

I thank my agents Eve White and Jack Ramm, and my editors Clara Farmer and Parisa Ebrahimi. Your fingerprints are all over this book and working with you has been a privilege. I also thank Charlotte Humphery and everyone else at Penguin Random House who has helped to bring this book together.

I thank Jon Day for believing in my writing and for pestering me to write a book about Travellers, and I thank William Kraemer for his matchless encouragement, energy and camaraderie.

I thank Anna Jean Hughes for her eagle eyes and big heart, and I thank Nell Leyshon for years of priceless advice and belief.

I thank all my other friends who have chipped in with thoughts and inspiration along the way, especially Jamie Berger, Anouar Chergui, Joolz Denby, Christopher Jones, Charles Newland, Phillip Osborne, Ian Pons Jewell, and all the other members of Poetry Club: Katie Abbott, Simon Bracken, Ellen Parnavelas and Dominic Walker. I thank the late Simon Evans for showing me there are many ways of looking at 'Gypsiness'. I thank Kirsten Norrie for her inspiration, collaboration and alchemy.

I thank the Romany writers who have been my role models, especially Dan Allum, David Morley, Chris Penfold-Brown, and Jess Smith.

I thank the editors of *The Junket*, who commissioned the essay from which this book would grow: Jon Day (again), Susanna Hislop, Arthur House, Thomas Marks, James Purdon, Peter Scott, and Kristen Treen.

I thank the Arvon Foundation and especially Becky Swain, Claire Berliner and Oliver Meek, for allowing me and the Romany Theatre Company to do a week-long creative writing course in the summer of 2009. It changed my life. I thank the Royal Society of Literature and the Jerwood Foundation for the huge morale boost they gave me in the form of a Jerwood Award for Non-Fiction. I thank Arts Council England, and especially Milica Robson, for their assistance with my work, and I thank the Society of Authors for their help and support.

I thank everyone who helped me out when I was on the road, especially Jake and Claire Bowers; Ben and Shona Coffer; Natalya Dragicevic; Barney and Jackie Dowling; Max Hildebrand; Ludo Hughes; Julie and Paul Colman; Jane Jackson and 'Gab' Garbutt; Rob and Steph Lomax; Dom McGuire; Nic and Ruth Millington; Clem and Bethan Mitchell; Pete and Jemima Mitchell; Simon Moriarty; Charles and Christina and Charlie and Vicky Newland;

Yseult Ogilvie; Bruno Travers, and Rob and Tom Wolframm. I thank Andrew and Elizabeth Cairncross for kindly letting us use their place in France.

I thank Essex Book Festival, especially Ros Green and Jo Nancarrow, for letting me stay on site in the van as a writer in residence. I thank Robert Teed and Paula Jackson for their work on the *Grace in thy Sight* residency in York, which also fed directly into the concept of this book. I thank Meg Reid of Felixstowe Book Festival for her warm encouragement.

I thank all the mechanics who've fixed the van, especially Mass at Parkway Motors.

If I should have thanked you by name, and I haven't, I thank you and I'm sorry.

Any mistakes in this book are solely mine.

Index